THIN-LAYER CHROMATOGRAPHY

JAMES M. BOBBITT
Associate Professor of Chemistry
The University of Connecticut
Storrs, Connecticut

With a Foreword by
J. G. KIRCHNER

REINHOLD BOOK CORPORATION
A subsidiary of Chapman-Reinhold, Inc.
NEW YORK   AMSTERDAM   LONDON

Printed in the United States of America
by The Guinn Co., Inc

Foreword

Thin-layer chromatography (as it is known today) was developed because of a specific need for a rapid method which would separate small amounts of compounds. Soon after its development it was apparent that the method was more than a micromethod for separating compounds. It was a means of (1) investigating absorbents and solvents from column work, (2) following the course of elution chromatography of colorless compounds, (3) checking the course of reactions and (4) carrying out certain reactions such as oxidations, reductions, dehydrations and so forth, directly on the strip or plate. By these means and other reactions applied directly to the unknowns, an insight into the type of compound could be gained. All these functions of thin-layer chromatography are enhanced by the speed of the method and the fact that only minute amounts of material are needed.

In general, a new technique that is developed for the separation and identification of compounds is not a method which, per se, displaces a previous technique. Rather it is an addition to the numerous tools available to the scientist for solving his problems.

A man that adopts the idea that a given technique is the solution to all his problems is missing an opportunity. Many times combinations of various techniques give results which surpass anything that can be attained with any of the individual techniques. Keeping this in mind it is to be hoped that this book will be an introduction to a method to those who have not used it and an aid to those who wish to further their knowledge of the subject.

J. G. KIRCHNER

Linden, N.J.
August, 1963

iii

Preface

Chromatography on thin layers of adsorbent was conceived as early as 1938 and developed largely during the early 1950's. However, it has been used more extensively since about 1958 and now appears to be in an era of rapid development and almost universal adoption. At such a time, a book setting forth the basic technical details and surveying the field is in order. The author first observed the technique in the laboratory of Professor Hans Schmid in Zürich, Switzerland and was much impressed. This impression and the successful application of the method in his own laboratory have prompted the writing of this book.

The text and the bibliography cover the majority of the literature through December 1962 and a few particularly pertinent papers in 1963.

It is the intention of the author to write a condensed and non-theoretical description of this simple laboratory technique. Thus, the experimental aspects and "tricks" will be taken up, catalogued and discussed in considerable detail. In the last Chapter, an attempt will be made to tabulate, in a concise and meaningful way, as many specific applications of the method as possible. Any theoretical treatment of the subject must consist of two portions. The first is a discussion of general chromatographic theory and the second is a consideration of the deviations from the theory which arise in thin layers. Such a discussion is beyond the scope of this book.

The author would like to express his appreciation to the following persons who have made his career—and, thereby, this book—possible: Professors James L. Hall, C. L. Lazzell, L. A. Pursglove, Katherine Wilson and Elizabeth Frost Reed who are or were on the Staff of

v

West Virginia University; Professor Carl Djerassi of Stanford University; Professor Hans Schmid of the University of Zürich; Dr. Ulrich Weiss of the National Institutes of Health, and, finally, his parents, Mr. and Mrs. J. S. Bobbitt of Bluefield, West Virginia. Beyond doubt, the author owes his greatest debt to Professor Melville Lawrence Wolfrom of the Ohio State University and to him this book is respectfully dedicated.

The actual writing of the text would have been impossible without the assistance of the author's wife, Jane Ann Hickman Bobbitt, Drs. Roy J. Gritter, Ana Rother and R. G. Jensen of the University of Connecticut, Dr. H. K. Mangold of the Hormel Institute, University of Minnesota, and Mr. Herbert R. Simonds of the Reinhold Publishing Corporation who read portions of the manuscript at various times. The following co-workers actually carried out most of the thin-layer chromatography and assisted in the final checking and proofreading of the text: Mr. Christopher Allen, Dr. Robert Doolittle, Mrs. Judith Douville, Dr. Robert Ebermann, Dr. K. L. Khanna, Mr. Donald Kiely, Miss Judith McNew, Dr. Sardar Mahboob, Dr. Ana Rother and Mr. David W. Spiggle. The author is further indebted to his secretary Mrs. Jean Jemielity for typing the manuscript, to Mrs. Eileen Stock who made all of the drawings and to Mr. Ernest F. Spitzer and the Chas. Pfizer Co. of Groton, Connecticut for the use of their fine library.

JAMES M. BOBBITT

Storrs, Conn.
September, 1963

Contents

CHAPTER 1

Introduction, History and General Applications

INTRODUCTION

Since the very beginning of the science of chemistry, its practitioners have been plagued by two technical problems. The first is to learn the purity of a given preparation or, conversely, how many components are in a given system. This information is necessary regardless of whether the system is a mineral mixture, an extract of some plant or animal, or the result of a chemical reaction. The second problem is to resolve the system into its pure components so that they can be characterized and studied. The earlier chemists performed phenomenal feats by fractional crystallization and distillation, but it has only been in the last fifty years or so that the various techniques of chromatography have promised true solutions to these problems.

It follows from the stated problems that chromatography can be considered from two viewpoints. One is *diagnostic** or qualitative and the second is *preparative.** The object of the former is to determine the number of components in a system and to learn, if possible, what they are without actually isolating them. The latter viewpoint involves the separation of a mixture into its components in such a way that reasonable amounts can be isolated and studied. Still a third aspect is *quantitative,* or concern about how much of each component is present.

---

* These concepts and others in this section have been well reviewed by Keulemans[187] and will be only briefly discussed in this volume.

1

All of the techniques of chromatography are based upon the same simple principle. They involve a moving system of some type (liquid or gas) which is in equilibrium with a stationary phase. These phases are so designed that the mixture to be separated will be distributed between the two. When the stationary phase is a solid and the forces acting between it and the mixture are adsorptive in nature, the technique is called *adsorption chromatography*. When the stationary phase is a simple liquid or a liquid held on some type of support, the chromatography is considered to be *partition chromatography*.

In general, adsorption chromatography involves a relatively non-polar moving phase and works best when the substances to be separated are not very polar. The major advantages over partition chromatography are that larger quantities can be separated in comparable systems and that a controlled temperature is not necessary. Partition chromatography, on the other hand, generally involves polar solvents and mixtures of very polar compounds such as carbohydrates or amino acids. Since it is basically dependent upon the distribution coefficients of the substances in question, which are, in turn, highly sensitive to temperature and other conditions, a carefully controlled atmosphere is required. The line of demarcation between adsorption and partition chromatography is, however, often blurred.

At this point, it would be appropriate to define some of the terms as they will be used throughout this book. The *adsorbent* will be the finely divided powder which makes up the stationary phase in adsorption chromatography, or holds the stationary liquid in partition chromatography. The *layer* will refer to a thin layer of absorbent, bound or unbound, deposited on a glass plate. The term *spotting* will refer to the application of the substance to be separated to the thin layer. The passing of a liquid through the layer to affect a separation will be referred to as *development* and the liquid itself will be consistently called the *developer*. The term *eluent* will be used only when the complete removal of a substance from the adsorbent is intended. The term *visualization* will refer to the rendering visable of the results of a developed chromatogram. The *Rf* will be the distance traveled by a given substance divided by the distance traveled by the solvent front. Both are measured from the origin.

Column chromatography, as originated by Tswett[409,410] and since practiced by legions of chemists, was primarily an adsorption technique used for preparative work. Column chromatography using an adsorbent such as silica gel or cellulose as a support for a liquid was conceived by Martin and Synge[241] and is partition chromatography for a preparative purpose. The countercurrent distribution of Craig and his co-workers[59,60] may or may not be defined as chromatography but at least involves similar phenomena. It might also be considered a partition technique with a preparative goal. None of the above techniques have been particularly successful as diagnostic methods due to the extensive labor involved in the preparation of a single chromatogram.

The first major development in diagnostic chromatography was the paper chromatography pioneered by Consden, Gordon and Martin.[57a,57b] The method was fantastically successful and was rapidly adopted all over the world and in every type of laboratory. The major advantages of paper chromatography are its extreme simplicity and the fact that relatively inexpensive equipment is needed. However, since it is a partition technique with the stationary liquid phase held on a piece of paper, it works best with polar developers and small amounts of polar substances. While techniques of preparative paper chromatography have been worked out and used successfully, they are laborious.

The second, primarily diagnostic technique of chromatography was gas chromatography. This was either an adsorption chromatography, as pioneered by Turner,[412] Claesson[56] and Cremer,[61,62] or a partition chromatography, as suggested by Martin and Synge[241] and introduced by James and Martin.[170] The advantages of gas chromatography are its speed of operation, its almost unbelievable degree of resolution and the fact that the results can be interpreted quantitatively. The disadvantages are that relatively expensive and complex equipment is needed and that the substances to be separated must have at least some vapor pressure at workable temperatures. The use of gas chromatography as a preparative technique has been quite successful although hampered by technical difficulties.

Thus, it would appear that a diagnostic technique which is adsorptive in nature and which combines the technical simplicity of paper chromatography and the speed of gas chromatography is lacking. Ideally, such a method should lend itself to quantitative interpretation and should be useful also as a preparative method. Most of the conditions are fulfilled by *thin-layer chromatography,* or, as it is sometimes called, "thin-film," "open-column," "chromatostrip" or "chromatoplate" chromatography. In essence, this is a type of adsorption chromatography where the adsorbent is a thin layer of some solid deposited on a glass plate support. In operation, it is analogous to paper chromatography; that is, the substance to be separated is placed a short distance from one end of the layer and is resolved by a solvent passing through the layer by capillary action. The development is carried out in a simple closed system as in paper chromatography, but is much more rapid. When the proper solvent mixtures are used, the method can become a partition technique. Thus far, the quantitative interpretation has involved errors of 3 to 5 per cent, but the method shows promise as a preparative means for quantities of one gram or less.

HISTORY OF THIN-LAYER CHROMATOGRAPHY

It is always difficult to sort out the various originators of some concept or technique and to assign credit, because any such development is the result of contributions and ideas from many people and laboratories. Such contributions vary from the initial flash of genius to the more practical aspects such as the introduction of new or more convenient equipment or materials. The historical development of thin-layer chromatography is best divided into two such phases. The first phase is the conception and initial development of equipment and techniques followed by their slow but steady adoption. The second phase is an extensive and rapid development following the invention of new equipment, the standardization of the method and, particularly, the commercial availability of apparatus and adsorbents. A third phase will surely follow in which the method becomes a routine technique applied universally and without particular thought and attention.

In 1938, Izmaïlov and Shraïber[169] described the use of thin layers of adsorbent on glass plates for the separation of galenicals. The English summary of this paper is as follows:

"A method for chromatographic adsorption analysis is elaborated, based on the observation of the division of substances into zones on a thin layer of adsorbent, using one drop of the substance. The results obtained by the method proposed are qualitatively the same as those obtained by the usual chromatographic adsorption method of analysis. The method enables one to obtain satisfactory results using one drop of the substance under test, very small quantities of the adsorbent and minimal time. The method may be used for the evaluation of galenical preparations and their identification, as well as for a preliminary test of the adsorbent and the kind of developer."

In 1941, Crowe[63] described the use of thin layers of unbound adsorbent to help predict the best solvents for column chromatography. In a book entitled "Introduction to Chromatography"[443] which was published in 1947, Williams reported the use of thin layers of adsorbent held between horizontal glass plates. The top plate had a small hole for application of the sample and the developer, and the chromatogram was made in a circular fashion.

The use of a binding agent (starch) to hold the layers in place was introduced by Meinhard and Hall[246] in 1949. The resulting layers of alumina–"Celite" prepared on microscope slides, were used for the separation, again in a circular fashion, of inorganic salts.

The next and, by far, the most extensive and comprehensive contributions to the development of thin-layer chromatography were made by J. G. Kirchner, J. M. Miller and their co-workers at the U. S. Department of Agriculture Laboratories in Pasadena. In an extensive series of papers (1951–1957) this group investigated various adsorbents and binding agents,[193] designed equipment for the preparation of "chromatostrips"[253] and used the technique for the investigation of the terpenoids.[190-194,251-253] Narrow glass plates called "chromatostrips" (0.5 by 5.25 in.) with a silicic acid-starch layer were found to be most useful for their work although they also introduced the use of larger plates.[191] The larger plates called "chromatoplates" by Reitsema[323] were used by him in extensive work on essential oils.[323-327]

Starting a little later, but roughly paralleling the work of Kirchner and Miller, Mottier and Potterat[268] worked out a method for analyzing food dyes on layers of nonbonded alumina and even separated amino acids by this technique.[267] Some of the other workers in the earlier phase (prior to 1956) were Ito, Wakamatsu and Kawahara,[167,168] Labat and Montes,[209] Grüner and Spaich,[131] Coveney, Matthews and Pickering,[58] G. Wagner,[426] Rigby and Bethune,[328] Bryant,[51] Lagoni and Wortmann,[210,211] Demole,[76] Fukushi and Obata,[108] Onoe[284] and Maruyama.[242] The earlier phases are well reviewed by Demole in French[77] and English.[78]

The major reason for the slow development and adoption of the technique during the time from 1951 to 1958 was the fact that equipment and chemicals were not commercially available. More inertia must be overcome in the construction of equipment and the preparation of adsorbents than in signing a check or placing an order.

This last obstacle was removed by Egon Stahl in Germany. Stahl, working with C. Desaga, G. m. b. H., in Heidelberg, devised a system involving standard-size glass plates (5 by 20 cm and 20 by 20 cm), a new apparatus for the preparation of layers, and a standard adsorbent (silica gel-plaster of Paris). Subsequently, the apparatus became commercially available from Desaga and the adsorbent became available from E. Merck, A. G., in Darmstadt. Stahl and his co-workers studied the variables of the technique in a thorough manner,[381] applied it to many new types of organic compounds[366-382] and pioneered the use of new adsorbents. These new adsorbents immediately became commercially available. Stahl called the method "Dünnschicht-Chromatographie" or "thin-layer chromatography" ("TLC") and this name seems to be widely accepted.

The applications of the thin-layer technique mushroomed after 1958 so that it is impossible to mention all of the people who have contributed. However, some of the more prominent workers in the field have been Stahl, of course, and Kaufmann, Demole, Gänshirt, Mangold, Stanley and Seiler. The contributions of these people and many others will be discussed later.

The use of thin-layer chromatography is now almost routine in natural product, pharamaceutical and lipid laboratories, but has not been so well accepted by the organic chemists as it might. The applications to various aspects of nonlipid biochemistry have been hampered by the very polar molecules involved, but these problems are rapidly being overcome by the introduction of new adsorbents.

The field has recently been reviewed again by Demole in French[79] and English;[80] by Stahl,[372] Schorn[346] and Wagner[428] in German; by Mangold[232] and Wollish, Schmall and Hawrylyshyn[452] in English; by Michalec[248] and Procházka[312] in Czech; by Vioque[418] in Spanish; by Kokoti-Kotakis;[205] and by Jensen.[176]

At present, three books have been published on the subject. Two of these, one edited by Stahl[375] with contributions from Bolliger, Brenner, Gänshirt, Mangold, Seiler and Waldi and one written by Randerath,[320a] are in German. The third, by Truter[404] is in English.

GENERAL APPLICATIONS

The motives for the application of thin-layer chromatography are many and varied. Some of these will be considered in the following discussion. The prejudices of an organic chemist with inclinations toward natural product work will be apparent. The various points will all be fairly obvious, but may, on occasion, suggest a solution to a research problem. Examples will be cited to illustrate the discussion, although it should be noted that they are chosen at random and no attempt has been made to cite all of the possible references.

Preliminary Study of a System or Situation

The small amounts of material involved and the speed with which results are obtained make thin-layer chromatography a valuable tool for preliminary explorations of many kinds. The pharmacognosist or plant chemist can learn something about the complexity and, by the judicious choice of spray reagents, even something of the components of a plant extract. He can then use the technique to follow his gross separation procedures and to learn where the products of interest are. The same reasoning applies, of course, to various aspects of plant and animal biochemistry.

The organic chemist, or indeed, any chemist, can explore a large number of reaction conditions, using small amounts of material, in a short time. This applies to both normal synthetic reactions and attempts to degrade a natural product or unknown substance. The operator can readily learn which reactions produce new products and which yield only starting material; which reactions produce complex product mixtures and which do not. If a given material is sought and is available for comparison, conditions can readily be found which produce it in the best yield and the cleanest form. The author and his co-workers have used this last general idea in the synthesis of the alkaloids, pilocereine[38] and anaferine.[332]

Intensive Study of a Single Reaction

After some idea of the best reaction conditions or best degradation scheme has been obtained for a given problem, thin-layer chromatography can be employed to learn considerably more about the reaction. A crude kinetic study of the reaction can be made by removing samples at timed intervals and chromatographing them simultaneously with starting material and the expected product, if available. This may tell whether stable intermediates are involved, whether the desired product is an end product or an intermediate and something of the course of reaction. At least, such a study will tell when all of the starting material is gone and will aid in establishing an optimum reaction time.

The author and his co-workers have used this approach extensively in the structure elucidation of the glucoside, catalposide.[40] An example from this work is shown in Figure 1.1. Others have used it in the study of the sequential methylation of phenolic acids,[225] the preparation of p-bromophenylosazones of xylose derivatives,[7] the glycerolysis of linseed oil[335] and the biogenetic production of terpenes in mint plants.[20] The presence of an unstable intermediate was shown in the synthesis of pseudoionone.[237]

The Isolation of Reaction Products

Thin-layer techniques can be applied to the isolation of reaction products in several ways. First of all, if acid-base partition, distillation or crystallization methods are to be used, one can easily learn something of the precision and completeness of the separations and the purity of the various fractions. Furthermore, the short times involved in learning where the product is will satisfy even the most impatient chemist.

If simple separation methods fail and the products must be separated by chromatography, thin layers offer several possibilities. Quantities less than one gram can be separated by preparative thin-

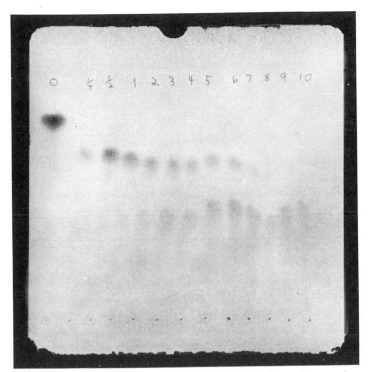

Figure 1.1. Kinetic study of the saponification and epoxide opening of the glucoside catalposide.[40] The starting material shown on the left at zero time is converted after one hour to a deshydroxybenzoyl derivative (middle spots) which is, in time, converted to a glycol (lower spots). The example clearly shows the presence of an intermediate and indicates the optimum reaction time for the preparation of either product. (Photograph by S. E. Wollman)

layer chromatography. This is, beyond doubt, easier, quicker and more precise than column chromatography and is discussed extensively in Chapter 9. In the author's laboratory, this has proved to be an ideal method for purifying samples prior to a final crystallization for microanalysis. Specific examples of this are noted in the tables in Chapter 11.

Applications to Column Chromatography

The simplest type of column chromatography involves the removal of small amounts of contaminants or tars by passing the sample, in a suitable solvent, over a short column of adsorbent. Such a process is adaptable to relatively large quantities and gives high yields. Thin-layer techniques can predict, in a short time, the ideal solvent and adsorbent. One needs only to find a system in which the product moves and the contaminant stays at the origin and to transpose this to a short column of the *identical* adsorbent. Normally, the adsorbents used for thin layers are of such small particle size that a pressure system or a vacuum system must be used when they are placed in columns. Such a scheme has been used by Kirchner and Miller[190] for the preparation of terpeneless essential oils. The reverse of this notion, that is, the isolation of small amounts of product from mixtures, has been used to isolate insecticide residues from plant material.

If the quantities involved and the degree of separation required are such that normal column chromatography cannot be avoided, thin-layer techniques can be used to predict the best solvent system and, above all, to analyze the effluent from the column. Several authors have stated or implied[90,251,365] that the solvents used to give good separations on thin layers can be used directly on a column of the same adsorbent. Duncan[90] has published the following formula for predicting whether two substances will separate on a column.

$$r = \frac{a}{b + 0.1a}$$

$a = Rf$ of faster moving substance on a thin layer
$b = Rf$ of slower moving substance on a thin layer
Separation can only be expected under the conditions prescribed by Duncan (very high adsorbent-material ratios) when r is greater than unity.

It should be pointed out, however, that all of these situations depend upon the actual magnitude of the thin-layer Rf values. This is particularly true in respect to the Duncan expression which would certainly not be valid when the substances run close to the solvent front. The separations on a column will depend primarily on the retention times of the substances involved and these retention times, as stated for thin-layer chromatography by Zoellner and Wolfram,[458] are inversely proportional to the Rf values of the substances on the same adsorbent. Thus, a small difference when Rf values are small can be expected to produce an acceptable difference in retention times and a separation, whereas a large difference when Rf values are close to unity will not give a separation. The author has had some success using the following scheme. A pair of solvents is found which will produce an acceptable separation on a thin layer. The polar component of the solvent system is then reduced until the substances to be separated show Rf's of about 0.2. This modified system is then used directly on a column of adsorbent identical in every way with that in the thin layer.

The monitoring of the effluent of a column is normally done by analyzing fractions obtained using a fraction cutting device. On a typical large layer (20 by 20 cm), as many as eighteen samples can be analyzed simultaneously. The fractions are then combined according to their components. Such applications are also noted in the tables in Chapter 11, and an example taken from the author's work on catalposide is given in Figure 1.2.

Routine Quantitative Assay

A number of procedures have been published for quantitative assay by thin-layer chromatography. These are discussed in Chapter 10 and documented in Chapter 11. Most of the work has been done in clinical chemistry where speed is an important factor. The major limitation of the technique is the error of about 3 to 5%.

Thin-Layer Chromatography in Conjunction with other Methods

The use of thin-layer chromatography in conjunction with gas chromatography has been especially useful in the lipid field.[178,232, 233,236] Normally, the class separations are made preparatively on thin layers and the classes are resolved, generally after chemical modification, by gas chromatography. In this manner, it is possible to take advantage of the ease of quantification and the high degree of resolution of the latter method. It should be noted, however, that the classes are also often resolved by "reversed phase" thin-layer chromatography.[181,182,184,230,232 and others]

A method has been suggested[147] for the combined use of thin-layer chromatography and the mass spectrograph. The silica gel taken

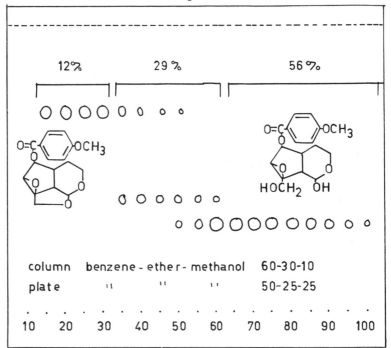

Figure 1.2. A thin-layer analysis of the chromatographic separation of two derivatives of catalposide.[40] The eluent from a Silica Gel G column was divided using an automatic fraction collector and every fifth tube was examined. The solvents for the column were predicted from thin-layer data as described in the text. The solvent systems used on the column and the analysis layer as well as the structure of the materials isolated are shown. The experiment clearly shows the degree of separation, the relatively short time involved (first sample came off after only fifteen 20 ml fractions) and which fractions contain pure compounds. The center spots represent an, as yet, unknown compound.

from the layer and containing the substance to be investigated is introduced directly into the instrument. The adsorbent does not appear to have any effect on the spectrum. The ratio of sample to adsorbent must be at least 1:100, however, and several micrograms of substance are needed.

The Use of Thin-Layer Patterns

Thin-layer chromatography, like paper chromatography, can be used to determine characteristic component-patterns for drugs, plant extracts and biochemical preparations. The comparison of these with patterns of adulterated or diseased samples can provide interesting results. Such techniques have been used to study "chemical races" in plants,[453] drug contaminants,[161] mint oils[323] and lipid components of multiple sclerosis patients.[157]

Classification Systems

In the alkaloids,[436] the estrogens[221] and mint oil constituents,[323] thin-layer chromatographic properties have been correlated to some extent with structural types, and classification procedures have been developed. Such systems make it easier to identify known compounds and to obtain information about unknown ones.

CHAPTER 2

Adsorbents

INTRODUCTION

The adsorbents most commonly used in thin-layer chromatography are, in the following order, silicic acid or silica gel,* aluminum oxide or alumina, kieselguhr or diatomaceous earth and powdered cellulose. Those which have been used to a lesser extent are polyamide powders, ion-exchange powders (modified cellulose), "Florisil," calcium sulfate, polyethylene, "Magnesol," hydroxyl-apatite, "Sephadex," zinc carbonate and various mixtures of these. Kirchner, Miller and Keller[193] explored several adsorbents using starch and plaster of Paris as binding agents. These data are shown in Table 2.1. Although they pertain only to the separation of essential oils by adsorption processes, they show the large number of substances which can be formed into usable layers. Only calcium hydroxide layers are really poor and, as will be discussed later, the addition of silica gel produces usable layers of this substance. Essentially any substance which has desirable adsorptive and chemical characteristics can be successfully used in thin-layer chromatography.

The four most widely used adsorbents, *silica gel, alumina, kieselguhr* and *cellulose*, however, offer a wide range of properties and can be used in most cases. Waldi, Schnackerz and Munter[436] made a comparative study of Silica Gel G, Aluminum Oxide G and Kieselguhr G with the following conclusions. Silica gel and alumina are, respectively, essentially acidic and basic in character while kieselguhr is

---

* The major difference between silicic acid and silica gel appears to be solely in the method of preparation. They are chemically identical, but the gel is prepared in such a manner as to enhance its adsorptive power.

TABLE 2.1. CHARACTERISTICS OF CHROMATOSTRIPS MADE
WITH VARIOUS ADSORBENTS[193]*

Adsorbent Coating	Physical Characteristics of Strip	Resolution of Essential Oils
Magnesium oxide	soft	none
Alumina	excellent	good
Alumina + silicic acid	excellent	good
Calcium hydroxide	soft, crumbly	none
Starch	good	none
Dicalcium phosphate	fair	some resolution
Bentonite	good	oils decomposed
Calcium carbonate	good	slight resolution
Magnesium carbonate	fair	slight resolution
"Filtrol"	good	separation, but oils decomposed
"Filtrol" X202	good	separation, but oils decomposed
"Filtrol," neutral E	good	separation, but oils decomposed
"Florisil"	good	fair separation
Talc	good	slight separation
Silicic acid	excellent	excellent

* Reproduced from Kirchner, Miller and Keller, *Anal. Chem.*, **23**, 420 (1951) through the courtesy of the au hors and The American Chemical Society.

neutral. Furthermore, silica gel has the highest capacity (the ability to separate the largest quantity of a mixture) followed by alumina and kieselguhr in that order.

Alumina chromatography is essentially adsorption chromatography; silica gel can function in both adsorption and partition chromatography depending upon the solvent system and kieselguhr is best characterized as a support for partition phenomena. Thus, alumina would be the adsorbent of choice for the separation of nonpolar basic or neutral mixtures. Silica gel can be used for nonpolar acidic mixtures and, because of its higher capacity, would even be preferred for the nonpolar neutral materials. Silica gel, kieselguhr and cellulose are all suitable for the separation, through partition processes, of polar molecules. Of course, the properties of these adsorbents can be extensively altered by addition of various acids, bases and buffers so that many purposes can be served which are not covered by the above generalizations.

Although artifact formation on thin layers is rare, it is not unknown. Steroid 16-β-esters have been shown to undergo reactions on alumina layers[347] and ethylene ketals have been hydrolyzed on silica gel layers.[363] Alumina in columns is known to catalyze ester hydrolysis, isomerization of double bonds and other reactions.[232] The chromatography of sugars on silica gel layers with ammonia solutions has been shown[439] to produce amination reactions.

The various adsorbents can be and are sometimes used in a pure form, but more frequently, they are used in combination with small amounts of added components. These additives can be blended with the solid adsorbent before it is made into layers, or they can be dissolved in the water portion of the slurry which, in most cases, is the vehicle for application to plates. In general the following purposes are served by the additives.

(1) They may serve as binders or substances to make the adsorbent more cohesive and to hold it to the plate. These make the layers much easier to handle and use and make it possible for them to be sprayed with visualizing reagents. The most common binder is plaster of Paris (calcined calcium sulfate, $CaSO_4 \cdot \frac{1}{2}H_2O$) which is added to the dry adsorbent in amounts up to 20 per cent. The first binder used by Meinhard and Hall[246] and by Kirchner and his group[193] was starch, which, although it gives the layers an added stability over plaster of Paris, limits the spray reagents which can be used to visualize the finished chromatograms. Other binders which have been used are polyvinyl alcohol,[284] collodion[317] and an alcohol-soluble polyamide, "Zytel 61."*[153] Two binders which have been added at later stages are decalin,[254] which is added to the developing system and dichlorodimethylsilane,[185] which is applied to the developed plates so that they can be washed like paper chromatograms. The relative advantages and disadvantages of these binders will be discussed in more detail in the section of this chapter devoted to silica gel.

(2) The additives may serve to alter the properties, both physical and chemical, of the adsorbents. Thus, acids, bases and buffers are commonly incorporated into the layers. Reagents which will complex or chelate to a greater or lesser extent with the substances to be sep-

* Du Pont de Nemours, Geneva, Switzerland

arated, are often added. The latter concept is a relatively recent one and will, in the author's opinion, become important.

The impregnation of layers with hydrophobic liquids so that "reversed phase" chromatography can be carried out will be discussed in Chapter 3.

(3) On occasion, materials are added to adsorbents as "fillers." These reduce the activity of the adsorbent and make it somewhat more porous, resulting in shorter developing times. This concept was originally used by Meinhard and Hall[246] who added "Celite" (see p. 24) to starch-bound alumina. More recently, Bennett and Heftmann[26,27] have added Kieselguhr G to Silica Gel G for a similar purpose.

(4) Finally, reagents may be added which will aid in the visualization of the completed chromatogram. The incorporation of phosphors or fluorescent compounds in the adsorbent so that unsaturated compounds can be seen or easily rendered visible in ultraviolet light is a common practice. On occasion, sulfuric acid is added to the adsorbent. This alters the character of the adsorbent and allows the visualization of the completed chromatogram by heating (to char the organic compounds).

Procedures have been developed by Stahl[373] and by Heřmánek, Schwarz and Čekan[144] for relating the activity of alumina layers to the Brockmann[50] activity scale.

A number of these adsorbents, both modified and pure, are commercially available. These sources will be listed in Table 2.4 at the end of this chapter, although, at the appropriate places, procedures will be given so that an investigator can prepare his own.

Silica Gel or Silicic Acid

Silica gel, used with a plaster of Paris binder is, by far, the most extensively used adsorbent in thin-layer chromatography. It forms a versatile layer which can serve as the solid stationary phase for adsorption chromatography, as a support for the polar liquid phase in normal partition chromatography and as a support for the nonpolar liquid phase in "reversed phase" chromatography. The distinction between the adsorption and normal partition chromatography in this case lies in the solvent system chosen for the chromatogram. If the system consists of solvents such as hexane, benzene, ether, methanol or similar substances, adsorption phenomena will result. If a system is chosen which contains both a nonpolar liquid and a polar liquid such as water, the result will probably be partition chromatography. In "reversed phase" chromatography, the silica gel layer is impregnated with a nonpolar liquid such as a Silicone oil or a hydrocarbon before use. This will be discussed in Chapter 3.

Two binders, starch and plaster of Paris, are commonly used with silica gel. Both originated with Kirchner, Miller and Keller.[193] Starch gives a more mechanically stable layer[8,120,193] which can actually be written on with a blunt lead pencil, but the inclusion of starch in the layer forbids the use of corrosive spray reagents for visualizing the finished chromatogram. (Cold concentrated sulfuric acid may be sprayed on the layers without difficulty, but the sprayed layers cannot be heated to char the spots.) The use of these corrosive spray reagents (sulfuric acid, chromic acid, nitric acid, etc.) as essentially universal reagents for organic substances, is one of the greatest advantages of thin-layer chromatography. On the other hand, the presence of calcium ion (from the plaster of Paris) in the layers has caused some difficulty in the chromatography of inorganic ions[355] and nucleotides.[317]

Silica Gel with No Binder. Silica gel has been used only rarely[1,51,312,322] without some sort of binder. This situation will surely change, however, due to the recent introduction of Woelm "Silica Gel for Thin-layer Chromatography," which contains no binder and depends, for the stability of its layers, on a small particle size. The commercial preparation "Anisil" has no binder as such, but does contain 10 to 15 per cent of magnesium oxide which enhances its layer stability *and makes it a basic adsorbent.*

A method for the preparation of a silica gel suitable for thin-layer chromatography has been given by Adamec, Matis and Galvánek.[1] The starting material was water glass (mixed, hydrated sodium silicates) and the adsorbent was used without a binder.

Silica Gel with a Plaster of Paris Binder. The commercial preparation Silica Gel G (G for *gips* or gypsum) is of this type. It is manufactured by Merck in Germany according to the specifications of

Stahl and, without doubt, is the most widely used adsorbent in thin-layer chromatography. Mangold[232] has stated that a reasonable approximation of the commercial product can be prepared by thoroughly mixing Mallinckrodt Silicic Acid, 200 mesh, with 10 to 15 per cent of newly calcinated calcium sulfate (prepared by heating reagent grade $CaSO_4 \cdot 2H_2O$ at 180° for 24 to 48 hours[296]) of the same grain size. A 200-mesh screen produces particles smaller than 0.12 mm.

Silica Gel G contains appreciable amounts of ferric ion. This does not interfere with the separations of organic compounds, but must be removed for successful work with inorganic ions.[355-360] Seiler and Rothweiler[358] give the following instructions (freely translated) for doing this.

"Five hundred grams of Silica Gel G is treated with 1000 ml of 6*N* hydrochloric acid (500 ml of concentrated hydrochloric acid and 500 ml of distilled water), stirred and allowed to stand. The supernatant liquid, colored yellow by the iron, is decanted and the silica gel is washed twice more with acid and then with three successive 1000-ml portions of distilled water. The adsorbent is then filtered and washed with distilled water until the filtrate is only slightly acidic. It is finally washed with 250 ml of ethanol and 250 ml of benzene and dried in an oven at 120°."

The material from the above treatment *now contains insufficient binder.* Two grams of plaster of Paris[359] or one gram of starch[358] are added to 28 g of purified silica gel to obtain a usable adsorbent.

When materials are to be recovered from thin-layer adsorbents by elution, it is suggested[244,394] that the adsorbent be prewashed. This can be done for Silica Gel G by extracting it three times with boiling methanol[244] or by allowing it to stand overnight with the same solvent.[394] Honegger found[158] that 50 g of Silica Gel G yielded the following amounts of impurity on elution: with chloroform, 6.8 mg; with benzene, 5.5 mg and with acetone, 10.5 mg. Or, the layers can be prewashed with the developing solvent.

Silica Gel With a Starch Binder. To the author's knowledge, no commercial preparation of this type is available. Kirchner, Miller and Keller[193] combine 19 g of Merck reagent grade silicic acid, 100 mesh, one gram of "Clinco"* starch,** 0.15 g of zinc silicate and 0.15 g of zinc cadmium sulfide. The latter two reagents are added as phosphors, but the same proportions would surely serve for the preparation of layers without them. The preparation of starch bound layers is inherently different from the preparation of plaster of Paris bound layers in that the slurry of adsorbent, starch and water is heated before it is applied to plates. This will be discussed in Chapter 3.

Silica Gel with Fluorescing Agents. Several reagents are commonly incorporated into thin layers so that the resulting spots on the developed chromatogram can be seen without using a spray reagent. This is particularly helpful in preparative work. The fluorescing agents, with one exception, are usually blended with the dry adsorbent before the layers are prepared. The exception is sodium fluorescein which is normally dissolved in the liquid used to make the slurry. When the developed plates are placed in short wave ultraviolet light, compounds containing conjugated double bonds show up as dark spots. The various fluorescent materials, the amounts used and their commercial sources are given in Table 2.2.

Acidic Silica Gel. Acids have been incorporated into thin layers for two reasons. The first is to modify the properties of the adsorbent and the second is to aid in visualization. Thus, Stahl[369] used $0.5N$ aqueous oxalic acid rather than pure water to prepare layers. The adsorption activity of such plates is slightly increased.

In contrast to this, Reichelt and Pitra[322] deactivated silica gel by adding 25 per cent water or 43 per cent of dilute (50 per cent) acetic acid to the dry activated powder. In this case, the silica gel was then used without a binder for the separation of cardenolides.

Layers prepared from adsorbents containing small amounts of sulfuric acid can easily be visualized by heating the developed chromatograms on a hot plate or in an oven to char the organic substances. Peifer[296] added 2.5 ml of concentrated sulfuric acid to 100 ml of chloroform-methanol, (70:30) v/v, which was subsequently slurried

---

* Clinton Foods, Inc., Clinton, Iowa.

** Dr. Kirchner has informed the author that still another starch binder is made from ordinary corn starch and "Superior AA Tapioca Flour" mixed in a ratio of 2 to 1. The tapioca flour is a product of Stein, Hall and Co., Inc. of New York. Furthermore, the amount of starch can conveniently be cut in half from the original proportions.

TABLE 2.2. FLUORESCENT AND PHOSPHORESCENT CHEMICALS USED
IN THIN-LAYER CHROMATOGRAPHY

Name	Amount Used	Commercial Source	Ref.
1. Zinc silicate luminescent material P 1, Type 118-2-7	2% in adsorbent	General Electric Co., Cleveland, Ohio	46
2. Rhodamine 6G	0.003% in adsorbent	Matheson, Coleman and Bell, East Rutherford, N.J.	323
3. Luminescent substance ZS-Super	2% in adsorbent	Riedel-de Haen, 3016 Seelze bei Hannover, Germany	117
4. "Ultraphor"	0.005% in adsorbent	Badische Anilin and Soda Fabrik, Ludwigshafen (Rhein), Germany	293
5. Luminescent chemical No. 601	1% in adsorbent	E. I. du Pont de Nemours & Co., Photo Products Dept., Wilmington 98, Delaware	232
6. "Sodium fluorescein"	0.04% sol. in water phase		366
7. Zinc silicate-zinc cadmium sulfide	0.75% of each in adsorbent	Du Pont phosphors No. 601 and No. 1502 respectively	193

with 50 g of Silica Gel G. The developed chromatograms (in this case on microscope or lantern slides) were visualized by heating.

Basic Silica Gel. Stahl[369] described the preparation of basic layers using 0.5N aqueous potassium hydroxide rather than water to make the slurry. The layers were found to be somewhat less active than normal. Such plates can be used to separate acids, which stay at the origin, from neutral compounds or bases which move with the solvent. Adsorbents consisting of 80 per cent calcium hydroxide and 20 per cent Silica Gel G[449] will be more properly considered as a separate adsorbent system. The commercial material "Anisil," as noted above, is a basic adsorbent.

Buffered Silica Gel. In general, buffered silica gel layers have been used for the separation of polar or ionic compounds by partition chromatography. The addition of the buffer is normally made in the same manner as with acids and bases, that is, by using the desired buffer solution in place of water to make the slurry. Such slurrys (at least those made with Silica Gel G) must be spread quickly since they thicken more rapidly than usual.[232] The layers should be allowed to stand several hours at room temperature before they are oven-dried.[232]

TABLE 2.3. THE USE OF BUFFERED LAYERS IN THIN-LAYER CHROMATOGRAPHY

Buffer Sol.	Concentration	Compounds Separated	Ref.
1. Sodium acetate	0.3 m	flavones	379, 380
	0.02 m	sugars	307, 377
2. Monopotassium phosphate and disodium phosphate	equal amts. of 0.2 M	amino acids	271
3. Citric acid-phosphate buffers	pH 7	sugars	307
4. Boric acid	0.1 N	sugars	307
5. Ammonium sulfate	10%	acidic lipids and amphoteric phospholipids	234

This helps to prevent flaking which is also more pronounced with buffered layers. Some of the uses of buffered layers will be summarized in Table 2.3.

The use of boric acid in the separations of sugars is interesting because of the formation of borate complexes between adjacent *cis*-hydroxyl groups. Such complexes are probably responsible for the effectiveness of the buffer.

The use of buffered layers for thin-layer ionophoresis by Honegger[156] is a rather special case since such solutions are normally used to carry current and to form complex ions which can be caused to migrate. Honegger used 0.1 M sodium citrate and acetic acid-formic acid solutions.

Silica Gel Containing Complexing Agents. The addition of complexing agents to thin layers to increase the power of resolution is an intriguing notion and will surely be further developed. At present, the only clear case of this is the use of silver nitrate on silica gel by Barrett, Dallas and Padley[16] and by Morris[260] to separate certain closely related lipids. The basis of this separation is the tendency of silver ion to complex with the pi electrons of double bonds to a greater or lesser degree. The former authors used 12.5 per cent silver nitrate to make a slurry with Silica Gel G. A similar result was produced by Morris[260] who sprayed layers with a saturated silver nitrate solution or a saturated methanolic boric acid solution (see p. 48) or both.

As previously stated, the use of boric acid layers for sugar separation may well be an example of complex formation. The use of 2,5-hexanedione in the moving phase for the separation of inorganic ions[359] is an example of the application of this notion in a reverse manner.

Alumina

Historically, alumina was the first adsorbent used for thin-layer work. Izmaïlov and Shraïber,[169] Meinhard and Hall[246] and the Kirchner group[193] all used or explored this adsorbent. It is strange, then, that alumina has not been more extensively used than it has. One possible reason for this is that alumina is a more reactive adsorbent than silica gel and is known to catalyze ester hydrolysis, isomerization of double bonds, and other reactions.[232] Also, alumina is a basic substance[436] in contrast to the acidic silica gel and has a somewhat lower capacity.[436] Thus, one would tend to choose it for the separation of basic or neutral substances only when silica gel separations were poor.

Alumina with No Binder. Again, in contrast with silica gel, alumina has been used to a large extent with no binder. The reasons for this are obscure but probably can be traced to the ready availability of chromatographic grades of alumina and the large body of knowledge which has accummulated on alumina chromatography. Furthermore, layers prepared by simply leveling dry alumina powder on plates give quite good separations. Thus, no slurries or elaborate application apparatus are needed. These layers are mechanically unstable and must be sprayed with caution.[70]

The alumina which is used in this manner is normal, commercially available alumina of any desired activity grade having a particle size of 0.1 mm or 200 to 300 mesh. Recently, Woelm has announced a special "Alumina for Thin-layer Chromatography" which is available in acid, basic and neutral grades and which is more cohesive than usual. This enhanced cohesiveness is produced by smaller particle size.

Huneck[165] has published directions for the preparation of a fibrous alumina which is quite cohesive and which forms stable layers with no binder.

Alumina with a Plaster of Paris Binder. This adsorbent is commercially available as Aluminum Oxide G and as Fluka Aluminum Oxide D5 but, strangely enough, few reports have been made on its application. It has, however, been used to separate alkaloids.[436] A reasonable approximation of the commercial product can be prepared[232] by blending Alcoa Activated Alumina,* 200 mesh, with 5 per cent of its weight of plaster of Paris (see p. 19 for preparation of this substance).

Alumina with a Starch Binder. This adsorbent was used by Meinhard and Hall[246] in the first recorded use of a bound adsorbent. However, it does not appear to have been used since and would seem to offer no particular advantage.

Kieselguhr or Diatomaceous Earth

Kieselguhr with a Plaster of Paris Binder. Silica gel is acidic and applicable in both adsorption and partition chromatography while alumina is basic and useful in adsorption chromatography. Kieselguhr completes this picture in that it is neutral[436] and is primarily a support for the stationary phase in partition chromatography. As such, it has a low capacity and is used for the separation of very polar molecules such as carbohydrates and amino acids. The commercial product, Kieselguhr G, has been used in a buffered form (with sodium acetate) for the separation of the simple sugars[377] with reasonable success. Furthermore, it has been impregnated with paraffin[6,183] and undecane[181,185,186] for "reversed phase" chromatography.

Kieselguhr Containing Complexing Agents. Halmekoski made slurries of Kieselguhr G with 0.01 mole of sodium molybdate, sodium tungstate or borax (per 30 g of adsorbent and 65 ml of water) and used the resulting layers for the separation of phenolic carboxylic acids.[136]

Cellulose

The use of powdered cellulose in thin layers was essentially an attempt to carry out "paper chromatography" in a short time. This has been successful. The cellulose is, of course, only a support for the stationary liquid phase and has been used in both normal (impregnated with formamide,[399,400]) and reversed phase chromatography. The capacity of the adsorbent is low.

* Aluminum Company of America, 230 Park Avenue, New York 17, New York

Cellulose without a Binder. The fibrous nature of powdered cellulose permits it to be shaped into stable layers without a binder.[321,450]

Cellulose with a Plaster of Paris Binder. The commercial product, Cellulose Powder MN 300 G, is of this type. Randerath[319] has systematically compared this material with paper for the separation of various nucleic acid derivatives. He found that the cellulose layers gave smaller, more compact spots and better separations in a shorter time (90 min) than paper (6 to 8 hr). Wollenweber[451] found similar results with food dyes.

Cellulose Ion-Exchange Powders. Two cellulose powders, modified to produce ion-exchange resins, have been used for the separation of nucleotides.[316-318,320] These are DEAE-cellulose (diethylaminoethyl cellulose) and ECTEOLA-cellulose (epichlohydrin linking triethanolamine with cellulose). They have been used with a collodion binder [316,317] or without a binder.[318]

A large number of cellulose powders, plain and modified, bound (G series) and unbound, are commercially available (Table 2.4). In fact, several are available which have not yet been mentioned in the literature.

Ion-Exchange Resins

Berger, Meyniel and Petit[29] have reported the use of "Dowex" 1 and "Dowex" 50 (both anion and cation exchangers, 200 to 400 mesh) for the separation of organic and inorganic compounds. They used a 1:1 mixture of the resin and commercial plaster of Paris-bound cellulose, Cellulose Powder MN 300 G.

Polyamide Powders

Polyamide powders are normally used without binders and have been developed by two groups. Davídek and his co-workers[69,71,74] have spread commercially available polyamide powder on plates and used the resulting layers for the separation of such polar molecules as flavonoids and gallic acid esters. Wang and his co-workers[219a,436a] allowed 20 per cent solutions of ϵ-polycaprolactam resin in 80 per cent formic acid to evaporate on glass plates and used the resulting thin layers for the separation of phenols.

A commercial product is now available from Woelm (see Table 2.4).

Hydroxyl-Apatite

Hofmann has reported the use of hydroxyl-apatite (a complex calcium phosphate hydroxide*) for the separation of 1- and 2-mono-
glycerides[155] and of proteins.[153] In the former case, he used plaster of
Paris as a binder and in the latter case, "Zytel 61" (see p. 16).

"Celite"

"Celite" No. 545 with a plaster of Paris binder has been used[414] for
the separation, by partition processes, of steroids. The layers were
impregnated with formamide. Such layers have extremely short developing times (3 to 7 minutes).

"Sephadex"

"Sephadex" G 25, a cross-linked dextran which differentiates according to the molecular weight of the molecules being separated,
has been used for the chromatography of proteins.[82] A modified
adsorbent, "DEAE-Sephadex" has been used for the separation, by
gradient elution, of proteins and nucleotides.[82]

Polyacrylonitrile "Perlon" Mixtures

Mixtures of polyacrylonitrile and "Perlon" (a polycaprolactam
powder) have been used, in a buffered state, to separate anthocyanins
and such very polar molecules as sugars.[36]

Zinc Carbonate

Zinc carbonate with 5 per cent starch as binder has been used for
the separation of 2,4-dinitrophenylhydrazones.[9]

Polyethylene Powder

Polyethylene powder, "Hostalen S," has been used[232] for the separation of fatty acids and their methyl esters.

Calcium Sulfate as Adsorbent

Layers prepared from pure calcium sulfate have been used for the
separation of steroids[243] and lipids.[180] The major advantage of such

---

* Prepared according to Anacker and Stoy[4b]

plates is that they can be mechanically washed like paper chromatograms. Thus, even more spray reagent systems can be used.

"Magnesol" (Adsorptive Magnesium Silicate)

This adsorbent with a starch binder was preferred by Bryant[51] and by Pryor and Bryant[313] for the separation of the essential oils. A commercial product containing no binder but especially prepared for thin-layer work is available.

Calcium Hydroxide with Silica Gel G

Layers prepared from a mixture of calcium hydroxide and Silica Gel G (6:1) and (4:1) have been found to produce good separations in the carotenoid field.[166,449]

"Florisil" (Mixed Silica Gel and Magnesia)

Peifer[296] has described a procedure for the preparation of microchromatoplates from "Florisil"-plaster of Paris (see p. 46).

CONCLUSION

Obviously, any finely divided material having the desired adsorptive, structural or chemical properties can be used as an adsorbent for thin-layer chromatography. Probably, the area which will be developed most fruitfully is the use of mixed adsorbents. Several of these are given above, and others, such as Silica Gel G-Kieselguhr G mixtures, have been reported.[26,27]

It is rather interesting that the one factor which delayed the development of this technique, that is, commercial availability of materials, has now progressed so far that several adsorbents are available (the various types of cellulose) for which no published uses are recorded.

The commercial sources of most of the adsorbents are given in Table 2.4 and the specific adsorbents which have been used for specific separations are detailed in Chapter 11.

TABLE 2.4. COMMERCIAL SOURCES OF THIN-LAYER CHROMATOGRAPHY ADSORBENTS

Commercial Name	Nature	Manufacturer	U. S. Source
"Anisil"	silica gel-magnesium oxide	Analytical Engineering Co., Hamden, Conn.	
Silica Gel Woelm	pure silica gel[1]	M. Woelm, Eschwege, Germany	Alupharm Chemicals, 616 Commercial Pl., P.O. Box 755, New Orleans, La.
Silica Gel G	silica gel with plaster of Paris	E. Merck, A. G., Darmstadt, Germany	Brinkmann Instruments, 115 Cutter Mill Rd., Great Neck, N.Y.
Silica Gel H	pure silica gel	E. Merck	Brinkmann Instr.
Silica Gel HF	pure silica gel with inorganic fluorescent material	E. Merck	Brinkmann Instr.
Silica Gel GF	silica gel with plaster of Paris and inorganic fluorescent material	E. Merck	Brinkmann Instr.
Silica Gel D5	silica gel with 5% plaster of Paris	Fluka, A. G., Buchs, S. G., Switzerland	Gallard-Schlesinger, Chemical Mfg. Corp., 1001 Franklin Ave., Garden City, N.Y.
Aluminum Oxide DO	pure aluminum oxide	Fluka	Gallard-Schlesinger
Alumina Woelm Basic	pure basic aluminum oxide[1]	Woelm	Alupharm
Alumina Woelm Neutral	pure neutral aluminum oxide[1]	Woelm	Alupharm
Alumina Woelm Acidic	pure acidic aluminum oxide[1]	Woelm	Alupharm
Aluminum Oxide G	aluminum oxide with plaster of Paris	E. Merck	Brinkmann Instr.
Aluminum Oxide D5	aluminum oxide with 5% plaster of Paris	Fluka	Gallard-Schlesinger
Aluminum Oxide D5F	aluminum oxide with 5% plaster of Paris and a fluorescence indicator	Fluka	Gallard-Schlesinger
Kieselguhr G	diatomaceous earth with plaster of Paris	E. Merck	Brinkmann Instr.
Cellulose Powder MN 300	pure cellulose powder	Macherey, Nagel & Co., Düren, Rhld., Germany	Brinkmann Instr.
Cellulose Powder MN 300G	cellulose powder with plaster of Paris	Macherey, Nagel & Co.	Brinkmann Instr.
Cellulose Powder MN 300 F254	cellulose powder with an inorganic fluorescent material	Macherey, Nagel & Co.	Brinkmann Instr.
Cellulose Powder MN 300 GF254	cellulose powder with plaster of Paris and an inorganic fluorescent material	Macherey, Nagel & Co.	Brinkmann Instr.
Cellulose Powder MN 300/AC	pure acetylated (10%) cellulose	Macherey, Nagel & Co.	Brinkmann Instr.

Cellulose Powder MN 300 G/AC	acetylated (10%) cellulose with plaster of Paris	Macherey, Nagel & Co.	Brinkmann Instr.
Cellulose Powder MN 300 CM	pure carboxymethyl cellulose	Macherey, Nagel & Co.	Brinkmann Instr.
Cellulose Powder MN 300 G/CM	carboxymethyl cellulose with plaster of Paris	Macherey, Nagel & Co.	Brinkmann Instr.
Cellulose Powder MN 300 P	pure cellulose phosphate	Macherey, Nagel & Co.	Brinkmann Instr.
Cellulose Powder MN 300 G/P	cellulose phosphate with plaster of Paris	Macherey, Nagel & Co.	Brinkmann Instr.
Cellulose Powder MN 300 DEAE	pure diethylaminoethyl cellulose	Macherey, Nagel & Co.	Brinkmann Instr.
Cellulose Powder MN 300 G/DEAE	diethylaminoethyl cellulose with plaster of Paris	Macherey, Nagel & Co.	Brinkmann Instr.
Cellulose Powder MN 300 ECTEOLA	pure anion exchange cellulose	Macherey, Nagel & Co.	Brinkmann Instr.
Cellulose Powder C-1000	cellulose powder with plaster of Paris	Excorna O. H. G., Mainz, Germany	Brinkmann Instr.
Magnesium Silicate Woelm	pure magnesium silicate[1]	Woelm	Alupharm
Polyamide MNP	pure polyamide powder	Macherey, Nagel & Co.	Brinkmann Instr.
Polyamide Woelm	pure polyamide powder[1]	Woelm	Alupharm
"Hostalen S"	polyethylene powder	Farbwerke Hoechst, A. G., Frankfurt a.M., Germany	
"Florisil"	activated magnesium silicate	Floridin Co., P.O. Box 989, Tallahassee, Fla.	
"Sephadex"	cross-linked dextrans	Deutsch Pharmacia, G.m.b.H., Frankfurt a.M., Germany	
Polyacrylonitrile		Farbenfabriken Bayer, Dormagen, Germany	
"Perlon"	polycaprolactam	Farbwerken Hoechst, Bobingen, Germany	
ε-Polycaprolactam resin		Toyo Rayon Co, Nakanoshima, Kita-ku, Osaka, Japan	
"Dowex" 1 and 50	anion and cation exchangers	Dow Chemical Co., Midland, Mich.	
"Celite" No. 545	diatomaceous earth	Johns-Manville, International Corp., New York	

[1] These adsorbents are of an especially fine particle size for thin-layer chromatography and produce mechanically stable layers without binders.

CHAPTER 3

Preparation of Thin Layers

INTRODUCTION

The thin layers of adsorbent used for thin-layer chromatography are supported and held in place by glass plates. The plates may, in theory, be any convenient size, but in fact the size is usually dictated by the apparatus used to prepare the layers. Layers are applied to the plates by spreading or spraying a slurry, by spreading a dry powder, or in the case of small plates, by dipping them in a slurry. The thin film of slurry is dried to produce the thin layer. The layer may then be treated in various ways before it is used.

THE VARIABLES IN LAYER PREPARATION

In general, the variables to be considered are the nature of the adsorbent (Chapter 2), the type of glass support plate, the thickness of the layer and the moisture content.

The Glass Plates

The glass plates used in thin-layer chromatography may be flat and smooth, flat and lightly ground[180,254,328,334] or ridged as shown in the cross-section diagram in Figure 3.1. Flat, smooth plates have been almost universally used, but the ground surfaces are said to increase the adhesion of the layers. The ridged plates are used solely to simplify layer preparation. Thus, one simply pours the adsorbent-water slurry on a ridged plate, wipes off the excess with a spatula and dries the finished layer. The squared-ridge plates (Figure 3.1a) have been advocated by Gamp, Studer, Linde and Meyer,[114] but the rounded ones (Figure 3.1b) are more readily available from normal glass shops,

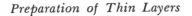

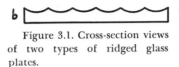

Figure 3.1. Cross-section views of two types of ridged glass plates.

where they are used to make semiopaque windows.* The ridged plates and the microchromatoplate system described later (p. 42) probably offer the most convenient systems for student use. To prevent accidents, all plates should have slightly beveled and smoothed edges.

The size and thickness of the glass plates are essentially dictated if a mechanical device such as those described below is chosen to prepare the layers. It has been found convenient to use, routinely, at least two sizes (exclusive of microplates). The smaller size should be wide enough to carry out concurrent, one-dimensional chromatography on three to four samples (about 2 in. or 5 cm minimum). Most workers allow the solvent front to rise 10 to 15 cm so that an over-all length of 20 cm or 8 in. is satisfactory. The larger size should be a square plate suitable for two-dimensional chromatography of a single sample or simultaneous, one-dimensional chromatography of eighteen or more samples. In a commercial apparatus system, the dimension of the square plate is equal to the length of the small plate (20 cm or 8 in.) and a multiple of its width. Such two-size systems are available with Stahl-type apparatus from Desaga-Brinkmann (p. 37) (5 × 20 cm and 20 × 20 cm) and Research Specialties Co. (p. 40) (2 × 8 in. and 8 × 8 in.). The Kirchner-type** apparatus manufactured by

---

* The author's attention was first called to the use of rounded plates by Dr. Louis Long of the Quartermaster Research and Development Laboratories in Natick, Mass.

** The author has elected to give this name to the type of apparatus in which the glass plate is passed under a stationary hopper because the Kirchner group was the first one to describe such an apparatus.[253]

Camag (p. 36) is normally designed for only one width, but two sizes of apparatus (10 cm and 20 cm width) are available. On the other hand, the Kirchner-type apparatus can be used with any type and thickness of glass, while the Stahl design works best with the plates supplied by the manufacturer. Although soft glass plates are routinely used, "Pyrex" plates are available from the manufacturers of the spreading apparatus.

If layers are prepared by spraying or by any of the simpler techniques discussed below, the plates can be of any size or type.

The original "chromatostrips" of Kirchner, Miller and Keller[193] were only wide enough for one sample (0.5 in.) although these workers also used wide plates. Such small strips are prepared in an apparatus designed by Miller and Kirchner[253] and are still used[383-389] by Stanley and his co-workers. However, they preclude a concentration study in which the sample is applied to a single plate in several concentrations, as well as a more precise comparison of two or three samples. The narrow plates are, however, more suitable for descending chromatography (p. 68).

The use of microscope slides for the preparation of "microchromatoplates" was described by Meinhard and Hall[246] in the first paper advocating the use of bound layers. Lately, the use of such plates has again become fashionable[152,437] and Peifer,[296] in an exceptionally fine paper, has described a complete system based upon microscope and lantern slides (see p. 42).

A somewhat different type of layer support was worked out by Lie and Nyc,[219] who coated the inside of test tubes with thin layers of adsorbent. Rosi and Hamilton[330] have prepared layers on both sides of glass plates so that they may be utilized more efficiently.

The Thickness of the Layer

Within a reasonably wide range (0.15 to 2.0 mm) the thickness of the layers is unimportant with respect to Rf's and the degree of separation. The thickness itself should be prescribed by the type of information or results sought. For diagnostic or qualitative work, very thin layers are best because the spray reagent is much more sensitive when it does not have to "search" for tiny amounts of substance in a large amount of adsorbent. On the contrary, when the work is preparative in nature, it is more efficient to use as thick a layer as possible so that the maximum amount of material can be separated in a single chromatogram.

The minimum thickness of about 0.15 mm was determined by Stahl, Schröter, Kraft and Renz[381] through a study of *Rf* vs. thickness. Only above this value were the *Rf*'s relatively constant (on silica gel layers). The maximum thickness is determined by the difficulty of drying thick layers without cracking and the degree to which there is unequal migration on the top and bottom of a layer. Honegger[158] investigated layers up to 5 mm thick and concluded that the best results were obtained between 1 and 3 mm. Ritter and Meyer,[329] in a similar study, obtained better results with 1-mm layers than with 2-mm layers. The vast majority of diagnostic work has been done with layers 0.25 mm thick because the original Stahl-Desaga apparatus produced layers of this thickness. The Kirchner group[193] used 0.02 in. (0.51 mm).

Thin layers of unbound adsorbents which are prepared by spreading the dry powders on a plate are generally somewhat thicker, ranging from 0.5 mm[269] to 1 mm.[52]

The Moisture Content

The activity of adsorbents to be used for adsorption chromatography is greatly reduced by small amounts of water. Since most thin layers are prepared from aqueous slurries, this variable is controlled largely by the length of time and the temperature used to dry and activate the layers. This will be discussed in detail in a later section entitled "Drying of Layers" (see p. 46).

LAYER PREPARATION

Cleaning the Glass Plates

It is essential that the glass plates be as clean as possible and that they be particularly free of grease. Normally, washing the plates with detergent and wiping them with cotton soaked with hexane just before application of adsorbent will suffice. Sometimes, however, it is necessary to clean the plates with some type of cleaning solution. Peifer[296] has recommended that his microchromatoplates be washed successively with detergent solution, water and finally with 50 per cent methanol-water slightly acidified with hydrochloric acid.

The Preparation of Slurries

As previously stated, the majority of thin-layers are prepared by spreading a uniform film of a slurry of the adsorbent on glass plates and allowing it to dry. Normally, the liquid portion of such a slurry is water, which may contain acids, bases, buffers or complexing agents, and the solid portion is adsorbent and binder. The major problem associated with these slurries is the obtaining of a viscosity suitable for the manner of spreading. If the slurry is too thin, it runs through the spreader too rapidly and produces excessively thin layers. When it is too thick, it does not run through the spreader rapidly enough and may clump.

When plaster of Paris is used as a binder, this viscosity is controlled by two factors: the relative amounts of adsorbent and water, and the time elapsing between the addition of water to adsorbent and the actual spreading operation. The hydration of plaster of Paris ($CaSO_4 \cdot \frac{1}{2}H_2O$) to gypsum ($CaSO_4 \cdot 2H_2O$) is so rapid that the slurry becomes unmanageable in two to three minutes. When buffers or other modifying reagents are added to the slurry, this time is appreciably shortened.[232] The actual mixing of adsorbent and water can be carried out by shaking them in a stoppered flask, by triturating them in a mortar or by stirring them in some other vessel. Table 3.1 shows the amounts of water suggested for various commercially available adsorbents. When possible, the type of spreading device is also given. Commercial sources of the adsorbents have been cited in the preceding chapter.

For the preparation of very thick layers, Honegger[158] suggests that these ratios be slightly modified by decreasing the amount of water. Furthermore, for layers from 3 to 5 mm thick, he added an additional 2 per cent of plaster of Paris and dried the layers under an infrared lamp. His data are given in Table 3.2.

The procedure for preparing a slurry containing starch as a binder is essentially different in that it involves a heating step. Kirchner, Miller and Keller[193] give the following procedure for such a preparation containing phosphors.

"The specified amounts of material [19 g of Merck reagent grade

TABLE 3.1. RECOMMENDED AMOUNTS OF WATER TO BE ADDED TO VARIOUS COMMERCIAL ADSORBENTS

Adsorbent	Adsorbent-water, w/v, g/ml	Apparatus	Ref.
Silica Gel G	30/60	Desaga	Manuf.
Silica Gel Woelm[1]	30/45	—	Manuf.
Silica Gel D5	20/50	Camag	Manuf.
Silica Gel, "Anisil"	15/30	Desaga	Manuf.
Aluminum Oxide G	25/50	Desaga	232
Aluminum Oxide D5	20/65	Desaga	232
	20/50	Camag	Manuf.
Aluminum Oxide D5F	20/50	Camag	Manuf.
Alumina Woelm[1,2]	35/40	—	Manuf.
Kieselguhr G	25/50	Desaga	377
Cellulose MN 300 G	15/100	Desaga	319
Magnesium Silicate Woelm[1]	15/45	—	Manuf.
Polyamide Woelm[1]	5 g in 45 ml of chloroform-methanol (2:3)	—	Manuf.

[1] These adsorbents contain no binder, but are of an especially small particle size.
[2] Same proportions for acid, basic or neutral.

TABLE 3.2. HONEGGER'S DATA FOR PREPARATION OF VERY THICK LAYERS[1] *

Adsorbent	Thickness, mm	Adsorbent—H₂O, g/ml	Air-dry, min	Infrared drying, min
Silica Gel G	1–1.5	1:1.7	5	
	2–3	1:1.6	30	30
	3–4[2]	1:1.6	30	30
	4–5[2]	1:1.57	30	30
Aluminum Oxide G	1–1.5	1:1	5	30
	4–5	1:0.9	10	30

[1] The data were obtained using the Camag apparatus.
[2] Added 2% more plaster of Paris.
* Reproduced from Honegger, *Helv. Chim. Acta*, **45**, 1409 (1962) through the courtesy of the author and Verlag Helvetica Chimica Acta, Basel, Switzerland.

silicic acid passing 100 mesh sieve, 1 g of "Clinco 15" starch, 0.15 g of zinc silicate and 0.15 g of zinc cadmium sulfide] thoroughly blended while dry, were mixed with 36 ml of distilled water in a 250 ml beaker. The slurry was then heated on a water bath held at 85° with constant stirring until it thickened (1.75 minutes) and was then held at this temperature for 30 seconds longer with stirring. The beaker was removed from the bath and 2 to 7 ml of water were added immediately to form a thin paste." As stated on p. 20, a mixture of corn starch and "Superior AA Tapioca Flour" is better than "Clinco" starch. If the amount of starch is decreased by half, it is not necessary to watch the temperature during the heating. The mixture must only be warmed thoroughly to thicken it.

Although water is the most common liquid for the preparation of slurries, several workers have preferred nonaqueous systems. In addition to the test-tube system of Lie and Nyc[219] and the microchromatoplate system of Peifer,[296] which are quoted elsewhere in this chapter, Hörhammer, Wagner and Bittner[160] have used ethyl acetate, Duncan[90] has used water-methanol, 1:1, v/v, and Müller and Honerlagen[270] have used acetone. None of these authors used the conventional spreading apparatus.

Mechanical Devices for the Preparation of Layers

At the present time, these devices fall into three major categories, the Kirchner type (see footnote on p. 31), the Stahl type and the spray type. While these "gadgets" are considerably more expensive and complicated than those used in some of the methods which will be described later, the author believes they have a distinct advantage. They produce uniform layers of any desired thickness in a very efficient manner.

The Kirchner Type. This type of spreading device is characterized by a stationary reservoir or hopper which deposits a thin film of adsorbent slurry on glass plates which are slowly passed under it. The layer-thickness is determined by the distance between the plate and the back edge of the hopper, and the width of the plates is predetermined by the size of the apparatus. The first such apparatus was designed by Miller and Kirchner in 1954[253] to produce "chromatostrips" 0.5 in. wide. The apparatus has since been modified by Applewhite, Diamond and Goldblatt[8] and shop drawings of the modification are available from the authors (Western Regional Research Laboratory, U. S. Department of Agriculture, Albany, Calif.).

A commercial model of this type of apparatus is shown in Figure 3.2 and is manufactured by Camag* in Switzerland. It is based upon the design of K. Mutter and J. F. Hofstetter at Hofmann-LaRoche A.

---

* Camag A. G., Homburger Str. 24, Muttenz, B. L., Switzerland. U. S. representatives: A. H. Thomas Company, Vine Street at 3rd, Philadelphia, Pa. and Microchemical Specialties Co., 1825 East Shore Highway, Berkeley 10, Cal.

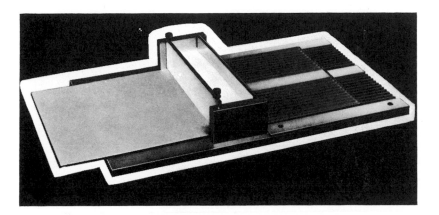

Figure 3.2. The commercial model of the Kirchner-type apparatus as designed by Mutter and Hofstetter. (Reproduced through the courtesy of Camag A. G.)

G. in Basel. Two models of this apparatus are available; one of these (Model A) coats plates 20 by 10 cm for one-dimensional chromatography and the second (Model B) coats plates either 10 cm or 20 cm in width. The Camag apparatus has been slightly modified by Wollish, Schmall and Hawrylshyn.[452] A similar apparatus is manufactured by the Kensington Scientific Corp.* in California.

It would appear to the author (who has had no experience with this apparatus) that the Kirchner type would be somewhat more tedious to use and less flexible with respect to plate width, than the Stahl type. On the other hand, it is less sensitive to plate thickness and probably yields more consistently uniform layers on small plates.

The Stahl Type. This type of spreading device is characterized by a moving slurry reservoir and stationary plates. The plates are arranged in a continuous surface on a support (the commercial models use plastic slabs) having a raised edge on two sides to hold the plates in position during the coating operation. The reservoir, machined in such a way that it produces the desired layer thickness, is then passed over the plates.

The first commercial model of this design was worked out by Stahl and is manufactured by Desaga** in Germany. The apparatus is pic-

* Kensington Scientific Corp., 1717 Fifth St., Berkeley, Cal.
** C. Desaga, G.m.b.H., Hauptstrasse 60, Heidelberg, Germany. U. S. representative: C. A. Brinkmann and Co., Inc., 115 Cutter Mill Rd., Great Neck, N.Y.

Figure 3.3. The Stahl-Desaga apparatus showing, in detail, the variable thickness applicator, a, and the standard applicator, b. (Reproduced through the courtesy of Brinkmann Instruments, Inc.)

tured in Figure 3.3. The spreader is available in two models; the Standard Model which gives layers 0.25 mm thick and the Model S 11 which gives layers of any thickness up to 2 mm. The standard plate sizes are 5 × 20 cm and 20 × 20 cm. Twenty of the small plates or five of the large ones can be coated in a single operation. While the technique works beautifully with the larger plates, the author has had difficulty obtaining uniform layers on small plates. This difficulty has also been encountered by Bennett and Heftmann[25] who solved it by placing a series of the large size plates (20 × 20 cm) under the small ones.* A glass slab or a smooth desk top can also alleviate

* Shandon Scientific Co., Ltd., 65 Pound Lane, London, N.W. 10 (U.S. representative, Consolidated Laboratories, Inc., P.O. Box 234, Chicago Heights, Ill.) manufactures an apparatus to avoid this difficulty. It contains a special leveling device and layer thicknesses are guaranteed to ±0.010 mm.

Figure 3.3a.

Figure 3.3b.

the problem. Sometimes wavy layers are produced by the "bump" caused by going from one plate to the next. As long as the developing solvent is passed in a direction parallel with the spreading operation, this is no problem.

A second commercial model similar to the Desaga apparatus is manufactured in the United States by Research Specialities Co.* This apparatus can also be purchased in a standard model or a variable thickness model. It is shown in Figure 3.4.

Home-made apparatus of the Stahl type has been devised by Barbier, Jäger, Tobias and Wyss,[13] Machata,[227]** Gamp, Studer, Linde and Meyer[114] and Schulze and Wenzel.[349]

Sprayed Layers. The notion of spraying a thin slurry of adsorbent on glass plates has been suggested, notably by Reitsema,[323] who used a small paint sprayer. Bekersky[24] has worked out a procedure using a normal laboratory spray bottle. Dilute slurries of Silica Gel G (15 g to 35 ml of water) or Aluminum Oxide G (20 g to 50 ml of water) are sprayed from a distance of 7 to 9 in. onto plates in a horizontal position. The method produces fairly uniform smooth layers, but the final thickness is unknown and only approximately controllable. The method has not yet been commercialized.

"Poor Man's Layers"

The development of a cheap method for the preparation of uniform, thin layers has challenged the ingenuity of chemists everywhere. This has resulted in the evolution of several acceptable methods. While the author is a firm believer in the more complex spreaders, these methods certainly offer possibilities for student use and for persons who wish to explore the system before investing in an apparatus.

The simplest way of preparing a layer of slurry is surely that of Lees and DeMuria[214] as shown in Figure 3.5. One to three layers of tape, either surgical or masking, but not "Scotch," are put on two opposite edges of a single glass plate or on the outside edges of the outside plates of a set arranged on a flat surface. The slurry is poured

* Research Specialty Co., 200 South Gerrard Blvd., Richmond, Calif.
** A plastic apparatus of this type is manufactured by Applied Science Laboratories, College Park, Penn.

on an open end and smoothed by drawing a glass rod over the plate or plates in a direction parallel with the taped edges. The tape supports the rod and determines the layer thickness. After a few minutes, the tape is removed and the layers are dried. The method is not very satisfactory for preparing thick (ca. 1–2 mm) layers. A similar method was devised by Duncan[90] who used removable metal strips on the edge of the plates to support the leveling rod. In this case, the thickness of the metal determines the thickness of the layer. Duncan used methanol-water, 1:1, v/v, to prepare his slurries. The detail of such a strip is shown in Figure 3.6. Boll[41] arranged a set of plates in an apparatus with raised edges. The slurry is poured on and leveled with a straight edge. Still another method is to machine out an indentation in a large spatula to a depth corresponding to the desired thickness. Such a spatula (Figure 3.7) is then used to level a slurry on a glass plate which is large enough to support the two ends of the blade.* As in many other aspects of thin-layer chromatography, the first mention of this type of thing was made by Kirchner, Miller and Keller[193] who used an arrangement of glass plates, some placed 0.02 in. above the others and serving as support for a leveling rod. Thus, this concept is as old as the method.

Still other workers prefer to pour a slurry of adsorbent in ethyl acetate on a plate and to level it by tipping it.[160] Such layers are said to require no activation and to function satisfactorily in a chamber which is not saturated. The same procedure has been used with aqueous starch-silica gel slurries.[43] A similar scheme was used by Wang to prepare polyamide layers.[436a] He prepared 20 per cent solutions of polyamide in 80 per cent formic acid, poured these solutions on glass plates, leveled them by tipping and allowed them to dry.

A special problem arises with the preparation of thin layers on the inside walls of test tubes.[219] Such layers were prepared and used by the following method. The test tube to be coated (13.5 × 150 mm) is filled with a suspension of silicic acid (no binder) and chloroform (1:2.5, w/v) and allowed to stand for about 5 seconds. The contents are then slowly poured out of the tube in one continuous slow tilting motion. After most of the slurry is discharged, the vessel is held in an

---

* This method was mentioned to the author by Mr. Robert Conkin of the Monsanto Chemical Co., St. Louis, Mo.

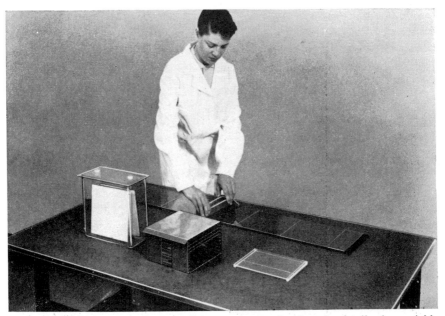

Figure 3.4. The Research Specialities apparatus showing, in detail, the variable thickness appiicator, a, and the standard applicator, b. (Reproduced through the courtesy of Research Specialities Co.)

inverted position for 2 to 3 seconds and then slowly tilted, without rotation, to a horizontal position for drying. The top portion (in the horizontal position) is marked because it is the linear surface where the sample will be placed. An additional coating is placed on the open end of the test tube by immersing the tip end about 5 mm, at an angle of 45°, in the adsorbent slurry. In this position it is rotated once. The sample is placed 1 cm from the open end on the side previously marked. The open end is dipped in a suitable developing solution.

Microchromatoplates

Thin layers have been prepared on microscope slides and lantern slides by spreading a paste with a spatula[246] with an especially designed gadget (for microscope slides only)[437] and using the Stahl apparatus with an alternate arrangement to hold the slides during the slurry application.[152] The author has prepared satisfactory layers using the complete Stahl assembly.

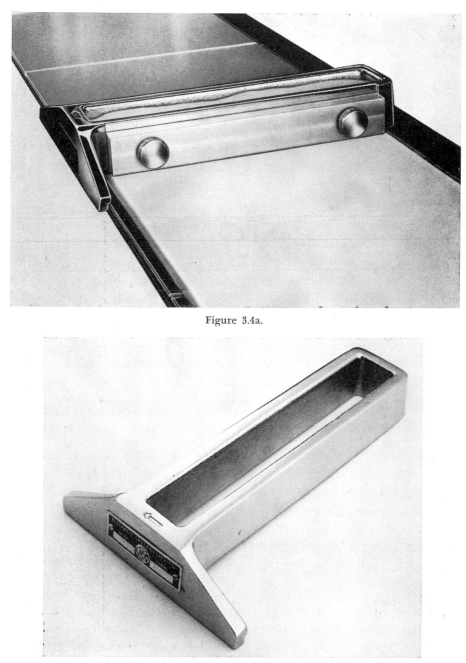

Figure 3.4a.

Figure 3.4b.

Figure 3.5. Preparation of thin layers using tape and a glass rod. (Reproduced from Lees and DeMuria, *J. Chromatog.*, **8**, 108 (1962) through the courtesy of the authors and the Elsevier Publishing Co.)

Peifer[296] has developed a complete scheme for chromatography on such small plates. He uses microscope slides for one-dimensional work and lantern slides for two-dimensional work. The slides, cleaned with detergent, water and water-methanol (50:50) acidified with hydrochloric acid, are *dipped*, two at a time, back to back, into a slurry of adsorbent in a nonaqueous medium. The slurry should be well stirred (about 1 min.) before dipping. They are then lifted slowly out of the slurry and allowed to drain on the edge of the container. They dry rapidly, are separated and the edges are wiped clean with tissue. In order to obtain a more durable layer, the plates are exposed briefly to steam to hydrate the plaster of Paris binder. The steam treatment is not actually necessary with silica gel layers. The layers are then

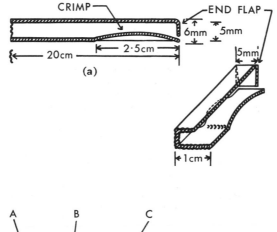

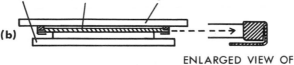

ENLARGED VIEW OF
PLATE WITH SIDE STRIP

Figure 3.6. Detail of Duncan side strips, a, and the side strips in use, b. The side strips are fastened to the opposite edges of a glass plate (B) and held in place by the 2.5 cm long indentation. Slurry is poured on the plate and leveled with a glass rod (C) which rests on the side strips. The apparatus is shown on a mounting board (A). The thickness of the metal in the strips determines the layer thickness. (Reproduced from Duncan, *J. Chromatog.*, **8**, 37 (1962), through the courtesy of the author and the Elsevier Publishing Co.)

Figure 3.7. A machined spatula for the preparation of thin layers.

activated by suspending them about 6 mm over a hot plate for 1 to 3 min. As mentioned previously, Peifer sometimes added sulfuric acid to his adsorbents to facilitate visualization. The recipes for Peifer slurries are summarized in Table 3.3. The chromatograms containing sulfuric acid are visualized by warming them over a hot plate and the others are sprayed in the normal manner.

TABLE 3.3. RECIPES FOR PEIFER SLURRIES[296]

Adsorbent	Slurry Medium	Proportions, g in ml
1. Silica Gel G	chloroform or chloroform-methanol (2:1, v/v)	35 g in 100 ml
2. Silica Gel G and sulfuric acid	chloroform-methanol-sulfuric acid (70:30:2.5, v/v/v)	50 g in 102.5 ml
3. Cellulose powder[1]	chloroform-methanol (50:50, v/v)	50 g in 100 ml[1]
4. Alumina[2]	chloroform-methanol (70:30, v/v)	60 g in 100 ml[2]
5. "Florisil"[3] (60–100 mesh)	chloroform-methanol-acetic acid (70:30:1, v/v/v)	55 g in 101 ml[3]

[1] 35 g of cellulose powder and 15 g of plaster of Paris are triturated with a minimum volume of methanol. The resulting viscous mixture is then diluted to give the above ratio.

[2] 45 g of activated alumina and 15 g of plaster of Paris are triturated with a minimum volume of chloroform-methanol and then diluted to the above ratio.

[3] 45 g of "Florisil" and 10 g of plaster of Paris are triturated with 1 ml of glacial acetic acid and a minimum volume of chloroform. The result is diluted to the above ratio.

Layers Prepared From Dry Powders

The preparation of layers from dry powders of unbound adsorbents is a slightly different problem. The first method was that of Mottier and Potterat[267,269] who used the apparatus shown in Figure 3.8. An even simpler affair is illustrated in Figure 3.9. A glass rod equipped with rubber or tape rings to hold it slightly above the plate and a larger ring to keep it centered is rolled over the plate containing an excess of alumina. This latter system is, of course, based upon the Mottier work, but has been more widely used.[52,71,74,144,146]

Drying of Layers

After the slurry is spread on a plate, it should be allowed to stand for at least 30 min. so that the binder can "set." Indeed it is even recommended by several workers[46,47,249,319] that more durable layers will result if they are allowed to stand in the air overnight. This would prevent cracking due to "casehardening." For adsorption chromatography, the layers are activated by heating them at 100 to 110° for various periods of time, generally one to several hours. There is little change in the activity when the time is lengthened beyond one hour or the temperature is raised above 110°. For layers containing plaster of Paris, the maximum drying temperature is 128° which is the point

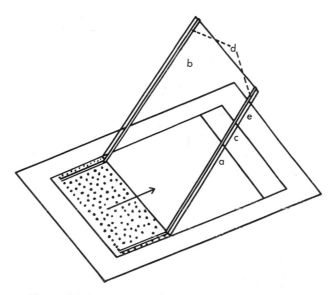

Figure 3.8. Preparation of thin layers of dry, adsorbent powders by the method of Mottier and Pottcrat. The dry alumina is placcd on the glass plate a in front of the moving and leveling guide b. Plate c is a stopping board and d is two rubber bands which determine the layer thickness. Guide b is then moved over the plate. (Reproduced from Mottier, *Mitt. Gebiete Lebensm. Hyg.*, **49**, 454 (1958) through the courtesy of the author and the Eidgenoessiche Drucksachen-und Materialzentrale, Bern, Switzerland).

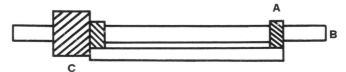

Figure 3.9. End view of a glass-rod leveling device for preparing layers of dry powders. The small spacers (A) are rubber tubing rings placed on a glass rod (B). The large ring (C) centers the gadget. Dry powder is placed on a plate and leveled by rolling the device back and forth.

at which gypsum again dehydrates. For partition chromatography, the layers are normally not activated since the residual water acts as the stationary liquid phase.

Better results with less cracking will be obtained if the layers are

dried in a vertical position as suggested by Desaga. All of the manufacturers of thin-layer equipment sell a metal drying rack which will
hold several plates and which can be placed in the drying oven in
either a horizontal or vertical position.

The activated plates should be stored in a desiccator or dry box of
some type until they are used. The manufacturers of thin-layer equipment provide such containers. However, in the author's laboratory,
the plates are carefully stacked in a normal desiccator over calcium
chloride or, if large, are kept in a large box containing a beaker of
sulfuric acid. After removal from the desiccator, the layers remain
active for a time which is inversely proportional to the relative
humidity. Normally, plates are active for ten minutes or more, but
it is not wise to leave a plate out for several hours during the monitoring of a reaction or the elution of a column.

Other Post-Preparative Operations

The adsorbent sticking to the edges of the plates should be carefully wiped off before using the layers. The layers may then be prewashed[388,389] with an appropriate solvent. A 0.5 per sent solution of
"Versene" (ethylenediaminetetraacetic acid trisodium salt) was used
by Schweiger[350] to prewash unbound cellulose layers. Figure 3.10
shows a suggested[389] apparatus for carrying out this operation.

The finished plates may, at this stage, be sprayed with a complexing
agent such as silver nitrate or boric acid.[260] This serves the same purpose as the incorporation of these substances in the slurry as discussed
in Chapter 2, but spraying is more convenient in that the plates can
be prepared one at a time as needed or in that only a portion of a
plate need be treated. Morris[260] sprayed with a saturated aqueous
solution of silver nitrate or a saturated methanolic solution of boric
acid or both. After spraying, the plates were dried at 110° for one
hour.

On occasion, it is desirable to use partition chromatography in
which the polar, stationary liquid is something other than water. To
this end, Teichert, Mutschler and Rochelmeyer[399,400] have impregnated cellulose layers by dipping them into a 20 per cent (v/v) solution of formamide in acetone. Vaedtke and Gajewska sprayed layers
of plaster of Paris bound "Celite" with formamide, propylene glycol

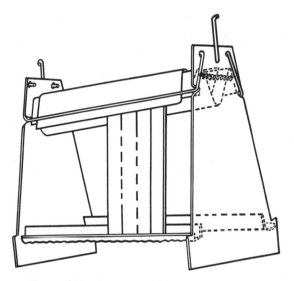

Figure 3.10. An apparatus for prewashing layers. The layers are placed in the apparatus and the washing liquid flows out of a reservoir by means of filter paper and over the layers in a descending manner. (Reproduced from Stanley, Vannier and Gentili, *J. Assoc. Off. Agr. Chemists*, **40**, 282 (1957) through the courtesy of the authors and the Association of Official Agricultural Chemists.)

or paraffin oil.[414] The plates were weighed before and after the spraying to determine the extent of impregnation. Knappe and Peteri[200] added polyethylene glycol (15 g to 30 g of Kieselguhr G and 45 ml of water) to the adsorbent slurry before the layers were prepared. In the latter case 0.050 g of sodium diethyldithiocarbaminate was also added to prevent peroxide formation in the polyglycol. Such chromatograms are developed with nonpolar solvent systems.

The Preparation of Reversed Phase Chromatograms

The impregnation of thin layers with a high-boiling, nonpolar liquid such as Silicone fluid or a hydrocarbon, leads to a partition chromatogram in which the moving phase is more polar than the stationary phase. Such chromatography is called reversed phase chromatography and normally gives improved separations in a homologous series of nonpolar compounds. This has been particularly adapted to the fatty acid series.

Malins and Mangold[230,232] prepared Silicone layers by slowly immersing Silica Gel G layers in a 5 per cent solution of Silicone Oil* in ethyl ether. The operation is carried out at room temperature and both the plates and the liquid must be at this same temperature. In addition, the operation must be carried out slowly. Failure to observe these precautions will produce crumbly layers.

Kaufmann, Makus and Khoe,[182,186] and Kaufmann and Ko[181] have used either a 10 to 15 per cent solution of undecane in petroleum ether (b.p. 40 to 60°) or a 5 per cent solution of tetradecane in the same solvent. Reversed phase layers have been made using paraffin by Winterstein, Studer and Rüegg[449] (5 per cent in petroleum ether) and by Michalec, Šulc and Měštan[249] (0.5 per cent in ether). All of these were prepared by dipping.

Purdy and Truter[315] prepared such layers by allowing Silica Gel G layers to be "developed" with a 15 per cent solution of decane in petroleum ether. A similar process was carried out by Wagner, Hörhammer and Dengler using 5 per cent paraffin in ethyl ether.[431]

After the impregnation, the layers are allowed to dry in the air for a few minutes. The development is carried out with polar solvents.

---

* Dow-Corning 200 fluid viscosity 10 cs. Dow-Corning Corp., Midland, Mich. This preparation is also available from Research Specialities Co. (p. 40) in a spray package for spraying layers.

CHAPTER 4

Application of the Sample

INTRODUCTION

The various factors to be considered in the application of samples to thin layers are the application solvent, the amounts to be applied and the mechanics of the application. These are largely controlled by the type of information or results desired. Thus, for diagnostic or qualitative chromatography a small amount of substance, which need not be accurately known, is applied to a single small spot. This is then developed simultaneously with spots containing possible components of the mixture (reactants, products or known constituents). For quantitative chromatography, a precise amount of the mixture to be analyzed must be applied. For preparative chromatography, large quantities of the mixture to be separated must be applied in a thin uniform band along one edge of a plate.

After the sample has been applied, it can be caused to undergo various reactions which will assist in its identification or will reveal something of its properties.

VARIABLES IN SAMPLE APPLICATION

Application Solvent

The solvent used for the application of samples to thin layers is not particularly critical, but the following factors should be considered. The ideal solvent should boil between 50° and 100° so that it does not evaporate too rapidly but can be easily removed at will. It should completely dissolve the sample to yield at least a one per cent solution, but should be as nonpolar as possible. This allows the sample to be concentrated at the center of the spot and not in a ring around the edge. The application solvents should, in any case, be removed as completely as possible before the chromatogram is developed.

Amount of Sample Applied

The easiest and best way to ascertain this quantity is by experimentation with the specific compounds in question. Every compound or mixture should be investigated at several different concentrations. This can be done on a single plate and, simultaneously, information about trace impurities, relative concentrations and separabilities can be obtained. An amount is then chosen which is large enough to be effectively visualized and to show trace impurities, and small enough to give discrete spots with a minimum of tailing. This amount will depend upon the layer thickness and the sensitivity of the visualization procedure which are inversely proportional to each other. Further, it will depend upon the adsorbent and whether the chromatography is adsorption or partition. The former has a much higher capacity. When the sample is too large, tailing[307] and high Rf values[352] will result.

For diagnostic and quantitative chromatography, samples ranging from 10 to 100 γ are normally used with layers about 0.25 mm thick. For preparative work, amounts ranging from 10 to 300 mg can be separated on a single chromatogram depending upon the size of the plate, the thickness of the layers, the ease of separation, and the type of chromatography.

Specific examples of quantitative and preparative thin-layer chromatography will be given in the chapters devoted to these subjects.

MECHANICS OF APPLICATION

The application of samples to bound layers is carried out by touching the tip of a filled capillary, micropipette, or microburette to the adsorbent layer in a manner analogous to that used in paper chromatography. Multiple applications with solvent evaporation after each are usually necessary. The sample is placed or "spotted" about 2 cm or 1 in. from the end of the plate so that the solvent level will be at least 1 cm below the center of the spot. The diameter of the spot should not exceed 0.5 cm and should be as small as possible. The spot can be kept small by a rapid evaporation of solvent using a stream of dry nitrogen[232] or a low-temperature hot plate.[223,244,253,329] Honegger[157] and Wagner, Hörhammer and Wolff[432] advocate the application of the sample in thin bands about 1 cm long rather than the conventional circular spots. The bands are at a 90° angle to the direction of development. Tate and Bishop[398] applied samples with a thin wire loop (about 1 mm in diameter) rather than the usual capillary and Metz[247] used a paper gadget to make the application point very small.

The manufacturers furnish a "spotting template" to help with the application of a large number of samples. This is a transparent sheet of plastic which fits over a thin-layer plate but does not touch the layer. It is suspended on two side pieces and is marked at 1 cm intervals. The Desaga-Brinkmann model is shown in Figure 4.1.

When a large number of samples must be applied over a long period of time, it is a good idea to cover the layer above the sites of application with a clean glass plate to protect it from moisture.[46]

Diagnostic Chromatography

For diagnostic work, the sample is usually applied through a melting point capillary tube of indeterminate size or a micropipette calibrated in microliters. Such a pipette is furnished by all manufacturers of thin-layer equipment.

Quantitative Chromatography

For this purpose, precise application methods are necessary. A microsyringe* used as such or with a mechanical push-button dispenser (Brinkmann, p. 37) is shown in Figure 4.2. The Agla** micrometer syringe has also been widely used. An appropriate microburette could be used.

Preparative Chromatography

The application of samples for preparative thin-layer chromatography is quite a different problem. Large quantities (50 to 300 mg)

* The Hamilton Company, Inc., Whittier, Calif.
** Burroughs Wellcome Co., The Wellcome Bldg., Euston Rd., London N.W. 1, England.

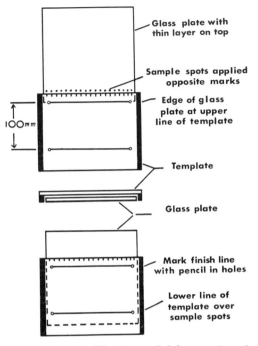

Glass plate with
thin layer on top

Sample spots applied
opposite marks

Edge of glass
plate at upper
line of template

100mm

Template

Glass plate

Mark finish line
with pencil in holes

Lower line of
template over
sample spots

Figure 4.1. The Desaga-Brinkmann "spotting template" in position (Reproduced through the courtesy of Brinkmann Instruments, Inc.)

must be applied in a reasonable time as a uniform band without destroying the layer. Multiple spotting with a single capillary is quite unsatisfactory because it is so tedious and almost always results in a disturbed layer.

The simplest approach to this problem is to blow a fine jet of sample and solvent into the layer from a suitable pipette while moving the pipette in a uniform motion over the plate. The pipette should have a small orifice and the operator needs a deft pair of hands.* Honegger[158] has suggested that the sample be applied in a shallow V-shaped ditch made on the starting line. Care must be taken so that the ditch does not go through to the glass plate.

In addition to these methods, two mechanical gadgets are commer-

* The author has seen this done by Mr. P. J. DeMuria at the Chas. Pfizer Laboratory in Groton, Conn. and it has been reported elsewhere.

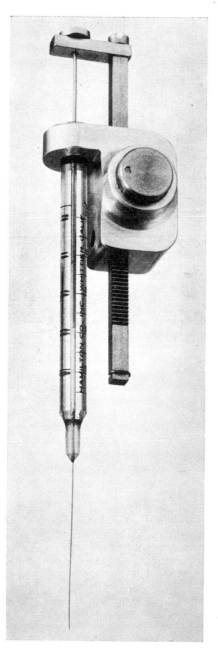

Figure 4.2. Microsyringe with push button dispenser for use in quantitative thin-layer chromatography. (Reproduced through the courtesy of Brinkmann Instruments, Inc.)

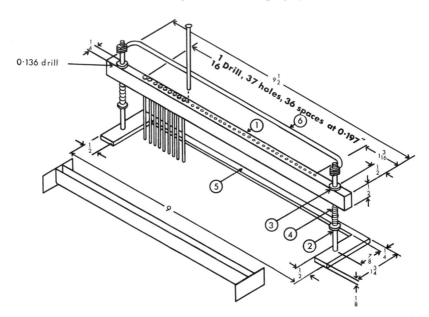

Figure 4.3. The Morgan apparatus for sample application in preparative thin-layer chromatography. The apparatus consists of an aluminum bar (1) with holes drilled near its ends which permit it to slide freely on two vertical ⅛ inch brass rods (2) and is held up against adjustable stop washers (3) by partially compressed springs (4). The top and bottom stop washers are ¼ inch OD and ³⁄₃₂ inch ID and are enlarged slightly with a punch so that they may be forced onto the vertical rods. The bottom washers which support the springs are soldered in place while the top washers remain in place by friction and may be adjusted by forcing either up or down. The two vertical rods threaded, screwed into tapped holes, and soldered in place in the cutout base plate (5) and the upper horizontal tie rod (6) form the rigid support for the apparatus. Thirty-seven precisely drilled ¹⁄₁₆ inch holes spaced 0.197 inch (0.5 cm) on centers in the aluminum crossbar carry the spotting pipettes. These are made from pieces of 1.5 mm OD Pyrex melting point capillary tubing (Corning #9530) selected so that they will just pass through the holes in the crossbar with no friction. A funnel stop is blown at the upper end of each tube, the tubes cut at a length such that the tips will extend to within ¹⁄₁₆ inch of the surface of the chromatographic plate when placed in the crossbar. The delivery tips are fire polished and squared off by grinding on a flat piece of fine carborundum wetted with water. Progress in the latter operation should be observed under suitable magnification and the grinding continued only until the contact surface of the tip is smooth.

A sample trough of suitable volume and design to be used with the apparatus in spotting preparatory plates may be constructed from metal, glass, or plastic depending upon the chemical nature of the samples and solvents employed. A trough of the design shown was constructed of No. 23 gauge Monel metal and has proven to be satisfactory for use with non-corrosive solvents. (Reproduced from Morgan, *J. Chromatog.*, **9**, 379 (1962) through the courtesy of the author and the Elsevier Publishing Co.)

cially available for sample application in preparative chromatography. These are the multiple capillary arrangement of Morgan[258] and the moving syringe system of Ritter and Meyer.[329]

The Morgan Apparatus. The Morgan apparatus is, simply, some thirty-seven capillary tubes arranged in a movable holder and is shown in Figure 4.3 with instructions for its construction. All of the tubes are filled by dipping them into a trough containing the sample in solution and they spot simultaneously when touched to a thin layer. It has been used with great success by the author and elsewhere at the University of Connecticut, and is commercially available from the A. H. Thomas Co.*

The Ritter and Meyer Apparatus. The Ritter and Meyer apparatus is a syringe equipped with a pressure valve that is supported by two bars on which it slides freely. The sample is placed in the syringe, a slight pressure is applied and the syringe is moved back and forth spraying a thin jet of sample. The plate holding the layer is placed on an asbestos-covered aluminum block which is heated to facilitate the removal of solvent. The apparatus is shown in Figure 4.4. It is commercially available from Desaga-Brinkmann (see p. 37).

Sample Application to Unbound Layers

The unbound layers (excluding the Woelm and Anisil special adsorbents) are not mechanically stable enough to touch so that samples are applied in small drops from a short distance away.[52] When unbound layers are developed in a near horizontal position, the sample can be adsorbed on a small amount of adsorbent and placed on the thin layer as such.[269] This latter technique is especially useful if one wishes to rechromatograph a sample on a new layer. The adsorbent containing the sample can simply be scraped off of one plate and applied to another without elution. Samples are applied to Woelm and Anisil layers in the same manner as with bound adsorbents.

CHEMICAL REACTIONS ON APPLIED SAMPLES

Sometimes, it is advantageous to modify or prepare a derivative of a sample after it has been spotted on a thin layer. This can be accom-

* Arthur H. Thomas Co., Vine Street at 3rd, Philadelphia, Pa.

Figure 4.4. The Ritter and Meyer apparatus for sample application in preparative thin-layer chromatography. (Reproduced from Ritter and Meyer, *Nature*, **193**, 941 (1962) through the courtesy of the authors and Macmillan and Co., Ltd.)

plished by adding the reagent to the developing solvent. Thus, bases can be regenerated from their salts and compounds can be brominated or oxidized by putting the appropriate reagents in the developing system. Alternately, a drop of reagent can be added to the spotted sample before chromatography. This technique has been used for oxidation, dehydration, hydrogenation and the preparation of derivatives. These reactions are carried out in the following manner.

Regeneration of Bases

The amine or alkaloid is spotted on the layer as its hydrochloride, and a base, diethylamine[436] or ammonia,[332] is added to the developing solution to the extent of 1 or 2 per cent. A similar reaction was performed in the thin-layer separation of the halide ions[357] by Seiler and Kaffenberger. The halides were spotted as their sodium and potassium salts, but the developing solution contained 10 per cent of concentrated ammonium hydroxide and the ions migrated as their ammonium salts. Mottier[266] neutralized dye solutions before chromatography on alumina by placing a drop of 1 N sodium hydroxide solution on the layer, drying it and then spotting the sample.

Bromination[186]

The sample is spotted in the normal way and the chromatogram is developed by solvents containing 0.5 per cent (by volume) of bromine.

Oxidation

Oxidation is brought about by addition of an oxidizing agent to the developing system or by direct application over the sample spot. Thus, Mangold[230,231,232] separated saturated and unsaturated fatty acids on reversed phase layers with a mixture of acetic acid-peracetic acid-water (15/2/3). The unsaturated compounds were oxidized and moved to the solvent front whereas the saturated compounds were separated in a normal manner.

In an alternate technique,[252] the sample to be oxidized is spotted in the normal way and covered with a drop of glacial acetic acid, saturated with chromic anhydride. The chromatogram is then developed with solvents which are not easily oxidized.

Dehydration[252]

The sample, spotted as usual, is covered with a drop of concentrated sulfuric acid and developed with solvents such as hexane which are resistant to sulfuric acid.

Phenylhydrazone Formation[252]

The sample, spotted as usual, is covered with a drop of phenylhydrazine and then developed with a noncarbonyl solvent.

Semicarbazone Formation[252]

A 10 per cent solution of semicarbazide hydrochloride is neutralized with sodium hydroxide and spotted with the sample. The chromatogram is developed with a noncarbonyl solvent.

Hydrogenation[186]

The spotting region of a layer is sprayed with a colloidal solution containing 1 to 2 per cent palladium in an electrolyte free solution.* The plate is dried in an oven, the sample is spotted in the region containing the palladium, and the layer is exposed to a hydrogen atmosphere in a vacuum desiccator. The plate is developed in the normal manner.

Irradiation[371]

The spotted sample is irradiated with a suitable energy source in the desired atmosphere and developed in the normal manner.

Salt regeneration and bromination normally go to completion but the other reaction products are contaminated with starting materials which can be used, untreated, on the chromatograms as standards. The reactions listed certainly represent only a small portion of the possibilities for this technique.

* The solution is commercially available from Firma Dr. Th. Schuchardt, Ainmillerstr. 25, München 13, Germany.

CHAPTER 5

Choice of a Solvent System

INTRODUCTION

The type of solvent system chosen to make a given separation will depend primarily upon whether the chromatography is adsorption or partition. Adsorption chromatography is the simpler of the two because the solvents are completely miscible in one another and their ability to move a sample follows the normal cluotropic series. On the other hand, partition chromatography involves a selection of a two-phase system which will have desirable partition coefficients for the particular sample to be separated. Furthermore, partition chromatography can be of two types depending upon whether the stationary phase is polar (normal) or nonpolar (reversed phase). An even more complex situation involving various ionic species arises with ion-exchange chromatography on thin layers.

It is sometimes advantageous to add a small amount of some special reagent to developing systems to bring about a desired chemical reaction, to improve separations or to change the layer in some manner.

ADSORPTION CHROMATOGRAPHY

The normal worker will spend more time searching the literature for solvent systems to use in adsorption chromatography than he will in determining these systems by experimentation. This is particularly true since the exact adsorptive properties of layers tend to vary from one laboratory to another. The classic eluotropic series of Trappe,[403] Strain[393] and Knight and Groennings[202] apply to thin-layer chromatography[232] and are given in Table 5.1. The more polar solvents producing the greatest migrations are at the bottom of the columns.

A preliminary study can be made in two ways. The first, devised by Izmaïlov and Shraïber,[169] Crowe,[63] and further developed by Stahl, [366,369,370] is the simpler. It involves the spotting of the sample in several places, an inch or so apart, on a single layer. Pure solvents of various polarities are deposited at the centers of these spots by means of a capillary and the outer edge of the solvent spot is noted. The layer is sprayed or visualized in some manner and the solvent which moves the sample about halfway between the origin and the outer edge is the best solvent. The second way to make a preliminary study is by running chromatograms with various solvents. In some laboratories, a series of chromatography jars containing certain key solvents like hexane, benzene, ether and methanol are kept ready for this purpose. In one of these ways, the ideal pure solvent or a pair of solvents whose properties "bracket" the material to be separated (one moving it less and one moving it more than desirable) are selected. In the latter case, various mixtures are investigated, or a gradient elution

TABLE 5.1. ELUOTROPIC SERIES OF SOLVENTS

Trappe[403]	Strain[393]	Knight and Groennings[202]
Light petroleum	light petroleum 30–50°	heptane
Cyclohexane	light petroleum 50–70°	diisobutylene
Carbon tetrachloride	light petroleum 50–100°	benzene
Trichloroethylene	carbon tetrachloride	isopropyl chloride
Toluene	cyclohexane	isopropyl ether
Benzene	carbon disulfide	ethyl ether
Dichloromethane	anhydrous ethyl ether	ethyl acetate
Chloroform	anhydrous acetone	*sec*-butyl alcohol
Ethyl ether	benzene	ethyl alcohol
Ethyl acetate	toluene	water
Acetone	esters of organic acids	acetone
n-Propanol	1,2-dichloroethane	methanol
Ethanol	alcohols	pyruvic acid
Methanol	water	
	pyridine	
	organic acids	
	mixtures of acids or bases, water, alcohols, or pyridine	

system[334] can be used. The gradient elution technique will be discussed more extensively in Chapter 6.

The author and others[144,232] strongly recommend that developing mixtures be kept as simple as possible. In most situations, a mixture of two components will produce satisfactory results. For example, the author has separated a wide range of compounds such as glycosides, aglycones and nitrogen heterocyclics with mixtures of methanol and ether.

One should not become too concerned about whether the substance to be chromatographed is soluble in the solvent system. There appears to be no direct relation between Rf and solubility. This is probably because migration involves solution from a molecular or amorphous state while normal solubility requires the breakup of a crystal structure. Thus, sucrose and glucose can be moved readily on silica gel by methanol-ether solutions in which they are apparently insoluble.

NORMAL PARTITION CHROMATOGRAPHY

In this case, the substances to be separated (generally very polar compounds like sugars or amino acids) are caused to distribute themselves between a polar stationary phase (water, acetic acid, phenol or formamide) on the layer and a moving nonpolar phase. The nonpolar phase normally consists of two organic liquids having different polarities. Since the actual developing solution must contain a miscible mixture of all three of these components, it is likely that the literature will provide easier information than random experimentation.

The two liquids constituting the nonpolar phase provide the major point of variation for partition chromatography. Within the bounds of mutual solubility, their ratio can be varied to provide a greater or lesser dissolving power for the moving phase. The literature on paper chromatography provides at least a starting point in search for a system and is directly applicable when the layer consists of powdered cellulose[319] or Silica Gel G.[44] The literature summarized in Chapter 11 cites many solvent systems which have been used in thin-layer work.

REVERSED-PHASE PARTITION CHROMATOGRAPHY

In this case, the stationary phase is nonpolar and is usually a high boiling hydrocarbon or a Silicone liquid which has been applied to the layers are described in Chapter 3, p. 49. The moving, more polar phase, might be water, acetic acid, acetonitrile, alcohol, or some combination of these solvents. The method is useful for separating compounds of a homologous series such as the fatty acids or their derivatives. Table 5.2, taken mainly from Mangold[232] suggests several possible solvent systems.

TABLE 5.2. DEVELOPING SYSTEMS FOR REVERSED PHASE
PARTITION CHROMATOGRAPHY*

Solvents[1]	Ratios, v/v	Stationary Phases[2]	Lipid Classes Fractionated	Ref.
Methanol	—	higher paraffins	carotenals	449
Acetic acid-water	24/1	undecane	fatty acids	182
—	3/1	Silicone oil	fatty acids and their methyl esters	230
—	17/3	Silicone oil	fatty acids and their methyl esters and aldehydic cores derived from lecithins	230
Acetic acid-acetonitrile	1/1	undecane	fatty acids	182
Acetic acid-acetonitrile-water	2/14/5	Silicone oil and squalane	methyl-esters of fatty acids	230
Methyl ethyl ketone-acetonitrile	7/3	higher paraffins	cholesteryl esters of fatty acids	184
Chloroform-methanol-water	5/15/1	undecane	diglycerides	182
Acetone-acetonitrile	7/3	undecane	triglycerides	182
Acetone-ethanol-water	6/1/3	polyethylene	methyl esters of fatty acids	232
Acetic acid-formic acid-water[3]	2/2/1	Silicone oil	fatty acids saturated/unsaturated	230
Acetic acid-peracetic acid-water	15/2/3	Silicone oil	fatty acids saturated/unsaturated	230

[1] All solvent mixtures must be saturated with the stationary phase.

[2] Silica Gel G served as a carrier for the stationary phases. Only polyethylene was applied directly to the plates.

[3] Chromatographed at 4–6°. (All others at room temperature.)

* Reproduced from Mangold, *J. Am. Oil Chemists' Soc.*, **38**, 708 (1961) through the courtesy of the author and The American Oil Chemists' Society.

ION-EXCHANGE CHROMATOGRAPHY

The modified-cellulose ion exchangers DEAE and ECTEOLA-celluloses have been used by Randerath[316-318,320] for the separation of nucleotides. He used dilute hydrochloric acid (0.02 to 0.04 *N*) to develop his chromatograms. Determann, Wieland and Lüben[82] used a gradient elution system, adding increasing amounts of sodium chloride to a phosphate buffer (*p*H 7.2), to separate enzymes and nucleotides on "Sephadex." Berger, Meyniel and Petit[29] used 1 *M* sodium nitrate to develop halogen ions on "Dowex 1" and acetic acid-methanol-acetone to separate fluorescein dyes on the same resin.

MISCELLANEOUS SPECIAL ADDITIVES

Several substances have been added to developing solutions for one reason or another. As mentioned (p. 58), bases,[332,436] bromine[186,295] and oxidizing agents[230-232] are added to bring about some reaction with the sample or some part of it. Seiler and Seiler[359] have added small amounts (0.4 per cent) of the complexing agent, 2,5-hexanedione, to facilitate the separation of inorganic cations. Mistryukov[254] added a small amount of decalin to developing solutions to be used on nonbound layers. The decalin increased the mechanical stability of the layer so that it could be visualized by spraying.

Small amounts of acidic or basic solvents are often added to developing systems to facilitate the separation of acids and bases, respectively, and to prevent "tailing" or smearing. "Tailing" is due, among other things, to the presence of more than one ionic species of the substances being chromatographed.[274] Thus, Mangold[232] and others[264] suggest the addition of 1 to 2 per cent of acetic acid to systems for developing chromatograms of fatty acids. In a similar manner, systems containing ammonia[232,256] and diethylamine[332,436] are used for separating nitrogenous lipids and other bases. These additives buffer the system and keep the material being separated exclusively in the nonionic form.

CHAPTER 6

Development of Thin-Layer Chromatograms

INTRODUCTION

The development process, that is, the actual passing of solvents through thin layers to cause separations, is a major point of variation in thin-layer chromatography. Like the preparation of layers, it challenges the imagination of the laboratory worker and many ingenious techniques have resulted.

Thin-layer chromatography has been carried out in an ascending manner on vertical or near horizontal plates, in a descending manner on vertical plates, or in a linear or circular manner on horizontal plates. The development can be performed discontinuously, one pass or multiple pass, in a stepwise fashion with different solvents, continuously or by gradient elution methods. The layers can be scored in such a way that the chromatography is carried out in wedge or modified wedge-shaped areas. The process can be carried out in a two-dimensional fashion with different solvent systems being used in each direction. The layer or the sample may also be modified between two developments. These techniques will be discussed in detail in this chapter.

Finally, the various factors which influence the development or, more precisely, the Rf values resulting therefrom will be considered. These include the nature of the adsorbent and of the developing system, the nature and amount of the sample, the chamber saturation, the use of multicomponent solvent systems and the temperature. Some methods of reporting Rf values and the causes and alleviation of tailing will be briefly discussed.

METHODS OF DEVELOPMENT

Ascending Chromatography

Most thin-layer chromatograms are developed by placing a glass plate, containing the sample on a bound, thin layer, in a vertical position in a closed, saturated system such that the bottom of the layer dips into the developing solvent. After the solvent ascends 10 to 15 cm, the plate is removed, dried, and visualized in some manner. Two or more layers can normally be processed in the same container provided that care is taken to completely saturate the system.

Kirchner, Miller and Keller[193] found that when water is a component of the developing system, the adsorbent layer tends to slide off of the plate below the solvent level. This problem was solved by standing the plate containing the layer on a cotton wad saturated with solvent. The author has observed a similar effect with very polar solvent systems, but found that even though the adsorbent below the liquid surface slides off, enough remains to carry the solvent into the layer satisfactorily.

While the plates are normally leaned against the side of the chromatographic jar or tank, several pieces of apparatus have been devised for holding them. A stainless-steel rack which will hold two large plates (20 × 20 cm) is available from Desaga-Brinkmann (p. 37), but a more versatile apparatus is available from Kensington Scientific Corp. (p. 36). This apparatus, pictured in Figure 6.1, is constructed from glass rods and will hold two plates (10 × 20 cm). It is suspended in a chromatographic chamber such that it can be raised or lowered without opening the chamber and thus allows the equilibration of a layer with the solvent before actual development. Such an equilibration step is recommended for partition chromatography.

When unbound layers are used (p. 46) they must be kept in a near-horizontal position (10 to 20° from horizontal) so that the adsorbent does not slide off. While other schemes have been devised,[254] the simplest method for supporting these plates is that of Mottier and Potterat.[269] As shown in Figure 6.2, the plates are propped in a large

a   b

Figure 6.1. Chromatographic chamber containing a movable plate holding device which can be used to equilibrate thin-layer chromatograms prior to development. It is shown in a raised position, a, and a lowered position, b. (Reproduced through the courtesy of the Kensington Scientific Corp.)

Petri dish or crystallizing dish and the dish is tilted so that the solvent is confined to the portion touching the layer.

Descending Chromatography

The technique of descending thin-layer chromatography has essentially been worked out and applied by W. L. Stanley and his co-workers.[383-385,388] They suspended 0.5 in. wide "chromatostrips"[193] coated with a silicic acid starch layer in an especially designed chamber as shown in Figure 6.3. The developing solvent is carried from the reservoir by a piece of coarse filter paper which is clipped to the top

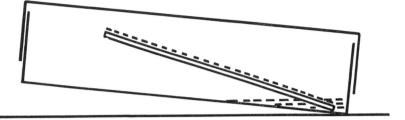

Figure 6.2. Development of a thin layer of unbound adsorbent. (Reproduced from Mottier and Potterat, *Anal. Chim. Acta*, **13**, 46 (1955) through the courtesy of the authors and the Elsevier Publishing Co.)

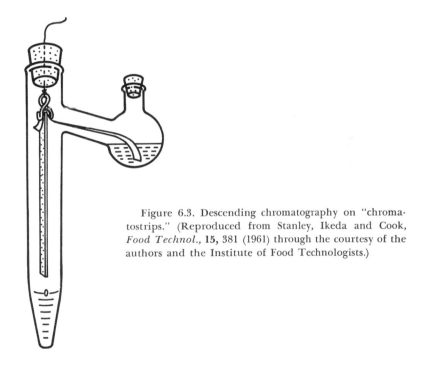

Figure 6.3. Descending chromatography on "chroma-tostrips." (Reproduced from Stanley, Ikeda and Cook, *Food Technol.*, **15**, 381 (1961) through the courtesy of the authors and the Institute of Food Technologists.)

end of the layer. Such a system is advantageous in that it permits a continuous chromatography from which samples of eluent can be removed for analysis.[385] Furthermore, it allows the use of relatively nonpolar solvents over a long time period and gives better separations.

Descending chromatography on wide plates containing the somewhat more fragile Silica Gel G layers has been carried out by Birkofer, Kaiser, Meyer-Stoll and Suppan[36] and by Zöllner and Wolfram.[458] The apparatus of the latter authors is much the simpler of the two and is shown in Figure 6.4. The solvent is carried to the surface of the layer (facing down) by a piece of paper which also helps to saturate the atmosphere. The apparatus has an additional advantage in that a paper chromatography jar can easily be modified for the purpose.

Mistryukov[255] has described an apparatus for the development, by descending chromatography, of unbound layers.

Horizontal Chromatography

Linear. Mistryukov[254] has published a method for carrying out linear chromatography on completely horizontal unbound layers and the continuous chromatography of Brenner and Niederwieser[45,46] as described below is on horizontal layers.

Circular. The original publication on bound layers by Meinhard and Hall[246] involved circular chromatography of inorganic ions and since then, the technique has been used extensively.[51,210,211,246,306,313,368] The sample is placed at the center of a layer and the solvent is fed into the center of the spot with a pipette[210,211,246] or a cotton wick[51] held in contact with the layer. The resulting chromatogram consists

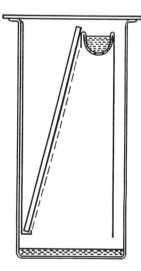

Figure 6.4. Descending chromatography on wide plates. The dotted line represents the layer. (Reproduced from Zöllner and Wolfram, *Klin. Wochschr.*, **40**, 1098 (1962) through the courtesy of the authors and Springer Verlag).

of concentric rings. An alternate method which allows the comparison of several samples involves the placement of samples around and equidistant from a center point. Solvent is fed into the center point and the result consists of a series of chromatograms radiating from the center point. Figure 6.5 shows one arrangement for circular chromatography by Stahl.[368] The apparatus requires a plate with a small hole in it.

Discontinuous Development

Single Pass. The vast majority of thin-layer chromatography has been carried out by allowing a single solvent system to pass through the layer one time. As discussed below, however, there is some reason to believe that better results could be obtained by different techniques.

Multiple Pass. Under the proper conditions, the development of a layer several times with the same solvent (with drying between developments) offers considerable advantage. The technique has been extensively used[158,179,222,269,380,398] and has, in itself, been the subject of two important papers.

The first paper[175] dealt with paper chromatography, but should be equally applicable to thin layers. In it, Jeanes, Wise and Dimler state that the optimum number of passes, n_{max}, can be predicted using Equation (6.1) where Rf_1 and Rf_2 are the values of individual com-

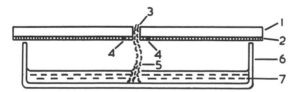

Figure 6.5. Circular thin-layer chromatography.

1 glass plate (20 × 20 cm)   5 cotton wick
2 Silica Gel G layer (0.25)   6 Petri dish cover
3 2 mm hole   7 developing solvent
4 sample spots

(Reproduced from Stahl, *Parfüm. Kosmetik,* **39,** 564 (1958) through the courtesy of the author and Dr. Alfred Huethig Verlag, Heidelberg, Germany).

$$n_{max} = \frac{\log Rf_1 - \log Rf_2}{\log (1 - Rf_2) - \log (1 - Rf_1)} \qquad (6.1)$$

pounds or Equation (6.2) where R_F is the average Rf value of the

$$n_{max} = \frac{1}{R_F} - 1 \qquad (6.2)$$

compounds. In the second paper[401] which does discuss thin-layer chromatography, Thoma gives Equation (6.3) for the calculation (using the same symbols as 6.1 and 6.2). It is apparent from these equations

$$n_{max} = \frac{-1}{\ln_e (1 - R_F)} \qquad (6.3)$$

that systems with low Rf values (0.2 or less) can be greatly assisted by repeated developments while those systems with high Rf values cannot. Thoma was able to show that better separations were, in fact, obtained by several developments with a less polar solvent system than by one development with a more polar one.

Stepwise Development. Stahl and his co-workers[369,378] devised a technique in which the layer was developed twice to differing heights with different solvent systems. Such a system is ideal when the sample contains a group of similar polar molecules and a group of similar nonpolar molecules. The chromatogram is first developed halfway (about 6 to 7 cm) with a polar system which deposits the nonpolar compounds at the solvent front about halfway up the layer and resolves the polar mixture in the bottom half of the chromatogram. The chromatogram is removed, dried and developed with a nonpolar solvent system. This system passes over the separated polar substances and resolves the nonpolar mixture in the top half of the chromatogram. This method is illustrated in Figure 6.6[378] by the separation of a mixture of glycosides (polar) and aglycones (nonpolar). Similar schemes have been used by Billeter and Martius[35] for the separation of the K vitamins and by Mangold and Kammereck[233] for the separation of lipid derivatives.

Weicker[438] used still a third step for the separation of complex lipid mixtures. He first developed silica gel layers to 3 cm with propanol-ammonia (2:1). This carried the fatty acids, cholesterol and cholesterol esters to the solvent front and resolved lecithins and polar

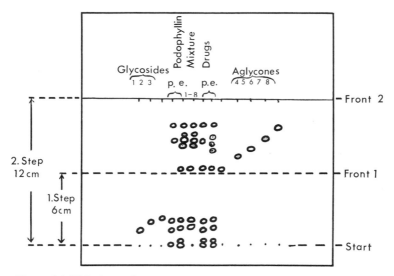

Figure 6.6. Thin-layer chromatography of *Podophylum* components using a stepwise technique. 1. α-Peltatin-β-D-glucoside, 2. Podophyllotoxin glucoside; 3. β-Peltatin-β-D-glucoside; 4. 4'-Demethylpodophyllotoxin; 5. α-Peltatin; 6. Podophyllotoxin; 7. β-Peltatin; 8. 1-Deshydroxypodophyllotoxin. The plant extracts (marked podophyllin) and the drugs of two species of *Podophyllum, peltatum* L. (p) and *P. emodi* Wall (e) are shown along with a synthetic mixture of the eight compounds. The adsorbent was Silica Gel G and the solvent systems for steps 1 and 2 were 10% methanol in chloroform and 35% acetone in chloroform respectively. (Reproduced from Stahl and Kaltenbach, *J. Chromatog.*, **5**, 548 (1961) through the courtesy of the authors and the Elsevier Publishing Co.)

lipids. A second development with chloroform-benzene (3:1) to 10 cm resolved the fatty acids and free cholesterol and carried the cholesterol esters to the solvent front. The layer was then rotated 180° and developed to a height of 4 cm with carbon tetrachloride to resolve cholesterol esters.

Still another variation[413] involves replacement of old adsorbent with new, and subsequent chromatography. Thus, in the separation of lipids, the crude mixture is developed first with ether-petroleum ether (5:95) on an unbound alumina layer. This moves the triglyceride fraction and the cholesterol esters. The adsorbent containing these components is removed and they are then assayed. The portion of the plate which contained these components is then cleaned and a new layer added. Development with petroleum ether-ether-acetic acid (94.5:5:0.5), then moves and separates cholesterol, fatty acids and phospholipids on the new layer and they are subsequently removed and assayed.

Gradient Elution. Rybicka[334,335] and Determann, Wieland, and Lüben[82] have developed apparatus for gradient elution of thin-layer chromatograms, that is, for changing the solvent during the actual course of development. In this case a chromatography jar equipped with a magnetic stirrer is used. The chromatogram is dipped into one solvent (the less polar) in the bottom of the jar. Simultaneously, a second solvent (the more polar) is added from a burette which is connected to a glass tube extending through a hole in the top of the jar to the solvent surface. As the development and the addition continue, the properties of the solvent system slowly approach those of the added solvent. Using this technique, Rybicka separated glycerides[334,335] on silica gel layers, Hofmann[153] separated proteins on hydroxyl-apatite and Determann, Wieland and Lüben[82] separated enzymes and nucleotides on "DEAE-Sephadex."

Chromatography in Shaped Areas. Sometimes, layers are scored or divided with a sharp object into various shaped areas such as is shown in Figure 6.7. These shapes are such that the solvent enters through a narrow area of the layer and is forced to expand into the wider areas. The method was introduced by Mottier[266] who used shape 6.7a in unbound alumina layers. Shapes 6.7b and 6.7c have been used by Stahl[368] and Peereboom and Beekes[295] and a wedge shape, 6.7d, is preferred by Prey, Berbalk and Kausz.[307] The result of such a chromatogram is that the horizontal dimension of the spots is increased and the vertical dimension is decreased. The resulting narrow bands allow a greater number of compounds to be more completely separated than usual. An additional advantage of this technique is that small quantities of one component can be found in the presence of a large amount of another.[307] The chromatogram 6.7c is the result of the separation of a mixture of one hundred parts of saccharose to one part of raffinose.

Two-Dimensional Chromatography. Sometimes, more components are in a mixture than will separate clearly on a one-dimensional strip. Or, perhaps, the mixture contains substances that differ from one

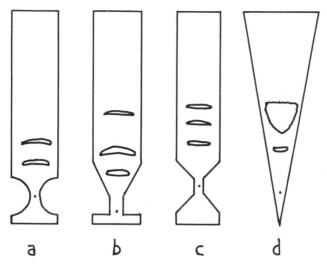

Figure 6.7. Chromatography in shaped areas according to Mottier,[266] a, Stahl,[368] b, Peercboom and Beekes,[295] c, and Prey, Berbalk and Kausz,[307] d.

another so much that two solvent systems should be used. In these situations chromatography is often carried out in two directions which are perpendicular to one another. The general procedure is as follows. The sample is spotted in one corner of a square layer and developed so that the components are resolved along one edge of the plate. The chromatogram is then removed from the developing jar, dried and placed in a second solvent so that the previously formed component spots along the bottom of the plate are again submitted to chromatography. Such a system has been used extensively in thin-layer chromatography.[21,44,46,87,182,184,193,221,269,317,352,371] The major point of variation in this technique is what is done to the solvent system or to the layer between the two developments.

Normally, two different solvent systems are used in the two developments so that the sample is exposed to the broadest possible conditions. The layer can be modified between the developments by dipping it in a hydrocarbon or a Siliconc oil solution[232] to make a reversed phase chromatogram. The latter system has been especially useful in the lipid field where adsorption chromatography is used in one direction to separate the lipid classes and reversed phase chromatography is used in the second direction to resolve the classes. Anet[5] has actually changed the adsorbent between developments. He first chromatographed 2,4-dinitrophenylhydrazones on Silica Gel G in one direction with toluene-ethyl acetate (3:1); then scraped off the adsorbent above the row of spots and replaced it with Aluminum Oxide G, and finally developed with the same solvent in the new adsorbent. The layers were made in each case with the modified[452] Camag apparatus (see p. 36).

Any of the modifying reactions listed in Chapter 3 (p. 57) can be carried out after the first development. Thus, hydrogenation,[186] bromination[186] or irradiation[371] sometimes modifies a mixture in such a way that the compounds which did not separate in the first development will do so in the second. This technique, called separation-reaction-separation by Stahl,[371] is clearly shown in the chromatogram in Figure 6.8 prepared by Stahl, where an irradiation reaction was carried out between separations. The chromatogram also shows the use of standards.

Continuous Development

Continuous development, or elution through a thin layer of adsorbent, offers two advantages. First, samples can be eluted off the end of the chromatogram, thus allowing the separation of mixtures containing components of widely differing polarities. Second, it allows the use of a relatively nonpolar solvent system over a long period of time. In this respect, it should be noted that a very polar developer tends, not only to move things too fast, but to override small differences between mixture components. Of course, with increased developing times, the spots diffuse more and separations become less sharp.

One method which has been used for this purpose (p. 68) is descending chromatography.[385,388] In this technique, the solvent drips from the bottom of the layer into the chromatography chamber and can be collected easily. A commercial apparatus is available from Research Specialities Co. (see p. 40) for this purpose. The apparatus is similar to that shown in Figure 6.3 except that there is an opening in the bottom of the chamber.

A second approach for continuous development has been described

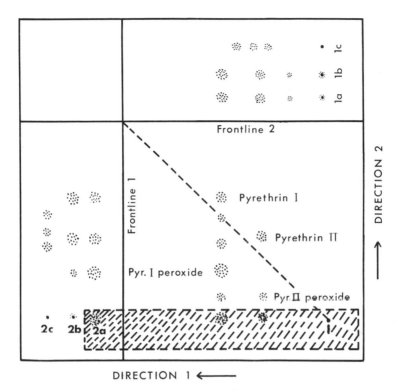

Figure 6.8. Thin-layer chromatography of pyrethrins by the separation-reaction separation-technique. The irradiation (dotted line area) was performed after the first separation. The same solvent system, 25% ethyl acetate in hexane, was used for both separations. The sample was initially placed at 1. Spots 1a, 1b and 2a and 2b are different concentrations of the starting mixture which will be developed in only one direction in order to orient the results of the two dimensional chromatogram. Spots 1c and 2c are a commercial (Desaga-Brinkmann) dye mixture of butter yellow, indophenol and Sudan Red G which is used to calibrate the layer and validate the *Rf* values given. The adsorbent was Silica Gel G. (Reproduced from Stahl, *Arch. Pharm.*, **293/65,** 531 (1960) though the courtesy of the author and Verlag Chemie.)

by Brenner and Niederwieser.[45,46] In this technique, the solvent is carried by a paper wick to one edge of a thin layer, passes through it and evaporates at the opposite edge. Samples cannot be taken from the end of the layer in this apparatus, which is illustrated in Figure 6.9. This has been used for the separation of amino acids[99] and for

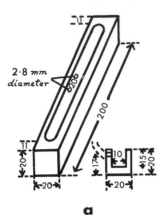

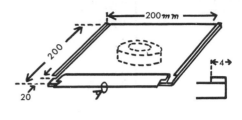

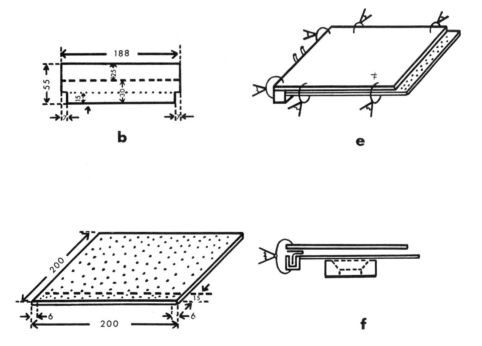

Figure 6.9. Brenner-Niederwieser apparatus for continuous, horizontal thin-layer chromatography. All measurements are in mm. Drawing a shows the steel solvent trough and the holes which feed solvent into it. Drawing b is the filter paper wick which carries the solvent to the layer. Drawing c shows a thin layer which has been spotted on a line 15 mm from the bottom and from which the adsorbent has been removed on the outermost 6 mm of the sides. Drawing d shows the layer in place on a cork ring with the wick in place and a detail of the edge strip which will support the cover plate. Drawing e shows a top view of the assembled apparatus and drawing f shows a side view (without the edge strips). In operation the sample is applied, the apparatus is assembled and the solvent is added. (Reproduced from Brenner and Niederwieser, *Experientia*, **17**, 237 (1961) through the courtesy of the authors and Birkhaeuser Verlag).

preparative separations.[158] A commercial apparatus is available from Desaga-Brinkmann (see p. 37).

Essentially the same thing has been accomplished in a simpler fashion by developing in chambers without lids or by using a chamber shorter than the layer is long. In the latter case, a cover with a slit for the plate is used as shown in Figure 6.10a. The solvent evaporates after it emerges from the slit. The author has carried out continuous development by placing a piece of filter paper over the top of the plate as shown in Figure 6.10b. The filter paper is held in place with rubber bands or paper clips and leads the solvent over the top of the plate.

Layer Electrophoresis

Electrophoresis has been carried out on thin layers by Honegger[156] and by Pastuska and Trinks.[291] Honegger used Silica Gel G, Kieselguhr G and Aluminum Oxide G for the separation of amines and amino acids and combined the two processes of thin-layer chromatography and electrophoresis. That is, he separated a mixture by chromatography in one dimension and subjected the results to electrophoresis in the second dimension. Pastuska and Trinks investigated amino acids, phenols, amines and dyes. In both cases, the layer was

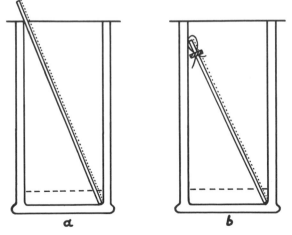

Figure 6.10. Simple arrangements for continuous thin-layer chromatography.

impregnated with an appropriate electrolyte and current was transmitted to the layer with filter paper moistened with electrolyte.

REPRODUCIBILITY OF R*f* VALUES

One of the major disadvantages of thin-layer chromatography is that R*f* values of substances are not exactly reproducible, at least from one laboratory to another. Furthermore, different samples of the same compound sometimes show slightly different behavior *even on the same layer.* These difficulties are more common in adsorption thin-layer chromatography and are probably traceable to the complexity of surface adsorption or to the fact that no two laboratories prepare layers in exactly the same manner. Many workers[47,112,144,146,227,252,290] have commented extensively on this problem and their remarks will be summarized by considering the various factors which determine and affect R*f* values.

Nature of the Adsorbent

The nature of the adsorbent and the thickness and moisture content of the layers are major factors in the determination of R*f* values and have been discussed previously in this book. The use of standard, commercial adsorbents, layer thicknesses over 0.15 mm and consistent drying times will largely reduce the variations. It has been noted,[47] however, that there is an appreciable difference between batches of Silica Gel G. The worker should also remember that an activated layer becomes less active after exposure to a moist atmosphere for appreciable times.

Developing System

The nature of the developing system is, of course, a prime factor in any discussion of R*f* values and should be controlled as closely as possible by the use of reagent grade solvents. Solvent mixtures should be made up frequently. This is especially true when very volatile solvents such as ether or pentane are being used. The mere opening of a chamber containing such a volatile solvent in a mixture can change the concentration appreciably.

Nature and Amount of Applied Sample

The nature of the sample, that is the properties of its components, is the third major factor in the determination of Rf values and is not controllable. The amount of sample does not have too much effect so long as it does not exceed the capacity of the system. Above this point, the Rf increases[352] or decreases and tailing or bearding results, depending upon whether the substance has a convex or a concave adsorption isotherm (see p. 82). The worker is urged to look at a given compound or mixture at several concentrations since the capacity of a layer will vary from one substance to another.[47]

The Rf of a given substance may not be exactly the same in a mixture as it is in the pure state.[288] If a given compound is suspected to be present in a mixture, this should be confirmed by chromatographing a pure sample against a mixture of the pure compound and the substance under investigation. The appropriate spot should increase in size if the compound is, in fact, a component.

Saturation of the Chamber

Care should be taken to saturate the chromatographic chamber with solvent as completely as possible before use.[369] This is normally accomplished by partially lining the walls with filter paper which dips into the solvent and, when possible, by shaking the chamber before the introduction of the chromatogram.[47] Such saturation (called oversaturation by Stahl) will speed up development by about one-third,[232] will give lower, but more consistent Rf values and will produce straighter solvent fronts and rounder spots.

The so-called "edge effect,"[42,369] that is, the difference in Rf values between the center and the edge of the plate, can largely be cured by complete chamber saturation if the layers have a fairly consistent thickness.

Multicomponent Developing Systems

There are two factors which should be watched when the developing system consists of several solvents. The first, as noted above, is the evaporation of the more volatile components and the second is the variation in concentration which will occur as the solvent front moves up the layer. To alleviate this latter situation, Brenner, Niederwieser, Pataki and Fahmy[47] recommended that the ratio of the distance from the solvent level to the sample origin and the total distance traveled by the solvent front be kept constant when precise Rf values are being measured.

Temperature

Variations in temperature have little effect on thin-layer chromatography.[47] This is in contrast to the situation with paper chromatography where it is quite important. This is understandable where adsorption chromatography is concerned, but less so when the chromatography is partition.

REPORTING R*f* VALUES

When reporting Rf values, it is a good idea to report the Rf values of some universally available substance or substances in the system used. The dye system of Stahl (butter yellow-indophenol-Sudan Red G)[369] is readily available (from Desaga-Brinkmann) and is satisfactory for certain ranges of adsorption chromatography. As an alternate method, Dhont and de Rooy[84,85] reported R_B values (sample migration/migration of butter yellow) for 2,4-dinitrophenylhydrazones and 3,5-dinitrobenzoates; Peereboom[293] reports R_A values (sample migration/migration of dibutyl sebacate) for various esters used as plasticizers; and Lisboa and Diczfalusy[221] report R_{OE1} values (sample migration/migration of estrone) for steroids.

TAILING

This bothersome phenomenon can normally be attributed to two factors, both of which have been discussed previously. The first, that is, the presence of various ionic species of acids and bases, can be alleviated by the addition of small quantities of acids and bases to the developing system (p. 65). The second factor is sample overloading such that one is working in the nonlinear portions of the isotherms of the substances being separated.* If the isotherms are convex, tail-

---

* This is discussed in considerable detail by Hagdahl on pages 63 and 64 and by Giddings and Keller on page 96 in Heftmann's book "Chromatography."[142]

ing will occur in concentrations above the linear range. If they are concave, bearding or tails which precede the sample will result. In any case, the situation can be improved by working at lower concentrations.

CHROMATOGRAPHY CHAMBERS

Any wide-mouth jar or bottle which can be completely sealed will serve as a chromatography chamber. The ideal chamber is not too much larger than the plates which are to be developed so that chamber saturation is rapid and, further should have a fairly flat bottom so that the plate will be straight. Special chambers are available from all of the manufacturers of thin-layer equipment.

CHAPTER 7

Visualization

INTRODUCTION

The visualization of developed thin-layer chromatograms can be carried out in many ways. The method used in a specific case will depend upon the type of compounds to be visualized, the nature of the adsorbent and the purpose of the chromatogram. Most visualization methods involve a spray reagent, but other techniques are available.

The inorganic character of most thin layers permits the use of corrosive spray reagents such as sulfuric acid, nitric acid, chromic acid or mixtures of these. These acids will convert almost any organic compound to carbon and thereby serve as universal reagents. The applicability of such reagents constitutes one of the major advantages of thin-layer chromatography. In addition, those specific spray reagents which have been developed for paper chromatography and which do not involve a mechanical washing step can be used.

The majority of spray reagents are destructive in that they destroy or modify the materials which they visualize. In preparative thin-layer work or in quantitative work where the sample is to be eluted before assay, such destructive methods cannot be used. Techniques for surmounting this problem will be discussed in Chapters 9 and 10.

Visualization techniques involving the presence of phosphors or fluorescent substances in thin-layer adsorbents have been developed as well as methods depending upon the relative transparencies of adsorbent and adsorbed compounds when sprayed with the proper reagent. Finally, techniques of radiochemistry and bioassay have been applied to the problem of visualization.

CORROSIVE AND UNIVERSAL SPRAY REAGENTS

With the exception of iodine, these reagents are strong dehydrating and oxidizing systems which function by converting organic compounds to carbon. The reagents are sprayed on the chromatograms which are subsequently heated to about 100°, and the organic compounds appear as black spots. The system is not without flaws, however. When layers containing silver nitrate are sprayed with sulfuric acid,[260] a very strong oxidizing system is produced which oxidizes the organic compounds to carbon dioxide. A second difficulty arises when the compound is very unreactive or volatilizes before it chars. In the case of camphor,[193] this difficulty was solved by spraying the chromatogram with concentrated sulfuric acid containing 5 per cent nitric acid. The sprayed chromatogram was placed, face down, on a glass cloth and heated on a hot plate registering approximately 500°. After the acid fumes ceased to come off, the glass plate was removed and the layer (which had come loose from the plate) was turned over with the glass cloth. The compounds showed as black spots. Such a volatility has been utilized by Baehler,[10] who visualized chromatograms by subliming the resolved compounds out of the adsorbent layer on to a cooled plate held 1 mm above the heated layer (see p. 115).

Iodine, either in a spray or as a vapor, is an exceptionally fine universal reagent and has been used extensively (see Table 7.1). It appears to concentrate itself in the region containing an organic compound,[219,244] thus producing a brown spot. The normal technique is to spray with 1% solution of iodine in methanol or to place the layer in a closed container with a few crystals of iodine. In either case, the spots fade rapidly and must be marked quickly. Under normal conditions, the reagent does not appear to modify the adsorbed substances.[17,230,244] If one wishes more permanent spots, the layers can be sprayed with a 0.5 per cent solution of benzidine in absolute ethanol while the iodine spots are still visible.[6]

A number of universal reagents are given in Table 7.1.

SPECIFIC SPRAY REAGENTS

In general, paper chromatographic spray systems which do not require mechanical washing are applicable to thin layers. If, however,

TABLE 7.1. UNIVERSAL SPRAY REAGENTS USED IN
THIN-LAYER CHROMATOGRAPHY

Reagent	Composition and Use	Ref.
1. Conc. H_2SO_4	Spray with acid and heat to 100–110°.	193 and many others
50% H_2SO_4	Spray with reagent and heat to 200°. Observe in daylight and U.V.	25, 26, 27, 262, 264, 310, 420
2% H_2SO_4 in H_2O-EtOH (1:1)	Spray with reagent and heat to 100°.	221
H_2SO_4 in acetic anhydride	Spray with H_2SO_4-acetic anhydride (1:3) and heat.	363, 368, 378
2. H_2SO_4-$KMnO_4$	Sol. A: 0.5 g $KMnO_4$ in 15 ml conc. H_2SO_4[1] a. Spray with A. b. Heat.	19, 98
3. H_2SO_4-$Na_2Cr_2O_7$	Sol. A: 3 g $Na_2Cr_2O_7$ in 20 ml H_2O diluted with 10 ml conc. H_2SO_4 a. Spray with A. b. Heat.	98
H_2SO_4-$K_2Cr_2O_7$	Spray with sat. sol. of $K_2Cr_2O_7$ in conc. H_2SO_4 and heat.	95
H_2SO_4-chromic acid	Spray with a sat. sol. of chromic acid in conc. H_2SO_4 and heat.	232
4. H_2SO_4-HNO_3	Spray with H_2SO_4-HNO_3 (1:1) and heat.	110,
	Spray with 5% HNO_3 in H_2SO_4 and heat.	190, 191, 193, 252
5. $HClO_4$	Spray with 2% (or 25%) sol. and heat to 150°.	247, 296
	Allow 70% acid to diffuse into the layer at right angle to developing direction.	70
6. I_2	Spray with 1% of I_2 in MeOH. Place in closed chamber containing I_2 crystals.	119, 130, 183, 186, 230, 232, 234, 235, 244, 249, 292, 361, 397, 420
I_2-benzidine	Spray I_2 treated layer with 0.5% sol. of benzidine in absolute EtOH.	6

[1] Large quantities of $KMnO_4$ can lead to the formation of explosive manganese heptoxide.

Silica Gel G layers are treated with dichlorodimethylsilane,[185] they are stable enough to be washed. The procedure is to place the layer in a vacuum desiccator with the silane and evacuate it to 300 mm for fifteen minutes. The layer is removed and allowed to stand for thirty minutes. It is then stable enough to be dipped in aqueous solutions.

A number of specific spray reagents are given in Table 7.2. Table 7.3 is a cross reference for Table 7.2.

Explanation of Table 7.2

Reagent. The reagents are listed alphabetically according to the major component of the reagent or, on occasion, the name of the reagent. The minor components as well as some additional names are given in the cross reference, Table 7.3.

Preparation and Use. When several similar preparations have been used, the author has chosen one to put in the table. However, the references apply to all documented applications of the reagents.

The following abbreviations are used to conserve space:

HOAc	acetic acid	PrOH	*n*-propanol
NaOAc	sodium acetate	BuOH	*n*-butanol
EtOAc	ethyl acetate	pet. ether	petroleum ether
EtOH	ethanol	EtOEt	ethyl ether
MeOH	methanol		

Type of Compounds. The types of compounds given cover most, but not all, of the total uses of a given reagent.

Color. The colors are generally taken from a single paper and should not be taken too seriously.

References. The references apply to the main bibliography.

METHODS INVOLVING FLUORESCENCE AND PHOSPHORESCENCE

The preparation of fluorescent and phosphorescent thin layers by the incorporation of chemicals in the adsorbent has been discussed in Chapter 2. Several fluorescent reagents such as 2',7'-dichlorofluorescein (0.2 per cent in ethanol,[232]), fluorescein (0.04 to 0.004 per cent sodium salt in water,[144,227,366]) Rhodamine B (0.05 per cent in water,[165]) and morin (0.05 per cent in methanol[341]) can also be sprayed on thin-layer chromatograms.

In any case, the treated layers cause compounds containing conjugated double bonds to show up as colored spots when viewed in an

TABLE 7.2. SPRAY REAGENTS

	Reagent	Preparation and Use	Type of Compounds	Color	Ref.
1	Acid Violet-7B (6BN)	Sol. A: 1.5% aqueous sol. of reagent. Do not heat over 60° a. Spray with A b. Warm to 100° for 20 min.	cations of the alkali and alkaline earth metals	varies	315, 358
2	Aluminum chloride	Sol. A: 5% alcoholic sol. of reagent a. Spray with A b. Observe in daylight and U.V.	flavonoids	yellow spots	286
3	Ammonia vapor	Expose to vapor.	flavonol glycosides		126
4	Ammonium molybdate-HClO$_4$	Sol. A: 3 g of ammonium molybdate in 25 ml H$_2$O, 30 ml of 0.1 N HCl and 15 ml 60% HClO$_4$ a. Spray with A b. Heat to 110° for 15 min.	universal for lipids	blue-black spots	157
	Ammonium molybdate-SnCl$_2$	Sol. A: 1% aqueous sol. of ammonium molybdate Sol. B: 1% SnCl$_2$ in 10% HCl a. Spray with A b. Dry c. Spray with B d. Heat to 105°	phosphates (inorganic)	blue spots	355
5	Aniline phthalate	Sol. A: 0.93 g aniline and 1.66 g phthalic acid in 100 ml of 1-BuOH saturated with H$_2$O[375] a. Spray with A b. Heat to 105° for 10 min.	reducing sugars	various colors	439
6	Anisaldehyde in H$_2$SO$_4$ and HOAc	Sol. A: 0.5 ml of reagent in 0.5 ml conc. H$_2$SO$_4$, 9 ml of 95% EtOH and a few drops of HOAc a. Spray with A b. Heat to 105° for 25 min. Sol. A: 0.5 ml of reagent in 50 ml of HOAc and 1 ml conc. H$_2$SO$_4$ a. Spray with A b. Heat to 120° for 6 min.	carbohydrates steroids	various blues	377, 441 247

			honeybee larval foods		292
7	*p*-Anisidine				
8	*p*-Anisidine phthalate	Spray with an alcoholic sol. 0.1 M in both *p*-anisidine and phthalic acid	reducing sugars	various colors	350
9	Antimony pentachloride in CCl₄	Sol. A: 20% (also 12 and 16) sol. of reagent in CCl₄ a. Spray with A b. Heat to 120° c. Observe in daylight and U.V.	terpenoids, steroids and essential oils	various colors	117, 171, 286, 299, 368, 394
10	Antimony trichloride in CHCl₃	Sol. A: sat. sol. of reagent in alcohol-free CHCl₃ a. Spray with A b. Heat to 100° for 10 min. c. Observe in daylight and U.V.	steroids, steroid glycosides, aliphatic lipids, vitamin A and others	various colors	13, 21, 67, 68, 128, 129, 141, 145, 171, 223, 247, 257, 287, 368, 371, 382, 392, 415, 416, 457, 460
	Antimony trichloride in CHCl₃ with acetic anhydride	Sol. A: sat. sol. of reagent in alcohol-free CHCl₃-acetic anhydride (5:1) a. Spray with A b. Heat to 130° for 5-10 min. c. Observe in daylight and U.V.	steroids and steroid glycosides		322
	Antimony trichloride in HOAc	Sol. A: equal parts, by weight, of SbCl₃ and HOAc a. Spray with A b. Heat to 95° for 5 min.[375]	steroids		348
	Antimony trichloride in CHCl₃ with SOCl₂	Spray with a sat. sol. of reagent in alcohol-free CHCl₃-SOCl₂ (10:1)	Δ⁴-steroids		145
11	*Aqua regia*-ammonium molybdate-vanadyl chloride	Sol. A: *aqua regia* (3 parts conc. HCl and 1 part conc. HNO₃). Sol. B: 3 ml of 5% ammonium molybdate and 7 ml 5 N HCl diluted to 100 ml with acetone Sol. C: 2 g V₂O₅ and 20 ml conc. HCl boiled until blue green, then diluted to 37 ml with 6 N HCl and to 400 ml with H₂O; 20 ml of this is then shaken with zinc powder until it becomes brown; decant and use immediately a. Spray with A, B and C consecutively	phosphorus in phosphates	blue spots	174

TABLE 7.2—*Continued*

	Reagent	Preparation and Use	Type of Compounds	Color	Ref.
12	Benzidine, diazotized	Sol. A: 0.1 to 0.085 M Na$_2$HPO$_4$ Sol. B: 0.18 g benzidine in 50 ml 0.5 N HCl Sol. C: 2 ml of B diluted with 2 ml 1% NaNO$_2$, allowed to lose its color (3–5 min), treated with 2 ml of 5% urea and finally diluted with 14 ml H$_2$O a. Spray with A b. Spray with C[134a]	phenols which couple		288, 290, 291
13	Bial's reagent	Sol. A: 40.7 ml conc. HCl mixed with 0.1 g orcinol, 1 ml of 1% FeCl$_3$ and diluted with H$_2$O to 50 ml a. Place in HCl atmosphere at 80° for 1.5 hr. b. Spray with A c. Place in HCl atmosphere at 80° until reaction occurs	glycolipids	violet	127, 197, 427, 43*l*
14	Boute reaction	a. Expose to NH$_3$ vapor b. Expose to nitrogen dioxide (from Cu and HNO$_3$)	estrogens with phenol groups	yellow	221
15	Bromcresol green	Spray with a 0.3% sol. of reagent in H$_2$O-MeOH (20:80) containing 8 drops of 30% NaOH per 100 ml.	carboxylic acids	yellow spots on green	42, 105, 106, 107, 193
16	Bromcresol purple	Spray with a 0.1% sol. of reagent in EtOH made just basic with NH$_4$OH or NaOH	a. halogen ions, except F^{-1} b. dicarboxylic acids	yellow spots on purple	357, 200, 201
17	Bromphenol blue-citric acid	Sol. A: 0.5 g of bromphenol blue and 0.2 g of citric acid in 100 ml H$_2$O a. Spray with A	aliphatic carboxylic acids	yellow spots on blue	302
18	Bromthymol blue	I. *alkaline* Spray with a sol. of 40 mg of reagent in 0.01 N NaOH (100 ml) II. *buffered* Spray with a sol. of 50 mg of reagent and 1.25 g of boric acid in 8 ml of 1 N NaOH and 112 ml H$_2$O	universal for lipids	yellow spots on blue	134, 173, 174, 208, 459

No.	Reagent	Procedure	Detects	Color	Ref.
19	Ceric sulfate-trichloroacetic acid	Sol. A: 0.1 g Ce(SO$_4$)$_2$ suspended in H$_2$O; add 1 g of trichloroacetic acid; boil and add, drop by drop, 1.84 ml of conc. H$_2$SO$_4$ until it becomes clear a. Spray with A b. Heat to 110°[375]	tocopherols	various colors	354
20	Chloramine T-HCl-NH$_3$	Sol. A: 10% reagent in water Sol. B: 1 N HCl a. Spray with A b. Spray with B c. Heat to drive off Cl$_2$ d. Expose to NH$_3$[375]	caffeine	rose red	117
21	Chlorine-KI-starch	a. Expose to Cl$_2$ for 0.5 hr. b. Drive off excess Cl$_2$ by waving in air c. Spray with sol. of KI and starch	esters of carbobenzoxy-amino acids	blue spots	456
	Chlorine-toluidine-KI	Sol. A: 160 mg toluidine in 30 ml HOAc; add 1 g KI and make up to 500 ml. a. Expose to Cl$_2$ for 5–10 min. b. Allow to stand in air 3–5 min. c. Spray with A[375]	3-phenyl-2-thiohydan-toins of amino acids		46
22	Chromotropic acid in H$_2$SO$_4$	Sol. A: 10% aqueous sodium 1,8-dihydroxy-naphthalene-3,6-disulfonate-23 N H$_2$SO$_4$ (1:5) a. Spray with A b. Heat to 105° for 30 min.	methylenedioxy group	blue	32
23	Chlorosulfonic acid-HOAc	Sol. A: ClSO$_3$H-HOAc (1:2) a. Spray with A b. Heat to 130° for 5 min. c. Observe in U.V.	triterpenes and cardiac aglycones	violet-brown	405, 406
24	Copper acetate-dithiooxamide on stabilized layers	Sol. A: 20 ml of sat. aqueous copper acetate diluted to 1000 ml Sol. B: 0.1% dithiooxamide in EtOH a. Dip layers in H$_2$O b. Dip layers in A for 10 min. c. Wash with H$_2$O for 30 min. d. Dip in B for 10 min. e. Wash in H$_2$O	fatty acids	green spots on white	180

TABLE 7.2—*Continued*

	Reagent	Preparation and Use	Type of Compounds	Color	Ref.
25	Cyanogen bromide-benzidine	Sol. A: 0.05% benzidine in 2 N HOAc a. Expose to CNBr vapor b. Spray with A	nicotinic acid derivatives	red to brown	117
26	α-Cyclodextrin-I$_2$	Sol. A: 1.0% sol. of reagent in H$_2$O-EtOH (70:30) a. Spray with A b. Expose to I$_2$	monochain lipids	white spots on purple	230, 231, 232
27	*o*-Dianisidine	Spray with a 1% sol. of reagent in HOAc	aldehydes and ketones	yellow-brown	193, 252, 328, 368
28	Dibromo-R-fluorescein	Sol. A: 0.2% sol. of reagent in EtOH a. Spray with A b. Observe in U.V.	glycerides	yellow fluorescent	16
29	2′,7′-Dichlorofluorescein	Sol. A: 0.2% sol. of reagent in 96% EtOH a. Spray with A b. Observe in U.V.	nonpolar lipids, saturated and unsaturated	green spots on purple	8, 28, 120, 230, 232, 234, 235, 236, 264, 333, 334, 364, 420, 423
30	2,6-Dichloroquinone-chlorimide-NH$_3$	Sol. A: 0.1% sol. of reagent in EtOH a. Spray with A b. Expose to NH$_3$	Vitamin B$_6$	blue spots	116, 117
31	2,6-Dichloroquinone-chlorimide-borax	Sol. A: 2% quinone in EtOH Sol. B: 2% borax in water a. Spray with A and B consecutively	phosphate esters	blue spots	293
32	N,N-Dimethyl-*p*-phenylenediamine-2HCl-NaOMe-irradiation	Sol. A: 0.5 g of diamine in 100 ml MeOH with 1 g Na a. Spray with A b. Moisten with H$_2$O c. Expose to U.V. without filter	chlorinated hydrocarbons	green-violet spots	23
	p-Dimethylaminobenzaldehyde in HCl (van Urk reagent)	Sol. A: 0.1 to 1% reagent in 50 ml of conc. HCl and 50 ml 96% EtOH a. Spray heavily with reagent b. Spray lightly with *aqua regia* (for alkaloids)	sulfonamides alkaloids (indole)	blue rose spots	452 376
	p-Dimethylaminobenzaldehyde in H$_2$SO$_4$	Spray with a 1% sol. of reagent in 2% sol. of H$_2$SO$_4$ in EtOH	a. essential oils b. morphine		287, 437

	Reagent	Procedure	Used for	Color	References
33	2,4-D.nitrophenylhydrazine (2,4-DNPH)	Spray with a 0.5% sol. of reagent in 2 N HCl	aldehydes and ketones	yellow to red spots	2, 13, 105, 106, 107, 165, 171, 192, 287, 323, 326, 328, 368, 376
33a.	DPNH-(reduced diphospho-pyridine nucleotide)		enzymes		82
34	Diphenylamine	Sol. A: 1% sol. of reagent in EtOH a. Spray with A b. Expose to U.V.	nitramine explosives	blue spots	216
	Diphenylamine in HCl and HOAc	Sol. A: 10% sol. of amine in EtOH a. Dilute 20 ml of A with 100 ml conc. HCl and 80 ml HOAc b. Spray with diluted A c. Cover with another plate and heat to 110° for 30–40 min.	glycolipids	blue	157, 174
35	Diphenylboric acid-β-amino-ethylester	Sol. A: 1% of reagent in MeOH a. Spray with A b. Observe in U.V.	flavanols, coumarins and their glycosides	varies	379
36	s-Diphenylcarbazone	Spray with a 0.1% sol. of reagent in 95% EtOH	acetoxymethoxymercury adducts of unsaturated lipids	purple to blue spots on rose	177, 232, 233
36a.	Diphenylthiocarbazone	Sol. A: 0.01% of reagent in CHCl$_3$ a. Spray with A	organotin derivatives	orange-red	411
37	Dragendorff's reagent	I. Sol. A: 1.7 g of basic bismuth nitrate in 100 ml of H$_2$O-HOAc (80:20) Sol. B: 40 g KI in 100 ml H$_2$O a. Spray with sol. made from 5 ml of A, 5 ml of B, 20 g of acetic acid and 70 ml H$_2$O II. Sol. A: Warm 2.6 g of bismuth carbonate and 7 g of NaI in 25 ml of HOAc. After 12 hr, filter sol. and dilute 20 ml of the filtrate with 8 ml EtOAc Sol. B: 10 ml of A diluted with 25 ml HOAc and 60 ml EtOAc a. Spray with B b. Colors can be enhanced by spraying with 0.1 N H$_2$SO$_4$[476]	alkaloids and choline containing compounds	orange	88, 157, 188, 227, 273, 332, 344, 427, 430, 444

TABLE 7.2—*Continued*

	Reagent	Preparation and Use	Type of Compounds	Color	Ref.
38	Ehrlich reagent	Sol. A: 1% sol. of p-dimethylaminobenzaldehyde in 95% EtOH a. Spray with A b. Place in HCl atmosphere for 3–5 min.	a. tryptophane metabolites b. gangliosides	various colors	87, 208
39	a. Echt blue salt B (tetraazotized di-o-anisidine) b. Echt blue salt BB (diazotized 1-amino-4-benzoylamido-2,5-diethoxybenzene) c. Echt red salt B (diazotized 5-nitro-2-aminoanisole)	Sol. A: 5% aqueous sol. of reagent a. Spray with A b. Spray with 0.1 N NaOH	phenols and amines, which couple		288
40	Ferric chloride	Spray with a 1% aqueous sol. of reagent	phenols	various colors	287, 292
	Ferric chloride in HOAc	Sol. A: Equal volumes of 5% aqueous $FeCl_3$ and 2 N HOAc a. Spray with A	pyrazolones		227
	Ferric chloride-$K_3Fe(CN)_6$	Sol. A: 1 volume 5% aqueous $K_3Fe(CN)_6$, 2 volumes 10% aqueous $FeCl_3$ and 8 volumes H_2O a. Spray with A	phenacetin phenols chlorinated hydrocarbons	blue	117 98 43
41	Ferrous ammonium sulfate-potassium thiocyanate	Spray with a mixture of the two aqueous solutions	peroxides		242
42	Fluorescein	Sol. A: 0.004% aqueous sol. of sodium fluorescein a. Spray with A b. Observe in U.V.	conjugated double-bond systems		82, 227
	Fluorescein-Br_2	Sol. A: 0.04% aqueous sol. of sodium fluorescein a. Spray with A b. Observe in U.V. for conjugated systems c. Expose to Br_2 d. Observe in U.V. for unsaturates	unsaturated compounds	yellow spots on pink	105, 106, 107, 171, 190, 191, 192, 193, 232, 252, 328, 365, 368

43	Folin-Ciocalteau reagent	Sol. A: Mix 10 g sodium tungstate, 2.5 g of sodium molybdate and 70 ml H₂O. Add, consecutively, 5 ml 85% H₃PO₄ and 10 ml conc. HCl. Reflux for 10 hr and add 15 g Li₂SO₄, 5 ml H₂O and 1 dp Br₂. Dilute to 100 ml with H₂O. Reagent should not be green Sol. B: 20% aqueous Na₂CO₃ a. Spray with B b. Dilute A with 3 volumes H₂O and spray[271]	a. phenols b. estrogens		163, 221, 380
44	Fuchsin-H₂SO₄	Sol. A: 1 g parafuchsin is dissolved in 700 ml H₂O and 50 ml 2 N HCl, diluted to 1 l with H₂O and allowed to stand overnight with occasional shaking a. Add 1% HgCl₂ to A b. Spray with reagent[48]	plasmalogens	violet	134
45	Hydrazine sulfate in HCl	Spray with a 1% sol. of reagent in 1 N HCl	aromatic aldehydes	yellow	396
46	Hydrogen chloride	Hold over conc. HCl	chalcones	red	384
47	Hydroxamic acid-ferric ion	Sol. A: equal volumes of 12.5% NaOH and 5% hydroxylamine, both in H₂O Sol. B: acetic acid Sol. C: 10% FeCl₃ in H₂O a. Spray with A b. Allow to stand for 10 min (or heat to 100° for 10 min) c. Spray with B and C consecutively	esters of all types	varies	134, 207
48	8-Hydroxyquinoline-NH₃	Sol. A: 0.5% sol. of reagent in 60% EtOH a. Expose to NH₃ b. Spray with A c. Observe in U.V.	inorganic cations	various colors	359, 360

TABLE 7.2—*Continued*

	Reagent	Preparation and Use	Type of Compounds	Color	Ref.
49	Iodine-potassium iodoplatinate	Sol. A: 0.5% sol. of I_2 in $CHCl_3$ Sol. B: equal volumes of 1.1% aqueous KI and 0.135% aqueous chloroplatinic acid a. Spray with A and B alternating	nitrogen-containing drugs		279
	Iodine in KI and HOAc	Sol. A: aqueous sol. which contains 5% I_2 and 10% KI a. Dilute 2 ml of A with 3 ml H_2O and 5 ml 2 N HOAc and spray with diluted sol.	alkaloids and steroids		347, 227
	Iodine-benzidine	Sol. A: 5% benzidine in EtOH a. Expose to I_2 vapor b. Spray with A	glycerides	blue	6
50	Iodine azide	Sol. A: 3.5 g of sodium azide in 100 ml of 0.1 N I_2 (reagent is explosive when dry[276]) a. Spray with A	penicillins	yellow	103
51	Isatin in H_2SO_4	Sol. A: 0.4% sol. of reagent in conc. H_2SO_4 a. Spray with A b. Heat to 120°	thiophene derivatives	various colors	65
52	Isonicotinic acid hydrazide	Sol. A: 4 g isonicotinic acid hydrazide and 5 ml conc. HCl in 1 l H_2O a. Spray with A b. Allow to stand 3–16 hr. c. Observe in U.V. and daylight	steroids		414
53	Kedde reagent	Sol. A: 2% sol. of 3,5-dinitrobenzoic acid in MeOH Sol. B: 2 N KOH a. Mix equal volumes of A and B just before spraying b. Spray with mixture	cardiac glycosides		223

54	Morin (2',3,4',5,7-pentahydroxyflavone)	Sol. A: 0.05 to 0.005% sol. of reagent in MeOH a. Spray with A b. Heat to 100° for 2 min. (optional) c. Observe in U.V.	a. N-blocked amino acids b. conjugated double-bond systems	yellow	52, 341
55	N-(1-Naphthyl)ethylene diamine·2 HCl (diazotized)	Sol. A: 1 N HCl Sol. B: 5% NaNO$_2$ Sol. C: 0.1% reagent in EtOH a. Spray with A, B, and C (consecutively)	sulfonamides	reddish purple	196
56	Naphthoresorcinol in H$_3$PO$_4$	Sol. A: 100 ml of 0.2% sol. of reagent in EtOH and 10 ml H$_3$PO$_4$ a. Spray with A b. Heat to 105° for 5–10 min.	carbohydrates	various colors depending upon type	120, 289, 307, 308
57	Ninhydrin	I. Sol. A: 95 ml of 0.2% reagent in BuOH plus 5 ml of 10% aqueous HOAc a. Spray with A b. Heat to 120–150° for 10–15 min. II. Sol. A: 50 ml of 0.2% sol. of reagent in abs. EtOH mixed with 10 ml of HOAc and 2 ml of 2,4,6-collidine Sol. B: 0.1% Cu(NO$_3$)$_2$·3H$_2$O in abs. EtOH a. Spray with A-B (50:3) mixed just before use b. Heat to 105°	a. amino acids b. aminophosphatides c. amino sugars	blue	44, 95, 99, 116, 117, 134, 156, 292, 424, 438, 450
58	Osmium tetroxide	Expose to reagent vapors (caution, poison) in closed chamber	cmpds. with double bonds	brown to black	459
59	Palladium chloride in HCl	Spray with a 0.5% sol. of reagent in dilute HCl	thiophosphate insecticides	yellow spots on brown	23
60	Periodic acid-HClO$_4$-V$_2$O$_5$	Sol. A: 10 g H$_5$IO$_6$ in 100 ml of 70% HClO$_4$ and a few crystals of V$_2$O$_5$ a. Spray carefully dried layer with A	thiophosphate esters	blue	304
	Periodic acid-Schiff's reagent	Sol. A: 0.5% HIO$_4$ in 90% HOAc Sol. B: 30% sol. of sodium pyrosulfite-3 N HCl (1:1) (both kept at 0°) Sol. C: 5 ml of 10% sodium pyrosulfite, 85 ml H$_2$O and 0.2 g fuchsin. Allow sol. to stand 12 hr, treat with carbon and filter a. Spray with A, B, and C consecutively b. Heat to 90° for 15 min.	glycerides	violet	174

Thin-Layer Chromatography

TABLE 7.2—*Continued*

	Reagent	Preparation and Use	Type of Compounds	Color	Ref.
61	Phosphomolybdic acid	Sol. A: 1.5% (also 5 and 10%) sol. of reagent in EtOH or EtOH-EtOEt (1:1) a. Spray with A b. Heat to 150° for 5 min.	a. bile acids b. glycerides c. unsaturated fatty acids d. many others	blue	13, 115, 152, 154, 155, 157, 179, 181, 182, 183, 184, 186, 238, 249, 293, 295, 362
	Phosphomolybdic acid-$SnCl_2$ on stabilized layers	Sol. A: 1% sol. of acid in $CHCl_3$-EtOH (1:1) Sol. B: 1% $SnCl_2$ in 2 N HCl a. Spray with A b. Dry and dip in B	phospholipids	blue	185
62	Phosphomolybdic acid-NH_3	Sol. A: 20% sol. of acid in EtOH a. Spray with A b. Dry for 2–3 min and expose to NH_3	tocopherols	blue	354
63	Phosphotungstic acid	Sol. A: 10% sol. of acid in EtOH a. Spray with A b. Heat to 100° for 5–10 min.	cholesterol esters		249
64	Phosphoric acid	a. Spray with 50–70% acid b. Heat to 100° for 10–30 min. c. Observe in U.V.	pregnantriols and other steroids		247, 391, 414
65	*ortho*-Phosphoric acid-phosphomolybdic acid	Sol. A: 40% *ortho*-phosphoric acid Sol. B: 5% sol. of phosphomolybdic acid a. Spray with A b. Heat to 110° for 7 min. c. Observe in U.V. d. Spray with B e. Heat to 110° for 2 min.	steroids	blue-green	433, 434, 435

66	Potassium hydroxide	Sol. A: 5% KOH-acetone (2:1) a. Spray with A b. Heat to 100° c. Cool and spray (optional) with HNO_3-H_2SO_4 (1:1)	aromatic nitro compounds and amines		110
	Potassium hydroxide-urea	Sol. A: 1 N KOH in EtOH Sol. B: 50% aqueous sol. of urea a. Spray with A b. Heat to 60° for 15 min. (citrates are yellow) c. Spray with B d. Observe in U.V.	citrates		293
67	Potassium iodide	Spray with saturated aqueous sol.	peroxides		242
	Potassium iodide-NH_3-H_2S	Sol. A: 2% sol. of KI in H_2O a. Spray with A b. Observe colors c. Expose to NH_3 d. Expose to H_2S	copper series of inorganic cations	significant colors after each treatment	359
	Potassium iodide-HOAc-Na_2SO_3-starch	Sol. A: fresh sol. of 5 ml of 4% KI, 20 ml HOAc and a few drops of 1% Na_2SO_3 Sol. B: 1% aqueous sol. of starch a. Spray with A and B consecutively	peroxides	blue	371
68	Potassium iodoplatinate	Sol. A: mix 45 ml of 10% KI with 5 ml of 5% platinum chloride and dilute to 100 ml a. Spray with A	alkaloids and vitamins	various colors	57, 116, 117, 279, 285, 436
69	Potassium permanganate	Spray with 0.25% aqueous sol. of reagent	diterpenoids		213
	Potassium permanganate (alkaline)	Sol. A: equal portions of 1% aqueous $KMnO_4$ and 2% aqueous Na_2CO_3 a. Spray with A b. Note color after 1–2 hr.	phenols and plasticizers (esters)	yellow-violet	290, 293
	Potassium permanganate-HOAc	Spray with mixture of equal volumes of 0.1 N $KMnO_4$ and 2 N HOAc	oxidizable materials		227
	Potassium permanganate-$Fe(NO_3)_2$	Sol. A: 0.5% aqueous sol. of $KMnO_4$ Sol. B: 1% aqueous sol. of $Fe(NO_3)_2$ a. Spray with A and B consecutively	phenols		340

Table 7.2—*Continued*

	Reagent	Preparation and Use	Type of Compounds	Color	Ref.
70	Procházka reagent	Sol. A: 10 ml of 35% formaldehyde, 10 ml of 25% HCl and 20 ml 96% EtOH a. Spray with A b. Heat to 100° c. Observe in daylight and U.V.	indole derivatives	yellow	376
71	Pyridyl-azo-naphthol	Spray with a 0.25% sol. of reagent in EtOH	uranium ion		360
72	Resorcinol-SnCl₂-H₂SO₄-KOH	Sol. A: 20% resorcinol in EtOH with added $SnCl_2$ Sol. B: 4 N H_2SO_4 Sol. C: 40% aqueous KOH a. Spray with A b. Heat to 150° for 10 min. c. Spray with B d. Heat to 120° for 20 min. e. Spray with C	esters and plasticizers	various colors	293
73	Rhodamine B	Spray with a 0.05% (or 0.5%) sol. of reagent in EtOH	lipids	purple spots on rose	19, 165, 181, 182, 183, 232, 427, 430, 448
	Rhodamine B-KOH	Sol. A: 0.05% aqueous sol. of reagent Sol. B: 10 N KOH a. Spray with A and B consecutively	glycerides	bright spots on rose	6
74	Rhodamine 6 G	Sol. A: 8% aqueous sol. of reagent a. Spray with A b. Observe in U.V.	lipids		459
75	Silver nitrate-NH₃-NaOMe	Sol. A: 0.3% AgNO₃ in MeOH Sol. B: MeOH saturated with NH₃ Sol. C: 7% Na in MeOH a. Mix 5 parts of A, 1 part of B and 2 parts of C b. Spray with mixture c. Note color after few min.[61a]	acyl sugar	brown	75
76	Silver nitrate-NH₄OH-fluorescein	Sol. A: 1% sol. of AgNO₃ made basic with NH₄OH Sol. B: 0.1% sol. fluorescein in EtOH a. Spray with A and B consecutively	halogen ions		357

No.	Reagent	Procedure	Detects	Color	Ref.
77	Sodium periodate	Spray with a 1% aqueous sol. of reagent	ferrocenes	blue	345
78	Sodium periodate-KMnO₄	Sol. A: 4 parts of 2% aqueous NaIO₄ and 1 part of 1% KMnO₄ in 2% aqueous Na₂CO₃ a. Spray with A[215a]	sugars		454
	Sodium periodate-ethylene glycol-thiobarbituric acid	Sol. A: 0.02 *M* NaIO₄ Sol. B: ethylene glycol-acetone-H₂SO₄ (50:30:0.3) Sol. C: 6% aqueous sol. of 2-thiobarbituric acid sodium salt a. Spray with A, B, and C consecutively.[436b]	neuraminic acid sialic acid derivatives	red	127
79	Stannous chloride-HCl	Spray with a 10% sol. of SnCl₂ in conc. HCl	aromatic nitro compounds		110
80	Sudan Black B on stabilized layers	Sol. A: 0.1% sol. of reagent in EtOH-H₂O (1:1) a. Dip in A b. Wash with EtOH-H₂O (1:1).	saturated glycerides	blue	180

81	Sulfanilic acid, diazotized (Pauly's reagent)	Sol. A: 0.5 g of sulfanilic acid and 0.5 g of KNO₂ in 100 ml of 1 *N* HCl
		I. a. Spray with A
		  b. Spray with 1 *N* NaOH
		II. a. Spray with conc. KOH in MeOH
		  b. Spray with A
			phenols and aromatic amines which will couple	yellow-orange	11, 72, 74, 82, 396, 426

82	Tetrazolium blue or 3,3'-(3,3'-dimethoxy-4,4'-biphenylene)-bis-[2,5-diphenyl-2H-tetrazolium chloride]	I. Reducing steroids
		Sol. A: 1% sol. in EtOH
		Sol. B: Mix just before using 2 ml of A, 5 ml of H₂O and 3 ml of 4 *N* NaOH
		  a. Spray with A
		II. Δ⁴-3-oxosteroids
		Sol. A: 90 ml 2.7 *N* NaOH and 0.1 ml of sol. A above
		  a. Spray with A[51a]
			corticoids		1, 243

83	2,3,5-triphenyltetrazolium chloride-NaOH	Sol. A: Mix just before use one volume of 4% sol. of reagent in MeOH and one volume of 1 *N* NaOH a. Spray with A b. Heat to 110° for 5–10 min.[375]	a. steroids b. reducing sugars c. glycosides	red spots	30, 247, 414

TABLE 7.2—*Continued*

	Reagent	Preparation and Use	Type of Compounds	Color	Ref.
84	Trichloroacetic acid	Sol. A: 4% sol. of reagent in CHCl₃ a. Spray with A b. Allow to stand	menthofuran K-strophanthin (in U.V.)	pink reddish-brown	19 223
	Trichloroacetic acid-chloramine-T	Sol. A: Mix just before use 8 volumes of a 25% sol. of acid in EtOH with 2 volumes of 3% chloramine-T sol. a. Spray with A b. Heat to 100° for 10 min. c. Observe in daylight and U.V.	cardenolides		90, 223, 322
85	Trinitrobenzene		azulenes		108
86	Uranium acetate	Spray with a 1% sol. of reagent in H₂O	flavonoids	brown	286
87	Vanillin-H₂SO₄	Sol. A: 1% sol. of reagent in conc. H₂SO₄ a. Spray with A. b. Observe in daylight and U.V.	terpenoids	various colors	49, 167, 168, 368
	Vanillin-H₃PO₄	Sol. A: 1% sol. of reagent in 50% H₃PO₄ a. Spray with A b. Heat to 120° for 10–20 min.	steroids		247, 336, 338
88	Water on Silica Gel G	a. Spray thoroughly b. Observe in reflected light	alkaloids, steroids, sugar acetates and others	opaque areas on semi-transparent background	115, 128, 398
89	Zwikker's reagent	Sol. A: 0.5% sol. of cobalt acetate in MeOH Sol. B: 0.5% sol. of lithium hydroxide in MeOH a. Spray with A and B consecutively	barbiturates		227

TABLE 7.3. CROSS REFERENCES TO SPECIFIC SPRAY REAGENTS

Reagent or Name	Item in 7.2	Reagent or Name	Item in 7.2
Acetic anhydride	10	Iodine	26
Benzidine	25	Lithium hydroxide	89
Bismuth nitrate	37	Pauly's reagent	81
Bismuth carbonate	37	Perchloric acid	4
Borax	30	Potassium ferricyanide	40
Bromine	42	Potassium iodide	21
Chloramine-T	84	Potassium iodoplatinate	49
Cobalt acetate	89	Potassium permanganate	78
2,4,6-Collidine	57	Potassium thiocyanate	41
p-Dimethylaminobenzal-	38	Pyruvic acid	33a
dehyde		Schiff's reagent	60
3,5-Dinitrobenzoic acid	53	Sodium molybdate	43
Diphospho-pyridine nu-	33a	Sodium tungstate	43
cleotide (reduced)		Stannous chloride	4, 72
Dithiooxamide	24	Starch	21
Dithizone	36a	Thiobarbituric acid	78
Ferric chloride	47	Thionyl chloride	10
Fluorescein	76	Toluidine	21
Formaldehyde	70	Trichloroacetic acid	19
Hydrogen sulfide	67	Urea	66
Hydroxylamine-HCl	47	van Urk's reagent	32

ultraviolet light.[232] If fluorescein sprayed layers are then treated with bromine vapor, the fluorescein is converted to eosin except where unsaturated compounds were present. The result is that the unsaturated compound shows up as a yellow spot on a pink background. It is best viewed in ultraviolet light.[227,232,366]

TRANSPARENCY METHODS

If a developed layer is sprayed with or dipped into a liquid of the correct refractive index, the adsorbent and the compounds to be visualized will have relatively different transparencies and can be distinguished when held in a correct angle with respect to light. In this manner, spots or bands can be located without destruction and with great accuracy. The most commonly used system of this type is water on silica gel,[115,128,398] in which the bands or spots stand out as semiopaque areas on a translucent background. The method would obviously fail if the adsorbed materials were water soluble.

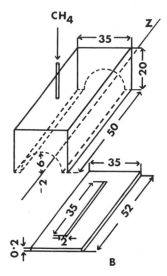

Figure 7.1. Gas flow counter with an extremely flat aperture plate (B) for measurement of weak β-emitters on thin-layer chromatograms. The aperture plate is attached to the counter tube without projecting parts. Z = counter wire (30 μ diameter). The measurements are given in mm. (Reproduced from Schulze and Wenzel, *Angew. Chem. Intern. Ed. Engl.*, 1, 580 (1962) through the courtesy of the authors and the publishers, Verlag Chemie and Academic Press.)

In a variation of this technique, Kaufmann, Makus and Khoe[185] dipped Silica Gel G layers (which had been stabilized with dichloro-dimethylsilane) in a mixture of ethanol-water (2:8) so that triglyceride spots became transparent. Hefendehl[141] sprayed already visualized Silica Gel G layers with a paraffin-ether mixture (1:1). The paraffin-impregnated layers became transparent after being stored in a desiccator for a few hours and the colored spots were easier to photograph.

RADIOACTIVITY METHODS

Chromatograms of radioactive compounds can be visualized by making X-ray prints.[20,232,234a] The layers are directly exposed to "No-Screen Medical X-Ray Safety Film"* for times varying from a few hours to a week. The films are developed with "Supermix Developer"** for 4 to 6 min. and fixed for 30 min. with "Acid Fixer." These methods have been applied mostly to lipids, although radioactive halides have also been detected by radioactivity.[29]

Schulze and Wenzel[349] developed a method for continuous auto-

* Eastman Kodak Company, Rochester 3, N.Y.
** General Electric X-Ray Dept., Milwaukee 1, Wisc.

matic measurement of radioactivity distribution of weak β-emitters on thin layers. Accurate measurements of C^{14} and tritium-containing compounds were made by passing the developed layer slowly under the aperture of the especially designed gas-flow counter shown in Figure 7.1.* The gas was methane. The method was also used for locating radioactive materials in preparative thin layer chromatography.

BIOASSAY METHODS

The developed chromatogram is covered with an agar plate containing an appropriate microorganism in good health. The spots which contain antibiotic inhibit the microorganisms and can thereby be detected. Thus, Nicolaus, Coronelli and Binaghi[275,276] located a number of penicillins, tetracyclines and rifomycins using *Sarcina lutea* and *Bacillus subtilis* in the presence of triphenyltetrazolium salts. The sensitivity was 0.01 to 0.1γ. The macrolides have been determined[33] using *Bacillus subtilis* as the revealing organism.

---

* A commercial model is available from Laboratorium Prof. Dr. Berthold, Wildbad (Schwarzwald) Germany.

CHAPTER 8

Documentation of Results

INTRODUCTION

Thin-layer chromatograms are normally too fragile for preservation as such and several techniques have been devised for making a permanent record of them. In general, these are to trace them or draw them in a laboratory book, to photograph or photocopy them, or to imbed them in a paraffin layer or plastic film of some type. The latter two, more exact, documentation methods offer the additional advantage that the photograph or films can often be quantitized.

PHOTOGRAPHY

The most positive way to record thin-layer chromatograms is to photograph them.[46,137,141,223,262,273,328,352,416] Chromatograms which are visible in normal light can be photographed with any available camera system. Hefendehl[141] found that better pictures resulted when the chromatograms were made semitransparent after normal visualization procedures (see p. 104).

Thin-layer chromatograms can also be copied with an office letter-copying device such as the "Zerox 914,"*[148] "Photorapid"**[121] or the "Copease" apparatus.†[232] A process using a direct positive blueprinting paper, Driprint HC (F speed)‡ has been suggested.[96] In some

---

* Manufactured by Zerox Corp., Rochester 3, N.Y.
** Manufactured by Bürogeräte, A. G., Zürich, Switzerland, Pronto model with Gevacopy paper GS, 8½ × 11 in.
† Manufactured by Copease Corp., 425 Park Avenue, New York, N.Y.
‡ E. Dietzgen Co., 407 10th Street, N.W., Washington, D.C.

cases[96,121] the layer is covered with cellophane film before photography to protect both the layer and the photocopying apparatus. It has also been suggested[148] that better copies will result if the spots are outlined with a stylus or even completely removed before duplication.

Sylvania F8T5/BLB, "Blacklite" blue tubes* and a yellow filter are recommended by Bürke and Bolliger[232] for black and white photography in ultraviolet light. Lukas has made photographs in ultraviolet light using an ultraviolet filter,[223] and Hansbury, Langham and Ott[137] have devised a method using a "Polaroid" system for the same purpose.

The use of X-ray film for recording chromatograms of radioactive substances was discussed in Chapter 7 (p. 104).

METHODS OF LAYER PRESERVATION

Meinhard and Hall[246] pressed a piece of "Scotch" or cellophane tape on thin layers to remove a portion of the layer. The tape was then placed directly in a laboratory book. The applicability of this technique is governed by the visualization procedure and the spray reagents used.

Mottier[265,267] and Machata[227] prepared semipermanent records of chromatograms by imbedding the layer in paraffin. In the case of unbound adsorbents, paraffin is applied to the plate as though it were another developing solvent, that is, by dipping the lower part of the layer in the melted paraffin and allowing it to rise by capillary action.[265,267] The bound layers are impregnated by dipping them in melted paraffin.[227] Semipermanent records can also be made by covering the layer with another glass plate and thus preserving it as a sandwich between two plates.[227,232] The sandwiches are sealed by taping them around the edges.

A more permanent preparation can be made by imbedding the adsorbent layer in a plastic film which can be peeled off of the glass plates and preserved as such. This is accomplished by spraying the chromatogram with a 4 per cent collodion solution containing 7.5

* Sylvania Electric Products, Inc., 500 5th Ave., New York, N.Y.

per cent glycerol,[18] aqueous dispersions containing 10 to 15 per cent of polyacrylic acid esters, polyvinylidene chloride and polyvinyl propionate,[218] Fisher Label Glaze,*[232] or "Neatan" (Brinkmann, see p. 37).

* Fisher Scientific Company, 633 Greenwich Street, New York, N.Y.

CHAPTER 9

Preparative Thin-Layer Chromatography

INTRODUCTION

The preparative separation of reasonable amounts of a mixture (10 to 1000 mg) on thin layers has been a relatively neglected aspect of thin-layer chromatography. The high capacities of the adsorbents (when used in adsorption chromatography), the high degrees of resolution obtained, and the over-all simplicity of the method make it a near ideal tool for the organic chemist. The technique itself involves the mechanical steps of normal thin-layer chromatography (Chapters 2 to 8) with slight modifications.

Thus, the layers are thicker (0.5 to 2 mm compared with 0.25 mm) than normal so that the maximum amount of material can be separated at once. The sample is not applied in spots but in a narrow band and developed in such a manner that the resolved components lie in bands. These bands are located by some nondestructive visualization technique; the adsorbent containing a single component is removed from the band area and the sample is removed from the adsorbent by elution with an appropriate solvent. Quantities ranging from 10 to 250 mg can be separated on a single chromatogram by this technique and a number of chromatograms can conveniently be carried out simultaneously.

The development of this aspect of thin-layer chromatography has been severely hampered by the lack of methods for sample application and for the nondestructive visualization of the developed chromatogram. The sample must be applied in large quantities to a relatively thin band without undue destruction of the rather fragile layer. It now appears that satisfactory, though not ideal, solutions have been found for these problems.

At least two attempts have been made to apply the concepts of thin-layer chromatography to large-scale separations. These involve chromatography in cast blocks or "chromatobars"[250] of plaster-of-Paris-bound adsorbent and chromatography in horizontal cellophane tubes filled with adsorbents.[66] A third similar technique is chromatography on layers of cellulose one inch thick packed between glass plates.[135] While each of these methods has certainly been successful in itself, the author believes that they are generally more laborious and inferior to the technique outlined below.

The various aspects of preparative thin-layer chromatography will be dealt with in the order and in the same manner as has been done in the preceding chapters for the general technique. Numerous examples of preparative work are cited as such in the tables of Chapter 11.

ADSORBENTS

Both bound and unbound adsorbents can be used with no special treatment other than perhaps a prepurification step (see pp. 19 and 48).

PREPARATION OF LAYERS

For the sake of convenience, most preparative thin-layer chromatography has been carried out on the usual square two-dimensional plates (20 × 20 cm or 8 × 8 in.). Larger plates could, of course, be used to separate larger quantities, but their use becomes awkward above this size and commercial apparatus is not available for preparation of the layers.

The adsorbent slurries have usually been made in the normal manner although Honegger suggests[158] the use of somewhat less water and a little more binder for very thick layers (see Table 3.2). Ritter and Meyer[329] found the optimum layer thickness to be about 1 mm although Honegger[158] gives a somewhat wider range of 1 to 3 mm. The very thick layers tend to crack and there is an appreciable difference between behavior on the open side of the layer and the side next to the glass. Layers up to 2 mm thick can be made with the adjustable Stahl applicator (see p. 37) and layers up to 5 mm thick can be made with the Camag apparatus (see p. 36).[158]

The layers are best allowed to dry at room temperature for several hours before final activation. This prevents casehardening and subsequent cracking. It is further recommended that, as the original Desaga instructions suggest, the layers be dried in a vertical position rather than horizontal.

SAMPLE APPLICATION

Sample application is made by applying the sample, in an appropriate solvent, in a thin band about 2 cm from one edge of the layer. A smooth application can be effected using the mechanical devices of Morgan[258] or of Ritter and Meyer[329] as discussed in Chapter 4. Alternately, the sample can be applied from a syringe moved manually along the layer. The operation is best carried out on a heated metal block[223,329] to evaporate the solvent. Honegger[158] applied the sample in a V-shaped trough cut in the layer.

The amount of sample applied will depend upon the specific mixture to be separated, the adsorbent involved and upon the type of chromatography. Much larger samples can be separated by adsorption than by partition chromatography. Mangold states[232] that up to 50 mg can be separated by adsorption chromatography on a layer of Morgan[258] or of Ritter and Meyer[329] as discussed in Chapter 4. Meyer[329] separated 75 mg on a plate of the same size with a 1-mm-thick layer. Honegger states[158] that 5 to 25 mg can be separated on such a 1-mm layer and Černý, Joska and Lábler[52] separated 20 to 100 mg of steroids on a layer of unbound alumina 20 × 10 cm and 1 mm thick. The author considers it "safe" to apply 50 mg of any mixture to a layer 20 × 20 cm and 1 mm thick and has applied as much as 300 mg of an easily separated mixture. For partition chromatography, only about one-tenth of these sample sizes should be used. Mangold[232] suggests 5 mg on a 20 × 20 cm layer 0.25 mm thick.

CHOICE OF DEVELOPMENT SOLVENTS

The solvents for preparative chromatography are the same as those used for normal thin layers.

DEVELOPMENT

The development of preparative chromatograms is carried out in the normal way with the following precautions. If several chromatograms are developed simultaneously, special care must be taken to saturate the chamber. The author prefers to develop such chromatograms with adsorbent turned toward the chamber wall and close to, but not touching, a layer of filter paper on the wall. If several chromatograms are to be developed in sequence in the same chamber, it should be remembered that thick layers remove more solvent than thin layers and the composition of the solvent may change appreciably.

All of the tricks of development discussed in Chapter 6 except those involving two-dimensional chromatography are applicable. Multiple-step and continuous development are particularly useful.[158]

VISUALIZATION

In the ideal case, the bands on a developed chromatogram will be colored or can be seen in ultraviolet light.[52,224] Bands containing conjugated double-bond systems can be located by using an adsorbent containing phosphors or a fluorescent additive as discussed in Chapter 2 (p. 21). Sometimes, small amounts of fluorescent or colored impurities will be present in a sample which will allow the orientation of a preparative plate with respect to a small plate (preferably with the same layer thickness) which has been visualized in a normal destructive manner. Schulze and Wenzel[349] used their gas-flow counter to find bands of compounds containing C^{14} and tritium labels.

Mistryukov[255] describes the use of "paper prints" to locate zones. Narrow paper strips (5 to 6 mm) are moistened and pressed against an unbound layer. After removal, the strips contain a layer of adsorbent and can be visualized with any spray reagent.

Iodine appears to be a good visualization reagent for most lipids[230] since it does not affect them appreciably. Gritter and Albers[128] have located steroids and other types of compounds by spraying the layer with water as discussed in Chapter 7 (p. 103). When all of these methods fail, an edge spray technique can be used. The preparative layer is covered with a glass plate except for 2 to 3 cm along one vertical edge and a line of adsorbent is scraped off along the edge of the cover plate to isolate the narrow edge strip.[329] The edge is then sprayed with an appropriate reagent, and the results are extrapolated across the layer.[230,333,420, and others]

ELUTION OF COMPOUNDS

Most workers simply scrape the adsorbent containing the desired components from the glass plate with a spatula and elute it with an appropriate solvent. However, this is difficult when using unbound layers and two gadgets have been devised for the purpose. Both operate on the vacuum cleaner principle. The first, as shown in Figure 9.1, is a piece of glass tubing with a constriction and holds a cotton wad to catch the adsorbent. It was devised by Mottier[267,269] and has the advantage that it can be used as an elution tube and no sample is lost in transfer. The Ritter and Meyer apparatus,[329] as shown in Figure 9.2, is more suitable for large quantities. The adsorbent is sucked into a Soxhlet extractor thimble from which it is eluted by extraction.

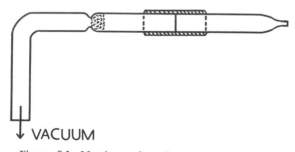

↓ VACUUM

Figure 9.1. Mottier gadget for removing adsorbent from a thin layer. (Reproduced from Mottier, *Mitt. Gebiete Lebensm. Hyg.*, **49**, 454 (1958) through the courtesy of the author and the Eidgenoessiche Drucksachen und Materialzentrale, Bern, Switzerland.)

Figure 9.2. Ritter and Meyer apparatus for removing adsorbent from a thin layer. (Reproduced from Ritter and Meyer, *Nature*, **193**, 941 (1962) through the courtesy of the authors and Macmillan and Co., Ltd.)

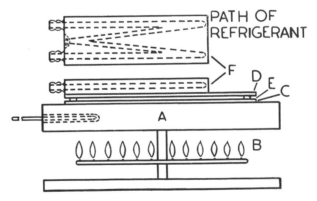

Figure 9.3. The apparatus of Baehler for direct sublimation out of thin layers. A refrigerant is passed through the metallic block (F) which rests on cover plate (D). The 1 mm spacer separates the cover plate from plate (C) which bears the thin layer. Block A is a piece of metal containing a thermometer which is heated by burners (B). (Reproduced from Bachler, *Helv. Chim. Acta*, **45,** 309 (1962) through the courtesy of the author and Verlag Helvetica Chimica Acta, Basel, Switzerland.)

The ideal elution solvent is one which moves the sample with the solvent front on a thin layer.[232] Aqueous eluents cannot be used with plaster-of-Paris-bound adsorbents because they will dissolve appreciable amounts of calcium sulfate. It is essentially impossible to avoid the solution of small amounts of silica gel in any eluting solvent. If the eluent is evaporated to dryness and taken up in a fresh solvent, preferably less polar than the original, most of the adsorbent will remain on the sides of the flask.

Sometimes, the substances on a chromatogram can be removed by direct sublimation to a cooled plate held about 1 mm over the adsorbent layer. Baehler[10] used the apparatus shown in Figure 9.3 for the visualization of chromatograms by sublimation, but the principle is mentioned for the purpose of isolation by Ener (as reported by Mangold[232]).

CHAPTER 10

Quantitative Thin-Layer Chromatography

INTRODUCTION

Quantitative evaluation of thin-layer chromatograms can be divided into two general categories. In the first, the mixture components are assayed *on* the thin layer while in the second, they are eluted from the adsorbent before being measured. Either technique can be used with about 5 per cent error or, in ideal cases, about 3 per cent error.

The assay on the layer can be carried out by measuring the spot area, or the spot area and density on a developed and visualized chromatogram. These values are then related to the amount of substance in the spots through the use of standards or calibration curves. Spot size or density can also be measured on photocopies or photographs of visualized chromatograms and related to substance amounts. Finally, the assay can be carried out visually[194] by measuring the minimum visable amount of the standard on a chromatogram and making successive dilutions of an unknown solution until this minimum value is reached. The major advantages of these techniques are their simplicity and the fact that the chromatograms can be visualized with destructive spray reagents.

The elution of substances from the adsorbent introduces several sources of error which will be discussed. A spectrophotometric or colorimetric method must be available for the assay of the eluted compounds since the simple weighing of eluted samples gives poor results.[442] The elution technique has been used more extensively than the layer assay method.

ANALYSIS ON THIN LAYERS

Spot Area

This type of determination is based upon the fact that there is a mathematical relationship between the spot area for a given substance and the weight of the substance contained in the spot. The method involves only a small number of mechanical operations and is widely applicable.[234,290,314,315,326,353,354]

There has, however, been some controversy over the type of mathematical relationship existing between these quantities. In fact, Stahl[374] questioned the existence of any precise relation at all. Seher [353,354] ignored the mathematics and obtained results with only 5 per cent error using calibration curves obtained by plotting spot area (from photostats) against weight. The calibration curves were not straight lines. Brenner and Niederwieser[44] and Pastuska and Petrowitz[290] obtained a linear relationship by plotting the logarithm of the weight of sample against spot area. This agrees with Giddings and Keller,[123] who derived such a relationship for paper chromatography from theoretical considerations. The most thorough and successful study of this technique was made by Purdy and Truter,[314,315] who found a linear relationship between the logarithm of the weight of a substance and the square root of the spot area. These authors noted, however, that a reasonably linear relationship resulted when the spot area or the logarithm of the spot area was used rather than its square root.

Purdy and Truter explored three general methods of analysis based upon spot size. Using quantities ranging from 1 to 100γ, they carried out analyses for potassium and magnesium ions, hexadecanol, cholesterol, palmitic acid, cholesteryl laurate and phenylazo-2-naphthol. Both adsorption and partition chromatography were involved. In all cases, it was necessary to have a pure sample of the substance in question for use as a standard.

The Graphical Method of Purdy and Truter. This method is similar to that of the Seher[353,354] technique, that is, it is based upon the preparation of a calibration curve by plotting spot area against weight with no regard to linearity. A standard deviation of 4.3 per cent (25 observations) was obtained and the major error was ascribed to the difficulty of duplicating conditions on the calibration chromatograms and the analysis chromatograms. In contrast, the second and third methods are algebraic and depend upon the linear relationship between $\log W$ and $\sqrt{A}$.

First Algebraic Method of Purdy and Truter. In this method, a standard solution of the compound to be assayed is spotted on the layer with a solution of the unknown and a solution prepared by precise dilution of the unknown. The chromatogram is developed and visualized and the spot areas are determined. The results are calculated using Equation (1) where W and A are the weight and spot area of the unknown, W_s and A_s are the weight and area of the standard, A_d is the area of the diluted unknown spot and d is the dilution fac-

$$\log W = \log W_s + \left(\frac{\sqrt{A} - \sqrt{A_s}}{\sqrt{A_d} - \sqrt{A}}\right) \log d \qquad (1)$$

tor. In essence, the unknown and its diluted sample establish the slope of the straight line used for the analysis and the standard establishes its intercepts. This method is the most accurate of the three, and yielded standard deviations of 2.7 per cent (540 observations) for adsorption chromatography and 3.6 per cent (982 observations) for partition chromatography.

Second Algebraic Method of Purdy and Truter. This method requires a pure sample of the substance to be assayed rather than a standard solution. The unknown solution is diluted in a precise manner and the diluted solution is divided into two portions. A known amount of the pure substance is added to one of the diluted samples and all three solutions are spotted on the same chromatogram. The chromatogram is developed and visualized; the spot areas are determined and the results are calculated using Equation (2). In this case,

$$\log \left(\frac{Wd + a}{W}\right) = \left(\frac{\sqrt{A_+} - \sqrt{A}}{\sqrt{A_d} - \sqrt{A}}\right) \log d \qquad (2)$$

W and A are the weight and spot area of the unknown; A_d and A_+

are the spot areas of the diluted sample and the diluted sample containing added substance, respectively; a is the amount of pure substance added to the diluted unknown and d is the dilution factor. This method is somewhat less accurate and yielded standard deviations of 3.9 per cent (374 observations) for adsorption chromatography and 3.9 per cent (982 observations) for partition chromatography.

Purdy and Truter found that it was necessary to spot the same volume of each solution on a single chromatogram. They used an Agla micrometer syringe suspended 2 mm above the thin layer for this purpose. The appropriate sample was squeezed out of the syringe and transferred to the layer by raising the layer until it contacted the solvent drop on the syringe. Chloroform was found to be an unsatisfactory spotting solvent. The chromatograms were developed in the usual manner and those containing colorless compounds were visualized by spraying with conc. sulfuric acid and charring at 160° for 10 minutes. The areas were determined by laying a sheet of transparent paper on the chromatograms, tracing the outline of the spots and measuring the areas of the figures by superimposing the tracing on millimeter graph paper.

In a related method, Eble and Brooker[93] measured the length of the streaks (actually the distance between the origin and the zone front) formed when tryptamine was chromatographed on Kieselguhr G with acetone-water (99:1). The method gave results that were reproducible to about 5 per cent.

Spot Area and Density

The size and intensity of spots formed by the acid spray and charring of a chromatogram provide a satisfactory basis for quantitative evaluation.[296,310,311] The method has an advantage in that the densities of the spots can be measured on a densitometer.

Additional variants are added, however, with respect to the spot-area methods discussed above. These are the carbon density of a given compound, its volatility and whether it chars in a uniform manner. These disadvantages can largely be nullified by the judicious use of internal standards and calibration curves[310] and results can be obtained with about 5 per cent error.

Before spotting, the thin layer, either the standard size of 5 × 20 cm[310,311] or microscope slide size,[296] is scanned in the densitometer to determine the degree and the uniformity of the background density. The chromatograms are then spotted, using a micropipette or microsyringe, with the sample containing the substance to be assayed. The chromatogram is developed, sprayed with 50 per cent sulfuric acid or 25 per cent perchloric acid and charred in an oven. It is then scanned by passing it through a densitometer and the amount of unknown substance is calculated using an appropriate calibration curve. The densitometers which have been used are the Photovolt* models 52C and 521A with a stage attached for semiautomatic plotting of curves for the standard size layers[310,311] and the Photovolt model 501A with transmission density unit no. 52 for the microchromatoplates.[296] The slit sizes were 1 × 5 mm for standard size and 1 × 3 mm for microsize. Glycerides[310,311] and cholesterol[296] have been analyzed by this technique.

Spot Area and Density on Photostats or Photographs

The spot area has been determined from photostats of thin-layer chromatograms and used as a quantitative measurement by Kammereck (as reported in Mangold[232]) and by Seher.[353,354] The error was about 5 per cent.

Neubauer and Mothes[273] photographed chromatograms of opium alkaloid mixtures and cut the photographs into strips which were passed through a densitometer. Hefendehl[141] made chromatograms transparent (see p. 104), photographed them and measured the density of the photographs against a calibration curve. He obtained results with about 5 per cent error in the analysis of menthofuran in an essential oil. Rybicka[335] followed the glycerolysis of linseed oil by this method and was able to determine the optimum reaction conditions by finding the concentrations of the glycerides at timed intervals.

Minimum Spot Visibility

In this technique,[194] a standard solution of the substance to be assayed is successively diluted and each dilution is chromatographed un-

---

* Photovolt Corp., 95 Madison Avenue, New York, N.Y. A commercial densitometer, especially designed for thin-layer work, is now available from Photovolt.

til the minimum visible amount is determined. This will, of course, depend upon the visualization method and the eye of the analyst and will vary from one compound to another. The unknown solution is then successively diluted and chromatographed until the minimum visible amount is determined. Knowing the dilution factor of the unknown and the minimum value, the amount of unknown in the original sample can be calculated. The average error for nineteen samples was 11.3 per cent.

Using a similar method, Waldi has carried out analyses for pregnandiol in urine as an early test for pregnancy[433,435] and for adrenaline (as its triacetyl derivative[434]) in adrenal extracts. He chromatographed the solution containing the material to be assayed on the same layer with a series of standard known concentrations and estimated the concentration of the unknown by comparison.

ANALYSIS AFTER ELUTION

Analysis by Spectrophotometry

Those compounds which possess a visible or ultraviolet spectrum are conveniently assayed in the following manner. After development of the chromatogram, the spot of adsorbent containing the substance to be analyzed is quantiatively removed; the substance is eluted with an appropriate solvent and assayed in a spectrophotometer. Thus, the spectroscopic properties of such compounds provide both a means of locating the spots on a developed chromatogram and a means of quantification. Substances which contain ultraviolet chromophores are more easily observed on phosphor-containing adsorbents (p. 21).

The methods involving elution contain several more sources of error than those in which compounds are assayed on the thin layers. First, the spots on the chromatogram must be located. This, however, is a minor problem when the substances have visible or ultraviolet chromophores. Second, the adsorbent containing the substance to be assayed must be completely removed from the glass support plate. Finally, the substance must be completely removed from the adsorbent before it is measured.

It has been suggested[194,383,389] that the thin layers be prewashed before being used for this type of analysis. This is carried out by allowing solvent to ascend (or descend) through the layers, perhaps in an apparatus similar to that shown in Chapter 3 (p. 49). The chromatogram is then spotted with a precise amount of substance to be separated and developed in a normal manner. The spots are located by viewing them in an appropriate light and the adsorbent containing the compound to be assayed is removed, normally with a razor blade. The compound is eluted from the adsorbent with a sufficiently polar solvent (one which will move the sample to the solvent front of a chromatogram) and measured in a spectrophotometer. The gadget described by Mottier[269] (Figure 9.1) could well be used in this technique since it provides both a method for the removal of adsorbent from the glass plate and an elution tube, thus minimizing transfer losses. The method requires the preparation of a calibration curve and compounds which follow Beer's law. It is also necessary to make "blank" readings on the adsorbent, preferably on adsorbent which has been developed in a thin layer and is removed from a point on the layer comparable to the one containing the sample to be assayed.

Normally, the method gives results with an error of 3 to 5 per cent. It was first used for the assay of biphenyl in citrus fruits (2.8 per cent error[194,389]) and has since been used for analysis of reserpine (about 5 per cent error [344]), coumestrol (5 per cent error[222]), menthyl salicylate,[383] estrogens (standard deviation, 10 per cent[394]), alkaloids (5 per cent error[400]), bile acids (standard deviation, 3 per cent[115]), and *p*-hydroxybenzoic acid esters (3 per cent error[118]). Quinine alkaloids[270] and 7-geranoxycoumarin[417] have been eluted and determined by fluorescence methods.

Analysis by Colorimetry

This technique is almost identical with the spectroscopic method described above except that a color-producing reagent is added to the sample before it is measured in the spectrophotometer. It is subject to the same disadvantages, although the location of the substances on the developed chromatogram is now a major problem. In general, the same nondestructive visualization techniques that are discussed in

Chapter 9 (p. 112) for preparative chromatography are applicable for the location of the spots to be eluted.

The method generally gives results with about 5 per cent error. It has been used for the analysis of esters (about 5 per cent error[420]), pregnanetriols (about 10 per cent error[391]), citral (2 per cent error[386]), coumarin compounds[388] and plasma phospholipids (about 5 per cent error[134]). Further, the method has been successfully applied to the assay of carbohydrates,[120,289] steroids,[244,278,391,460] lipids[413,430,458] and meprobamate.[102]

RADIOACTIVITY METHODS

Analysis techniques which depend upon radioactivity require prior labeling of the compounds to be analyzed. The chromatograms are spotted and developed in the usual way and have been evaluated by three methods. The first method is to make autoradiographs[231,234a] as described in Chapter 8 (p. 104) and to evaluate them using a densitometer and calibration curve. The second method[234a] is to locate the spots by such an autoradiograph or by nondestructive spray reagents and to elute the sample and measure it in a conventional counter. Scintillator solutions have been used[35,349,364] to aid the counting. Finally, Schulze and Wenzel[349] used a gas-flow counter (Figure 7.1) for the assay of C^{14} and tritium labeled compounds with about 3 per cent error.

The application of labeling techniques to lipids has been thoroughly discussed by Mangold.[232,234a]

CHAPTER 11

Specific Applications of Thin-Layer Chromatography

INTRODUCTION

This chapter will contain, in a tabular form, the majority of the specific applications of thin-layer chromatography which were recorded prior to January 1, 1963. Specific Rf values will not be given because of their notorious inconstancy on thin layers and because they are too numerous. It is hoped that this chapter will serve at least two purposes.

First, it will provide a general idea of the types of compounds which have been chromatographed on thin layers and, to some extent, the conditions of the separation. It would be hazardous, however, to assume that this compilation is complete because chromatographic conditions are usually incidental to a piece of research and are frequently buried in the experimental description.

Second, it will provide some idea of the adsorbents, solvents and visualization techniques which are commonly used in a given area or with a given class of compounds. In many cases, the same group of compounds has been treated in more than one fashion and the reader can choose the one which best suits his facilities and inclinations.

The numerous blank spaces in the tables are due to the failure of the original author to give specific details or to the present author's inability to obtain or translate the original atricle. In either case, they are given to make the compilation as complete as possible.

In many cases, a single reference will give details of several separate experiments such as the use of two adsorbents, the use of two techniques or the separation of two distinct groups of compounds. In other cases, two papers will report different aspects of the same experiments. This has been shown, as well as possible, by a system of partial lines. On occasion, a dotted line is used. This means that the regions on the ends of the dotted line are related and divided as shown but that the category crossed by the dotted line is the same for both experiments.

(EXPLANATION OF TABLES 11.1 TO 11.23)

Compounds

The various applications have, first of all, been arranged according to the class of compounds involved. This has been somewhat arbitrary at times and considerable overlapping could not be avoided. This is particularly serious between the sections devoted to amines, alkaloids and drugs and pharmaceuticals and between the essential oils and the terpenoids. In most cases, the applications are cross-referenced and the same example is reported in two places when it involves compounds falling in two classes. When the number of compounds in a specific entry is small, they are given by name. Otherwise, collective terms are used.

Within a given class, an attempt has been made to group the applications as much as possible according to the compounds involved. In most cases, the large comprehensive papers are given first and the others follow. The papers which came to the author's attention after the tables were first prepared, however, are given at the end of each section. The 2,4-DNPH's referred to in several cases mean the 2,4-dinitrophenylhydrazones.

Adsorbent

The adsorbent is given as a specific industrial product when it is reported as such in the original paper and when it is *especially prepared for thin-layer chromatography*. When a specific product is not named, it is implied that the original authors prepared their own adsorbent and the reader is referred to Chapter 2. In most cases where partition chromatography is involved, the adsorbent is equilibrated with the developing solution or some of its components. This is generally noted.

The various materials which have been incorporated into the adsorbent for one reason or another are given in the tables, but without details. The reader is referred to Chapter 2.

Developer

The solvents used for development are given as such except when the article gives a very large number. In these cases, a selected few are given, and the number not listed is mentioned in the last item. Unless noted, the different solutions represent separate experiments and are not successive.

The proportions of the various solvent mixtures, unless noted, are volume-volume. The abbreviations listed on p. 87 have been used to conserve space. Otherwise, the names or, sometimes, the formulas (CCl_4, $CHCl_3$, H_2O, etc.) are used.

Visualization

For the sake of brevity, only the names of the spray or visualization reagents are given. The reader is referred to the alphabetical listing in Chapter 7 for exact details. Two abbreviations are used in this section; 2,4-DNPH for 2,4-dinitrophenylhydrazine and U.V. for ultraviolet visualization.

Comments

The author has tried to give the basic purpose of the chromatography in each case and has, on occasion, added notes about especially interesting applications.

TABLES 11.1–11.23 FOLLOW

TABLE 11.1. ALDEHYDES, KETONES AND THEIR DERIVATIVES

	Compound	Adsorbent	Developer	Visualization	Comments	Ref.
1	Unsaturated aliphatic aldehydes and acyloins	Silica Gel G	a. pet. ether-EtOEt (90:10) (95:5) b. pet. ether-EtOEt-HOAc (70:30:1)	I₂ vapor	a. diagnostic b. monitored a synthesis	119
2	Long-chain (over eight carbons) aliphatic ketones	Silica Gel G	a. benzene-EtOEt mixtures b. toluene-EtOEt mixtures c. pet. ether-EtOEt mixtures	phosphomolybdic acid	diagnostic	238
3	Biologically active aldehydes					447
4	β-Dicarbonyl compounds	starch-bound silica gel	benzene-EtOAc (7:3)		diagnostic	14
5	Cyclohexanediones	see "Miscellaneous" No. 12				254
6	Aliphatic and aromatic aldehydes and ketones	unbound aluminum oxide	a. benzene b. benzene-EtOH (98:2)(95:5) (90:10) c. CHCl₃ d. EtOEt e. pet. ether-benzene (1:1)	reagents used for paper chromatography	diagnostic	144
7	Aromatic aldehydes and ketones	plaster-of-Paris-bound silica gel	hexane-EtOAc (4:1)(3:2)		diagnostic	113
8	Phenolic aldehydes	see "Phenols, etc." No. 12				290
9	Vanillin and other substituted benzaldehydes	Silica Gel G	a. pet. ether-EtOAc (2:1) b. hexane-EtOAc (5:2) c. CHCl₃-EtOAc (98:2) d. decalin-CH₂Cl₂-MeOH (5:4:1)	a. hydrazine sulfate in HCl b. methanolic KOH c. methanolic KOH followed by diazotized sulfanilic acid	diagnostic	396

10	Cholestanedione-1,3	see "Steroids" No. 45				397
11	Aldehydes and ketones in peppermint oil	see "Essential Oils" No. 6				323 324
12	Acetals and their determination in thin layers					206
13	2,4-Dinitrophenyl-hydrazones of aldehydes	Silica Gel G	a. benzene-pet. ether (3:1) for aliphatic b. benzene-EtOAc (95:5) for aromatic	colored	diagnostic	84
14	2,4-DNPH's of ketones	starch-bound SiO$_2$-Bentonite (4:1)	a. benzene b. benzene-pet. ether-EtOEt mixtures	colored	diagnostic	209
15	2,4-DNPH's of aliphatic aldehydes and ketones	Silica Gel G	benzene-EtOAc (95:5)	a. colored b. alcoholic KOH	a. diagnostic b. preparative	258
16	2,4-DNPH's of aliphatic aldehydes	polyvinyl alcohol-bound silica gel	benzene-H$_2$O (91.8:8.2)	colored	diagnostic	284
17	2,4-DNPH's of aldehydes and ketones	unbound aluminum oxide	a. benzene-hexane (1:1) b. EtOEt	colored	diagnostic	331
18	2,4-DNPH's of aliphatic aldehydes	starch-bound ZnCO$_3$	small amounts of pyridine in pet. ether-benzene mixtures	colored	a. diagnostic b. monitored column separation	9
19	2,4-DNPH's of hydroxy aldehydes and ketones	a. Aluminum Oxide G b. Silica Gel G	toluene-EtOAc (3:1)(1:1)	colored	diagnostic	5

TABLE 11.2. ALKALOIDS

	Compound	Adsorbent	Developer	Visualization	Comments	Ref.
1	Fifty-four misc. alkaloids	Silica Gel G	a. $CHCl_3$-acetone-diethylamine (5:4:1) b. $CHCl_3$-diethylamine (9:1) c. cyclohexane-$CHCl_3$-diethylamine (5:4:1) d. cyclohexane-diethylamine (9:1) e. benzene-EtOAc-diethylamine (7:2:1)	potassium iodoplatinate	a. diagnostic b. devised an identification system	436
		Aluminum Oxide G	f. $CHCl_3$ g. cyclohexane-$CHCl_3$ (3:7) plus 0.05% diethylamine			
		Silica Gel G-NaOH	h. MeOH			
2	Thirty-seven misc. alkaloids	unbound aluminum oxide	a. benzene-EtOH mixtures b. $CHCl_3$ c. EtOH	paper chromatography reagents	diagnostic	144
3	Twenty-one indole derivatives	Silica Gel G	a. MeOAc-2-propanol-NH_4OH ($Ca.$ 25% NH_3) (45:35:20) b. $CHCl_3$-HOAc (95:5)	a. Van Urk reagent b. Procháska reagent c. 2,4-dinitrophenylhydrazine	a. diagnostic b. two dimension	376
4	*Amaryllidaceae, Papaveraceae* and Bisbenzylisoquinoline alkaloids (total 57)	Silica Gel G Silica Gel G-NaOH	EtOAc-$CHCl_3$-MeOH (20:20:10)	Dragendorff's reagent	diagnostic	88
5	Alkaloid-containing drug mixtures	Silica Gel G with fluorescent material	a. MeOH-HOAc-EtOEt-benzene (1:18:60:120) b. EtOH-HOAc-benzene (12:5:80) c. EtOEt-$CHCl_3$-MeOH (50:50:1) d. benzene-EtOH (9:1) e. BuOH-HOAc (10:1)	a. $FeCl_3$-$K_3Fe(CN)_6$ b. chloramine T-HCl-NH_3 c. potassium iodoplatinate d. 2,6-dichloroquinone chlorimide e. ninhydrin f. $SbCl_3$ in CCl_4 g. CNBr and benzidine	diagnostic	117

6	Alkaloids and barbiturates in toxicology	Silica Gel G	a. MeOH b. CHCl₃-EtOEt (85:5)	a. Dragendorff's reagent b. I₂ and KI in HOAc c. sodium fluorescein d. FeCl₃ in HOAc e. Zwikker's reagent f. KMnO₄ in HOAc	a. diagnostic b. clinical	226 227
7	Sixteen alkaloids and nitrogen containing drugs	Silica Gel G	a. EtOH-pyridine-dioxane-H₂O (50:20:25:5) b. EtOH-HOAc-H₂O (60:30:10) c. EtOH-dioxane-benzene-NH₄OH (5:40:50:5) d. MeOH-BuOH-benzene-H₂O (60:15:10:15)	potassium iodoplatinate	a. diagnostic b. urine assay	57
		Aluminum Oxide G	e. BuOH-butyl ether-HOAc (40:50:10) f. BuOH-butyl ether-NH₄OH (25:70:5)			
8	Opium alkaloids	alumina buffered to *p*H 5 with acetate	H₂O-EtOH-BuOH (1:1:9)	U.V.	diagnostic	239
9	Opium alkaloids	Silica Gel G	benzene-MeOH (8:2)	Dragendorff's reagent	a. diagnostic b. quantitative c. preparative	273
10	Ergot alkaloids	a. cellulose powder impregnated with formamide b. Silica Gel G	a. benzene-heptane-CHCl₃ (6:5:3)	a. Dragendorff's reagent b. With formamide layers the excess formamide was first destroyed by spraying with 0.25% NaNO₂ in 0.5% HCl and Dragendorff's reagent was used. c. U.V. d. K₄Fe(CN)₆	a. diagnostic b. quantitative	399 400
	Morphine alkaloids	c. Silica Gel G-NaOH d. Cellulose powder impregnated with formamide	b. CHCl₃-EtOH (9:1) c. benzene-heptane-CHCl₃-diethylamine (6:5:3:0.03)			
11	Alkaloids of *Achillea* species	Silica Gel G	CHCl₃-MeOH (1:2)	a. potassium iodoplatinate b. H₂SO₄	diagnostic	285

TABLE 11.2—*Cont.*

	Compound	Adsorbent	Developer	Visualization	Comments	Ref.
12	Lysergic acid alkaloids				diagnostic	151
13	*Aspidosperma* alkaloids	Silica Gel G (not activated)	Methyl cellosolve	U.V.	diagnostic	215
14	Quinine alkaloids	Silica Gel G (prepared in acetone)	"Shellsol" T-diethylamine-acetone (23:9:9)	exposed to formic acid vapor and U.V.	a. diagnostic b. quantitative	270
15	An isomer of rhoeadin from *Papaver rhoeas*	Aluminum Oxide G	a. benzene-$CHCl_3$ (1:2) b. benzene-tetrahydrofuran (95:5) c. $CHCl_3$-MeOH (9:1)	Dragendorff's reagent	diagnostic	444
16	Morphine	Silica Gel G	BuOH-HOAc (9:1) saturated with H_2O	p-dimethylaminobenzaldehyde in H_2SO_4	a. diagnostic b. on microscope slides	437
17	Tropine and *pseudo* tropine	Silica Gel G	EtOH-NH_4OH (28% NH_3) (8:2)	Dragendorff's reagent	diagnostic	188
18	Anaferine (a piperidine alkaloid)	Silica Gel G	a. MeOH-$CHCl_3$-diethylamine (1:9:0.5) b. EtOH-NH_4OH (conc.) (8:2)	Dragendorff's reagent	diagnostic	332
19	Reserpine	Silica Gel G	MeOH-methyl ethyl ketone-heptane (8.4:33.6:58)	U.V.	a. diagnostic b. quantitative c. developed in dark	344

TABLE 11.3. AMINES AND THEIR DERIVATIVES

	Compound	Adsorbent	Developer	Visualization	Comments	Ref.
1	Simple aliphatic amines	Silica Gel G	a. EtOH (95%)-NH$_4$OH (25% NH$_3$) (4:1) b. phenol-H$_2$O (8:3) c. butanol-HOAc-H$_2$O (4:1:5)	ninhydrin	diagnostic	399
		Silica Gel G buffered to pH 6.8	d. EtOH-H$_2$O (70:30)			
2	Strong-base amines	unbound aluminum oxide	a. acetone-heptane (1:1) b. CHCl$_3$/NH$_3$ (sat. at 22°)-EtOH (96%) (30:1) c. acetone-MeOH-H$_2$O (8:2:1) d. methyl ethyl ketone-H$_2$O (15:1)	I$_2$ vapor-U.V.	a. diagnostic b. describes descending development with unbound layers	255 256
3	Diphenylamine derivatives	Silica Gel G	a. CHCl$_3$ b. toluene c. benzene	NaNO$_2$ and H$_2$SO$_4$	a. diagnostic b. analysis of powder	138
4	Tryptamine	Kieselguhr G	acetone-H$_2$O (99:1)	FeCl$_3$-K$_3$Fe(CN)$_6$	quantitative	93
5	Aromatic amines and nitro compounds	plaster-of-Paris-bound silica gel		a. KOH in acetone b. SnCl$_2$ in conc. HCl c. HNO$_3$-H$_2$SO$_4$	diagnostic	110
6	Nitramine explosives	see "Miscellaneous", No. 10				216
7	Piperidoles and quinolols	see "Miscellaneous", No. 12				254
8	Twelve pteridines	Silica Gel G	a. dimethylformamide-H$_2$O (190:10) (20:180) b. 5% citric acid c. NH$_4$OH (25% NH$_3$) d. twenty others	U.V.	diagnostic	274
9	Simple amines and diamines by electrophoresis	Silica Gel G buffered with borax	electrolyte: EtOH-H$_2$O (80 ml. plus 30 ml.) with 2 g. N$_2$OAc	ninhydrin	diagnostic	291

TABLE 11.4. CARBOHYDRATES, GLYCOSIDES AND THEIR DERIVATIVES

	Compounds	Adsorbent	Developer	Visualization	Comments	Ref.
1	Thirteen misc. sugars	Kieselguhr G buffered with NaOAc	EtOAc-2-propanol-H$_2$O (65:23.4:11.6)	anisaldehyde and H$_2$SO$_4$	diagnostic	377
2	Simple sugars	Polyacrylonitrile-Kieselguhr G-Aluminum Oxide G (5:6:1) buffered with Na$_2$HPO$_4$	n-amyl alcohol-2-propanol-HOAc-H$_2$O (55:15:110:30)	aniline phthalate	diagnostic	36
3	Simple sugars	Silica Gel G buffered with boric acid	a. benzene-HOAc-MeOH (1:1:3) b. methyl ethyl ketone-HOAc-MeOH (3:1:1)	naphthoresorcinol and H$_2$SO$_4$	a. diagnostic b. quantitative	289
4	Simple sugars	unbound Cellulose Powder MN-300	a. EtOAc-pyridine-H$_2$O (2:1:2) both phases b. phenol, equilibrated with 1% NH$_4$OH c. 2-propanol-pyridine-HOAc-H$_2$O (80:80:10:40)	anisidine phthalate	diagnostic	350
5	Simple sugars	Silica Gel G	n-PrOH-conc. NH$_4$OH-H$_2$O (6:2:1)	a. ninhydrin b. aniline hydrogen phthalate	a. diagnostic b. preparative c. noted sugar amination during development	439
6	Simple sugars	a. Silica Gel G b. Silica Gel G buffered with boric acid c. Kieselguhr G buffered with 0.02 N NaOAc	a. PrOH-EtOAc-H$_2$O (3:2:1) b. BuOH-acetone-H$_2$O (4:5:1) c. PrOH-EtOAc-H$_2$O (7:2:1) d. methyl ethyl ketone-HOAc-H$_2$O (3:1:1) e. Sol. b with 5% NH$_4$OH f. EtOAc-2-PrOH-H$_2$O (65:24:12) (5:2:0.5)	naphthoresorcinol and H$_3$PO$_4$	a. diagnostic b. used wedge-shaped chromatograms	307

No.	Substance	Layer	Solvent	Detection	Remarks	Ref.
7	Glucose and trehalose	Silica Gel G	sec-BuOH saturated with H₂O	NaIO₄-KMnO₄	a. diagnostic b. could not separate more complex mixtures	454
8	Ten sugar acetates and eight inositol acetates	Silica Gel G	benzene with 2-10% MeOH	a. H₂O b. ferric hydroxamate reagent	a. diagnostic b. preparative c. multiple development	398
9	Sugar acetates Sugar benzoates	starch-bound silicic acid —	a. EtOAc-benzene (3:7) b. MeOH-benzene (2:98) c. EtOAc-benzene (3:97)(4:6)	silver nitrate-NH₃-NaOMe	diagnostic	75
10	Partially methylated sugars, isopropylidene sugars and other derivatives	a. Silica Gel G b. Silica Gel G with boric acid	a. BuOH-acetone-H₂O (4:5:1) b. methyl ethyl ketone-HOAc-H₂O (3:1:1) c. pet. ether	naphthoresorcinol-H₃PO₄	diagnostic	308
11	Sucrose and raffinose Sucrose esters	Starch-bound silica gel —	a. 2-PrOH-toluene-EtOH-H₂O (10:2:5:2.5) b. toluene-EtOAc-EtOH (95%) (10:5:5)	naphthoresorcinol-H₃PO₄ 2',7'-dichlorofluorescein	a. diagnostic b. quantitative	120
12	Maltooligosaccharides up to ten glucose units	Kieselguhr G	a. BuOH-pyridine-H₂O (65:20:15) and six other combinations b. BuOH-EtOH-H₂O (50:30:20) c. BuOH-2,6-lutidine-H₂O (60:30:10)	anisaldehyde-H₂SO₄-HOAc	diagnostic	441
13	Aldose 2,4-DNPH's	a. Aluminum Oxide G b. Silica Gel G	a. toluene-EtOAc (1:1) b. toluene-EtOAc (3:1) (1:1)	a. colored compounds b. NaOH	a. diagnostic b. two-dimensional development on two different absorbents	5
14	Sugar derivatives	alumina				203
15	p-Bromophenylosazones of xylose derivatives	plaster-of-Paris-bound silica gel	benzene-MeOH (9:1)	colored compounds	diagnostic	7

Table 11.4—*Cont.*

	Compound	Absorbent	Developer	Visualization	Comments	Ref.
16	Cardiac glycosides	unbound, deactivated (H$_2$O or HOAc) silica gel	benzene-EtOH (3:1) saturated with H$_2$O	a. trichloroacetic acid-chloramine-T b. SbCl$_3$ and acetic anhydride in CHCl$_3$	diagnostic	322
17	Cardiac glycosides	Silica Gel G	EtOAc-pyridine-H$_2$O (5:1:4), upper phase	SbCl$_3$ in CHCl$_3$	diagnostic	392
18	Cardiac glycosides	Silica Gel G	a. CHCl$_3$-MeOH (9:1) b. CHCl$_3$-acetone (65:35)	H$_2$SO$_4$ and acetic anhydride	diagnostic	378
19	Glycosides of *atractylis gummifera*	Silica Gel G	a. BuOH-MeOH-H$_2$O (8:1:1) b. PrOH-xylene-H$_2$O (7:2:1)	conc. H$_2$SO$_4$	diagnostic	100
20	k-Strophanthin	Silica Gel G	BuOH-MeOH-formamide (17:2:1)	a. SbCl$_3$ in CHCl$_3$ b. trichloroacetic acid-chloramine-T c. Kedde reagent d. conc. H$_2$SO$_4$	diagnostic	223
21	Flavone and coumarin glycosides	Silica Gel G	EtOAc-methyl ethyl ketone-formic acid-H$_2$O (5:3:1:1)	diphenylboric acid, β-aminoethyl ester	diagnostic	379
22	Flavone glycosides	starch-bound silica gel	a. EtOAc-CHCl$_3$ (95:5) b. EtOAc-EtOH (95:5) c. 3-methyl-1-butanol-hexane-HOAc-H$_2$O (3:1:3:3)	a. AlCl$_3$ b. uranium acetate	diagnostic	286
23	Flavanol glycosides	Silica Gel G	a. HOAc-formic acid-H$_2$O-MeOH (10:2:2:1)	NH$_3$ vapor	diagnostic and quantitative	126
	Cardiac glycosides	---	b. methyl ethyl ketone-toluene-H$_2$O-HOAc-MeOH (40:5:3:1:2.5)	SbCl$_3$ in CHCl$_3$		

24	Rutin	a. unbound polyamide powder	a. MeOH b. MeOH-H$_2$O (8:2) 6:4)	a. diazotized sulfanilic acid b. U.V.	diagnostic	74
		b. Silica Gel G	c. BuOH-HOAc (9:) saturated with H$_2$O	p-dimethylamino-benzaldehyde in H$_2$SO$_4$	a. diagnostic b. on microscope slides	437
25	Brain gangliosidic substances	Silica Gel G	PrOH-1 N NH$_4$OH-H$_2$O (6:2:1)		a. diagnostic b. monitored column	440
26	*Catalpa* glucosides	Silica Gel G	a. MeOH b. MeOH-EtOEt mixtures	conc. H$_2$SO$_4$	diagnostic	39
27	Anthocyanins and their aglucones	polyacrylonitrile-"Perlon" (7:1) buffered with KH$_2$PO$_4$	1-pentanol-1-propanol-HOAc-H$_2$O (3:2:1) plus 2 parts 1-heptanol		diagnostic	36
28	Misc. glycosides					189

TABLE 11.5. CARBOXYLIC ACIDS AND THEIR DERIVATIVES (EXCLUSIVE OF FATTY ACIDS)

	Compound	Adsorbent	Developer	Visualization	Comments	Ref.
1	2,6-Dimethyl-2,6-octa-dienedioic acid (Hilde-brandt's acid)	Silica Gel G	$CHCl_3$:HOAc (97:3)	$KMnO_4$	diagnostic	428
2	Dicarboxylic acids	Silica Gel G	a. benzene-MeOH-HOAc (45:8:4) b. benzene-dioxane-HOAc (90:25:4)	bromphenol blue acid-ified with citric acid	diagnostic	302
3	Carboxylic acids (as am-monium salts)	Silica Gel G	a. EtOH(95%)-H_2O-NH_4OH(25% NH_3)(100:12:16)	bromcresol green	diagnostic	42
4	Methoxy-piperonylic acids	Silica Gel G	EtOAc-hexane-HOAc (50:50:0.5)	chromotropic acid-H_2SO_4	diagnostic	32
5	Phenolic acids	see "Phenols, Alcohols, etc.", No. 9 and No. 12				225 288 290
6	Aromatic acids	a. gelatin-bound Silica Gel G-"Perlon" (0.5:7:4)	a. n-amyl alcohol-n-BuOH-EtOAc-HOAc-H_2O (60:20:30:10:5)	U.V.	diagnostic	36
		b. polyacrylonitrile-"Perlon" (8:4)	b. n-octane-EtOAc-n-amyl alcohol-EtOEt-formic acid (40:50:15:15:10)			
7	p-Hydroxybenzoic acid esters	Silica Gel G with fluo-orescent material	pentane-HOAc (88:12)	U.V.	quantitative	118
8	Phthalates, phosphates and other esters as plasticizers	see "Miscellaneous," No. 14				293
9	Gallic acid and its esters	unbound polyamide powder	a. MeOH b. EtOH c. EtOEt d. CCl_4-MeOH (7:3) e. six others		a. diagnostic b. antioxidants	69

10	Lactones, lactams and thiolactones	Silica Gel G	a. isopropyl ether b. isopropyl ether-EtOAc (80:20) c. isopropyl ether-iso-octane (20:80) (60:40)	a. NaOH-hydroxyl-amine-HOAc-FeCl₃ consecutively b. Dragendorff's reagent	diagnostic	207
11	Dicarboxylic acids (from oxalic to sebacic) and carbocyclic acids	Kieselguhr G-Polyethylene glycol (M-1000) (2:1)	isopropyl ether-formic acid-H_2O (90:7:3)	bromcresol purple	diagnostic	200 201

TABLE 11.6. DRUGS AND PHARMACEUTICALS

	Compound	Adsorbent	Developer	Visualization	Comments	Ref.
1	Caffeine, theobromine and theophylline	Silica Gel G	a. EtOAc-MeOH-12 N HCl (18:2:0.05) b. EtOAc-MeOH-HOAc (8:1:1) c. CHCl₃-MeOH (19:1)	sublimation from layer	a. diagnostic b. preparative	10
2	Meprobamate	starch-bound silicic acid	EtOH-cyclohexane (15:85)	conc. H_2SO_4	a. diagnostic b. quantitative	102 240
3	Barbiturates	see "Alkaloids," No. 6				226 227
4	Nitrogen-containing drugs	Silica Gel G	a. organic solutions b. buffer solutions } depending upon drug	a. I_2 in CHCl₃ b. potassium iodoplatinate	a. diagnostic b. semiquantitative	279
5	Narcotics in forensic chemistry	see "Miscellaneous," No. 19				92
6	Alkaloidal drugs in urine	see "Alkaloids," No. 7				57
7	Urinary metabolites of psychotropic drugs	Silica Gel G	BuOH-HOAc-H₂O (65:15:20) (88:5:7)	conc. H_2SO_4	diagnostic	101
8	Chloramphenicol	aluminum oxide			monitored synthesis	217
9	Penicillin preparations	Silica Gel G	a. acetone-MeOH (1:1) b. 2-PrOH-MeOH (30:70)	sodium azide-I_2 solution	diagnostic	103
10	Tetracyclines, penicillins and rifomycins	a. Silica Gel G b. Silica Gel G buffered to pH 4.5 or 4.2	a. aqueous citric acid solutions b. pure alcohols c. many others	a. HCl and others b. microbiological assay	diagnostic	275 276
11	Antibiotics (macrolides)	Silica Gel G	acetone-H₂O (98:2)	microbiological assay	diagnostic	33

12	Sulfonamides	a. Silica Gel G b. Silica Gel G containing fluorescein	CHCl$_3$-EtOH-heptane (1:1:1) plus 1.0 to 1.8% H$_2$O	a. HCl-NaNO$_2$-N-(1-naphthyl) ethylenediamine b. U.V.	diagnostic	196
13	Sulfonamides	Silica Gel G	CHCl$_3$-EtOH-heptane (1:1:1)	p-dimethylaminobenzaldehyde, acidified	diagnostic	452
14	Sulfonamide, radioactive	Silica Gel G	BuOH sat. with conc. NH$_3$	radioactive method	a. diagnostic b. quantitative c. preparative	349
15	Misc. constituents of plant drugs					379
16	Pharmaceutical applications				review	122 340

TABLE 11.7. DYES

	Compound	Adsorbent	Developer	Visualization	Comments	Ref.
1	Food dyes	unbound aluminum oxide	a. BuOH-EtOH-H$_2$O (90:10:10) (80:20:10)(70:30:30) (60:40:40)(50:50:50)	colored compounds	a. diagnostic b. spot made alkaline before chromatography c. circular	266 269 306
2	Food dyes	Cellulose Powder MN 300 G and MN 300	a. aqueous sodium citrate (2.5%)-NH$_4$OH(25%) (4:1) b. PrOH-EtOAc-H$_2$O (6:1:3) c. t-BuOH-propanoic acid-H$_2$O (50:12:38) with 0.4% KCl	colored compounds	diagnostic	451
3	Food dyes	unbound aluminum oxide	a. MeOH b. EtOH c. CHCl$_3$ d. CCl$_4$ e. EtOEt f. seven others	colored compounds	a. diagnostic b. quantitative	73
4	Food dyes	Silica Gel G	a. CHCl$_3$-acetic anhydride (75:2) b. benzene c. methyl ethyl ketone-HOAc-MeOH (40:5:5)	SbCl$_3$ in CHCl$_3$	diagnostic	257
5	Carotenoid dyes	see "Vitamins," No. 2				210 211
6	Carotenoid dyes, synthetic	calcium hydroxide-Silica Gel G (6:1)	pet. ether-benzene (2:3)	colored compounds	a. diagnostic b. monitored synthesis	166
7	Dyes in gasoline	Silica Gel G	benzene	colored compounds	a. diagnostic b. to catch gasoline thieves	139
8	Test mixture dyes: butter yellow, Sudan red III and indophenol	see "Miscellaneous," No. 16				381

TABLE 11.8. ESSENTIAL OILS

	Compound	Adsorbent	Developer	Visualization	Comments	Ref.
1	Essential oils of Argentina	starch-bound silicic acid containing fluorescent material	a. hexane b. pet. ether-EtOAc mixtures	a. U.V. b. fluorescein-Br$_2$ c. bromcresol green d. 2,4-DNPH e. conc. H$_2$SO$_4$	diagnostic	105 106 107
2	Thirteen essences	starch-bound silicic acid	a. hexane b. benzene-ethanol mixtures	a. SbCl$_3$ in CHCl$_3$ b. 2,4-DNPH c. KMnO$_4$ d. p-dimethylaminobenzaldehyde-H$_2$SO$_4$	diagnostic	287
3	Misc. essential oils	Silica Gel G	benzene-CHCl$_3$ (1:1)	SbCl$_3$ in CHCl$_3$	a. diagnostic b. used with gas chromatography	382
4	*Perfume industry* a. Essential oils b. Single essences c. Balsams and resins d. Tar and tar products e. Phenols and phenol ethers f. Wool wax and derivatives g. Azulenes	Silica Gel G	a. hexane b. benzene c. CH$_2$Cl$_2$ d. CHCl$_3$ e. benzene f. benzene-MeOH mixtures g. CHCl$_3$-MeOH mixtures h. hexane i. benzene	a. SbCl$_3$ in CHCl$_3$ b. SbCl$_6$ in CCl$_4$ c. conc. H$_2$SO$_4$ d. varillin and other aldehydes in H$_2$SO$_4$ e. fluorescein-Br$_2$ f. 2,4-DNPH g. o-dianisidine h. SbCl$_6$ in CCl$_4$ i. acetic anhydride-H$_2$SO$_4$ j. chloranil in CHCl$_3$ k. Br$_2$ in CHCl$_3$	a. diagnostic b. circular c. in shaped areas	368
5	Misc. essential oils	see "Terpenoids," No. 1				190

TABLE 11.8—*Cont.*

	Compound	Adsorbent	Developer	Visualization	Comments	Ref.
6	a. Misc. essential oils	starch-bound silicic acid containing fluorescent material (Rhodamine 6 G)	a. hexane b. hexane-EtOAc mixtures	a. U.V. b. 2,4-DNPH	diagnostic	323
	b. Oils of *Mentha* genus				—	324
	c. Mint oils				quantitative	326,327
						325
7	Oils of Japanese mint	starch-bound silicic acid	hexane-EtOAc (85:15)	vanillin in H_2SO_4	diagnostic	167 168
8	Oils of *Mentha piperita*	Silica Gel G	hexane	a. $SbCl_3$ in $CHCl_3$ b. transparency method	quant. assay of menthofuran	141
9	Oils of peppermint					297
10	Oils of *Oleum menthae*	Silica Gel G	a. benzene-EtOAc (95:5) b. hexane	a. vanillin in H_2SO_4 b. $SbCl_3$ in $CHCl_3$ c. $SbCl_5$ in CCl_4 d. fluorescein-Br_2 e. 2,4-DNPH f. KI in HOAc with Na_2SO_3 and followed by starch g. HNO_3-HOAc (1:300)	diagnostic	171
11	Oils of peppermint	plaster-of-Paris-bound silicic acid	"Skellysolve" B-EtOAc mixtures, up to 10% EtOAc	a. transmitted fluorescent light b. U.V. c. trichloroacetic acid in $CHCl_3$ d. $KMnO_4$ in H_2SO_4 e. Rhodamine B	a. diagnostic b. study site and mode of terpene formation in plant c. preparative	19 20
12	Menthol in peppermint oil	alumina-silicate			quantitative	133

13	Oils of Eucalyptus	starch-bound silica gel	hexane-EtOAc (85:15)	conc. H_2SO_4	a. diagnostic b. circular	313
14	Oils of Eucalyptus	starch-bound magnesol			a. diagnostic b. circular	51
15	Oils of *Strobilanthopsis Limifolia*	a. silica gel-"Celite"-starch (16:4:1) b. plaster-of-Paris-bound silica gel	hexane-EtOAc mixtures		a. diagnostic b. monitored column	58
16	Oil of jasmine	see "Terpenoids," No. 13				76 81
17	Azulene of camphor blue oil	see "Terpenoids," No. 14				108
18	Oil of *Pogostemon patchouli* Pell	starch-bound silicic acid	a. hexane-EtOAc (85:15) b. solution a plus 5% CHCl₃	conc. H_2SO_4	a. diagnostic b. used "chromatobars"	124
19	Oils of *Arnica montana L.*	starch-bound silicic acid and *terra silicata*	CHCl₃	conc. H_2SO_4	diagnostic	131
20	*Oils of grapefruit* a. Hydrocarbons	a. starch-bound silicic acid b. plaster-of-Paris-bound silicic acid	a. hexane b. 2,2-dimethylbutane c. cyclohexane d. methylcyclohexane e. isopentane	a. fluorescein-Br₂ b. HNO₃-H₂SO₄ (5:95)	a. diagnostic b. predicted solvents for column work	191
	b. Oxygenated compounds	—	f. hexane-EtOAc mixtures g. EtOAc-CHCl₃ (alcohol free) mixtures h. EtOAc-benzene (15:85) i. hexane-nitropropane (50:50) j. isopropyl ether-hexane (50:50)			
21	Oils of orange juice	starch-bound silicic acid	hexane-EtOAc (85:15) plus a variety of others	a. fluorescein-Br₂ b. 2,4-DNPH c. o-dianisidine d. conc. sulfuric-nitric acid	diagnostic	192

TABLE 11.8—*Cont.*

Compound	Adsorbent	Developer	Visualization	Comments	Ref.
22 *Oils of lemon* a. Menthyl salicylates	starch-bound silicic acid with phosphors	a. EtOEt-pet. ether mixtures	a. U.V.	a. quantitative b. descending tech.	383
b. Coumarins	—	b. hexane-EtOAc (85:15)	b. 2,4-DNPH c. o-dianisidine in glacial HOAc d. U.V.	c. monitored column d. diagnostic	387 388 417
c. Hydrocarbons	—	c. heptane to develop and elute hydrocarbons from end of layer	e. Fluorescein-Br₂	e. quant. assay of hydrocarbons by gas chromatography	385
d. Citral	—	d. hexane-EtOAc (85:15)	f. fluorescein-Br₂, viewed under U.V.	f. diagnostic	386
e. Chalcones	—	e. hexane-EtOAc (75:25) f. EtOEt-pet. ether (65:35)	g. HCl gas h. U.V.	g. diagnostic	384
23 Oils of sage	Silica Gel G	benzene	vanillin in H₂SO₄	diagnostic	49
25 Volatile oil of grafted umbelliferous plants				diagnostic	198 199
26 Oils of *Curcuma*	Silica Gel G	benzene-CHCl₃-MeOH (200:100:3)	SbCl₃ in CHCl₃	diagnostic	445
27 Oils of *Acorus calamus*	Silica Gel G	benzene		a. diagnostic b. to relate plants	453
28 Oils of *coriander lavender* and muscat sage					298

		Silica Gel G	benzene-EtOAc (95:5)	a. SbCl$_3$ in CHCl$_3$ b. SbCl$_6$ in CCl$_4$ c. conc. H$_2$SO$_4$	diagnostic	
29	Oils of *Oleum rosmarini*, *O. Lavandulae* and *O. rosae*					172
30	2,4-DNPH's of aldehydes and ketones from essential oils	see "Aldehydes, etc." No. 14				209
31	Removal of hydrocarbons from essential oils	see "Terpenoids," No. 1				190

TABLE 11.9. FLAVONOIDS AND COUMARINS

	Compound	Adsorbent	Developer	Visualization	Comments	Ref.
1	Isoflavones	starch-bound silicic acid with phosphors	a. EtOAc-Skellysolve B (3:1) (1:1) b. acetone-EtOAc-Skellysolve B (4:3:3) c. EtOH-CHCl₃ (1:3)(1:1)	U.V.	a. diagnostic b. preparative	132
2	Flavonoids	unbound polyamide powder (Silon)	a. MeOH-H₂O (80:20)(60:40) b. MeOH	U.V.	diagnostic	71 74
3	Flavonoids and coumarins	Silica Gel G-NaOAc	toluene-ethyl formate-formic acid (5:4:1)	diphenylboric acid, β-aminoethyl ester	diagnostic	379
4	Flavonoids and coumarins of lemon	starch-bound silicic acid with phosphors	CHCl₃-acetone mixtures	U.V.	a. diagnostic b. monitored column	162
5	Coumarins	Silica Gel G	a. pet. ether-EtOAc (2:1) b. hexane-EtOAc (5:2)	KOH and diazotized sulfanilic acid	diagnostic	396
6	Coumarins in lemon juice	starch-bound silicic acid with phosphors	hexane-EtOAc (75:25)	U.V.	preparative	31
7	Coumestrol in plants	starch-bound silicic acid with phosphors	a. CHCl₃-EtOEt (1:1) b. EtOAc-"Skellysolve" B (3:1) c. acetone-"Skellysolve" B (1:3) d. EtOEt-"Skellysolve" B (7:3)	U.V.	a. diagnostic b. quantitative	222 224 34

TABLE 11.10. INORGANIC AND METALORGANIC COMPOUNDS

	Compound	Adsorbent	Developer	Visualization	Comments	Ref.
1	Fe^{+2}, Zn^{+2}, Be^{+2}, Ni^{+2}, and others	starch-bound alumina-"Celite"	a. H_2O b. dilute HCl c. organic liquids	a. I_2 b. U.V.	a. diagnostic b. circular on microscope slides	246
2	a. Copper family-Cu^{+2}, Cd^{+2}, Bi^{+3}, Pb^{+2}, Hg^{+2}	purified Silica Gel G	a. BuOH-1.5 N HCl-2,5-hexanedione (100:20 0.5)	a. KI b. NH_3 and H_2S	diagnostic	359
	b. Sulfide group-Zn^{+2}, Co^{+2}, Fe^{+2}, Ni^{+2}, Mn^{+2}, Cr^{+3}, Al^{+3}		b. acetone-conc. HCl-2,5-hexanedione (100:1:0.5)	c. NH_3 d. 8-hydroxyquinoline e. U.V.	theory	356
3	U^{+6}, Ga^{+3} and Al^{+3}	purified Silica Gel G	a. EtOAc (sat. with H_2O)-tributyl phosphate (50:2) b. acetone-conc. HCl (100:0.5)	a. pyridyl-azo-naphthol b. 8-hydroxyquinoline c. U.V.	diagnostic	360
4	Alkali metals-Na^{+1}, Li^{+1}, K^{+1}, Mg^{+2}	purified Silica Gel G	EtOH-HOAc (100:1)	acid violet	diagnostic	358
5	Halogens-F^{-1}, Cl^{-1}, Br^{-1}, I^{-1}	purified Silica Gel G	acetone-BuOH-conc NH_4OH-H_2O (65:20:10:5)	a. bromcresol purple and NH_3 b. ammonical $AgNO_3$ and fluorescein	diagnostic	357
6	Various phosphates	purified Silica Gel G	MeOH-conc. NH_4CH-10% trichloroacetic acid and H_2O (50:15:30)	ammonium molybdate followed by $SnCl_2$ and HCl	diagnostic	355
7	K^{+1} and Mg^{+2}	Silica Gel G	EtOH-MeOH (1:1) plus 1% HOAc	acid violet 6BN	quantitative	315
8	Radioactive halogens	"Dowex 1"-Cellulose Powder MN 300 G (1:1)	1 M aqueous $NaNC_3$	radioactivity	diagnostic	29

TABLE 11.10—*Cont.*

	Compound	Adsorbent	Developer	Visualization	Comments	Ref.
9	Twenty-four ferrocene derivatives	Silica Gel G	a. benzene b. benzene-EtOH (30:1)(15:1) c. propylene glycol-MeOH (1:1) d. propylene glycol-chlorobenzene-MeOH (1:1:1)	a. Br_2 b. $NaIO_4$	diagnostic	345
10	Chromium and cobalt complexes of o-hydroxy-o'-carboxyazo dyes	Aluminum Oxide Fluka	MeOH	colored compounds	diagnostic	342
11	Organo-tin stabilizers in polyvinyl chloride	Silica Gel G containing "Komplexon III"	H_2O-BuOH-EtOH-HOAc (10:5:5:0.15)	Diphenylthiocarbazone	diagnostic	411

TABLE 11.11. INSECTICIDES

	Compound	Adsorbent	Developer	Visualization	Comments	Ref.
1	a. Thiophosphate esters	Silica Gel D5	hexane-acetone 4:1	PdCl₂ in dilute HCl	a. diagnostic b. in forensic chemistry	23
	b. Chlorinated compounds	Aluminum Oxide D5	hexane	N,N-dimethyl-p-phenyl-enediamine hydrochloride in sodium methylate		
2	Dichlorophene and hexachlorophene	starch-bound silicic acid	heptane saturated with HOAc	FeCl₃-K₃Fe(CN)₆	a. diagnostic b. quantitative	43
3	Thiophosphate esters	starch-bound aluminum oxide	heptane-acetone (10:1)	H₅IO₆-HClO₄-V₂O₅	diagnostic	304
4	Pyrethrins	plaster-of-Paris-bound silica gel	EtOAc-hexane (20:80)	fluorescein-Br₂	diagnostic	365
5	Pyrethrins and their peroxides	Silica Gel G	a. benzene-methyl ethyl ketone (90:10) b. benzene-EtOAc (85:15) c. CCl₄-EtOAc 80:20) d. hexane-methylethylketone (80:20) e. hexane-EtOAc (75:25)	SbCl₃ in CHCl₃	a. diagnostic b. reaction on layer	371
6	Pentachlorophenol	Silica Gel G-oxalic acid	CHCl₃	U.V.	a. diagnostic b. quantitative	83
7	Chlorinated organic pesticides					455
8	Chlorinated hydrocarbons with insecticidal properties					300

TABLE 11.12. LIPIDS—CLASS SEPARATION

	Compound	Adsorbent	Developer	Visualization	Comments	Ref.
1	Misc. lipids	Silica Gel G	a. EtOEt b. isopropyl ether c. isopropyl ether-HOAc (98.5:1.5)	Phosphomolybdic acid	Class separation prior to analysis by reversed phase technique	182
2	Misc. lipids	Silica Gel G	pet. ether-EtOEt-HOAc (90:10:1)	2',7'-dichlorofluorescein	Class separation prior to analysis by reversed phase technique	230
3	Misc. lipids				monitored column	150
4	Radioactive lipids	silicic acid	pet. ether-EtOEt (92:8)	a. radioactivity b. α-cyclodextrin-I_2 c. I_2	class separation	231
5	Industrial aliphatic lipids	a. Silica Gel G b. Silica Gel G plus 10% $(NH_4)_2SO_4$	a. pet. ether-benzene (95:5) b. benzene sat. at 20° with 1 N NH_4OH c. $CHCl_3$ (sat. with 1 N NH_4OH)-MeOH (97:3) d. acetone-14 N NH_4OH (90-10) e. $CHCl_3$-(MeOH-0.1 N H_2SO_4, 95:5)(97-3)(80-20)	a. I_2 b. 2',7'-dichlorofluorescein c. $K_2Cr_2O_7$ in H_2SO_4	diagnostic	234
6	Misc. fats, oils and waxes	Silica Gel G	a. pet. ether-EtOEt-HOAc (90:10:1)(70:30:2)(70:30:1) b. hexane-EtOEt (95:5)	a. I_2 b. 2',7'-dichlorofluorescein	a. diagnostic b. class separation	235
7	Tissue lipids	Silica Gel G	hexane-EtOEt-HOAc (90:10:1)	2',7'-dichlorofluorescein	class separation prior to assay by gas chromatography	236
8	Serum lipids	unbound aluminum oxide	a. pet. ether-EtOEt (95:5) b. pet. ether-EtOH (98:2) c. pet. ether-EtOEt-HOAc (94.5:5:0.5) d. heptane-HOAc (98:2)		a. class separation b. quantitative	413

9	Serum lipids and phospholipids	plaster-of-Paris-bound silicic acid	a. CHCl₃-MeOH-H₂O (80:25:3) b. pet. ether-EtOEt-HOAc (90:10:1)(60:40:1)	2',7'-dichlorofluorescein	diagnostic	423
10	Serum lipids	Silica Gel G	a. PrOH-NH₄OH (2:1)-1st step b. CHCl₃-benzene (3:2) 2nd step c. CCl₄-reverse	SbCl₃ in CHCl₃	a. stepwise technique b. two dimensional c. quantitative	21 164 438
11	Serum, liver and adipose tissue lipids	Silica Gel G				86
12	Plasma lipids	Silica Gel G	CHCl₃-MeOH-H₂O (65:25:4)	a. bromthymol blue-NH₃ b. ninhydrin c. fuchsin-H₂SO₄ d. hydroxamate reaction	a. diagnostic b. quantitative for phosphates	134
13	Plasma lipids	Silica Gel G	a. pet. ether-diisobutylketone-HOAc (87:13:0.7) b. pet. ether-methyl ethyl ketone-HOAc (95:4:1)	a. 50% H₂SO₄ b. Rhodamine 6 G c. bromthymol blue d. osmium tetroxide	class separation prior to separation by reversed phase technique	459
14	Butter-fat lipid	Silica Gel G				245
15	Brain tissue lipids	Silica Gel G	a. CHCl₃-MeOH-H₂O (24:7:1)(60:20:3) b. CHCl₃ c. CCl₄	a. ammonium molybdate-HClO₄ b. phosphomolybdic acid c. ninhydrin d. Dragendorff's reagent e. diphenylamine	diagnostic on multiple sclerosis patients	157 159
16	Brain lipid constituents (pure test substances)	Silica Gel G	a. heptane b. CCl₄ c. 1,2-dichloroethane d. CHCl₃ e. 1,2-dichloroethane-MeOH (98:2) f. pet. ether-EtOEt (70:30) g. four others	a. bromthymol blue, buffered b. bromthymol blue c. conc. H₂SO₄-HOAc (1:1) d. phosphomolybdic acid e. HIO₄-Schiff reagent f. *aqua regia*-ammonium molybdate-vanadyl chloride g. diphenylamine	a. diagnostic b. system for exploring unknown lipids	174

TABLE 11.12—*Cont.*

	Compound	Adsorbent	Developer	Visualization	Comments	Ref.
17	Dogfish liver lipids	Silica Gel G	pet. ether-EtOEt-HOAc (90:10:1)		separated the alkoxy-glycerides class for assay	229
18	Lipids of feces and fecal-iths	Silica Gel G	pet. ether-EtOEt-HOAc (80:20:1)	50% H₂SO₄	a. class separation b. semiquantitative assay	442
19	Lipids				review review	104 232

TABLE 11.13. LIPIDS—FATTY ACIDS AND THEIR DERIVATIVES

	Compound	Adsorbent	Developer	Visualization	Comments	Ref.
1	Fatty acids	plaster of Paris impregnated with undecane	a. HOAc-CH₃CN (1:1) b. solution a with 0.5% Br₂	copper acetate-dithio-oxamide	separated "critical" pairs after hydrogenation and bromination on layer	180
2	Fatty acids	Kieselguhr G impregnated with undecane	HOAc-CH₃CN (1:1)	copper acetate-dithio-oxamide on layers "smoked" with dichlorodimethylsilane	diagnostic	185
3	Fatty acids	Kieselguhr G impregnated with undecane	a. HOAc-CH₃CN (6:4), 80% sat. with undecane b. HOAc-CH₃CN (30:70, 80% sat. with undecane and containing 0.5% Br₂	Rhodamine B	separated "critical" pairs after hydrogenation and bromination on layer	186
4	Fatty acids	Silica Gel G impregnated with undecane	a. 96% HOAc b. HOAc-CH₃CN (1:1)	phosphomolybdic acid	diagnostic	182
5	Fatty acids of Swiss Pharmacopoeia	see "Lipids-Glycerides", No. 16				6
6	Keto- and hydroxy-fatty acids and their lactones	Kieselguhr G impregnated with tetradecane or paraffin	a. HOAc-H₂O (80:20), 80% sat. with impregnating solution (5% of agent in pet. ether) b. HOAc-H₂O (90:10), 75% sat. with impregnating solution	a. Rhodamine B b. phosphomolybdic acid	diagnostic	181
7	Fatty acids of castor oil and oiticica oil	Silica Gel G	pet. ether-EtOEt-HOAc (70:30:1)(70:30:2)	2′,7′-dichlorofluorescein	diagnostic	235
8	Lignoceric, cerebronic and nervonic acids	Silica Gel G			diagnostic	109
9	Fatty acid methyl esters	starch-bound silicic acid with phosphors	a. "Skellysolve" F-EtOEt (90:10)(70:30)(50:50) b. benzene-EtOEt (75:2a)(50:50)	a. 2′,7′-dichloro-fluorescein b. U.V. c. fluorescein-Br₂	a. diagnostic b. monitored column	8

TABLE 11.13—*Cont.*

	Compound	Adsorbent	Developer	Visualization	Comments	Ref.
10	Fatty acid methyl esters	Silica Gel G impregnated with AgNO₃	EtOEt-hexane (10:90)(40:60)	2',7'-dichloro-fluoroescein	diagnostic	260
11	Fatty acid methyl esters	Silica Gel G	hexane-EtOEt-HOAc (85:15:1)	2',7'-dichloro-fluorescein	preparative separation prior to analysis by gas chromatog.	333
12	Fatty acid methyl esters	Silica Gel G	hexane-EtOEt mixtures (up to 30% EtOEt)	a. I₂ b. 2',7'-dichloro-fluorescein c. 50% H₂SO₄	a. quantitative b. preparative	420
13	Fatty acid methyl esters	Silica Gel G impregnated with Silicone oil	a. CH₃CN-HOAc-H₂O (70:10:25) b. peracetic acid-HOAc-H₂O (10:75:15)	a. I₂ b. α-cyclodextrin and I₂	a. diagnostic b. separated sat. esters by using an oxidizing developer	230
14	Fatty acid methyl esters	Silica Gel G	a. pet. ether-EtOEt (80:20) b. solution a plus 1% HOAc	50% H₂SO₄	diagnostic	262
15	Epoxy fatty acid methyl esters	Silica Gel G	hexane-EtOEt (95:5)(90:10)	50% H₂SO₄	monitored various separation methods	261 264
16	Fatty acids and esters	silicic acid on the inside of test tubes	a. hexane b. hexane-EtOEt (97:3)(85:15) c. CHCl₃	I₂	diagnostic	219
17	Fatty acid esters of orujo oil	Silica Gel G	hexane-EtOEt (90:10)	50% H₂SO₄	a. diagnostic b. monitored column	422
18	Fatty acid esters of cholesterol	a. Silica Gel G b. Silica Gel G impregnated with paraffin	a. tetralin-hexane (25:75)(1:1) b. CCl₄ c. methyl ethyl ketone-CH₃CN (7:3)	phosphomolybdic acid	a. diagnostic b. two-dimension	184

19	Fatty acids and their cholesterol esters	Silica Gel G	a. PrOH-NH₄OH (2:1) b. CHCl₃-benzene (3:2) c. CCl₄	SbCl₃ in CHCl₃	a. diagnostic b. stepwise technique c. two-dimension	438
20	Cholesterol and its esters	see "Steroids," No 28 and No. 27				228 249
21	Acetoxymercurymeth- oxy derivatives of un- saturated fatty acid methyl esters	Silica Gel G	a. pet. ether-EtOEt (4:1) b. PrOH-HOAc (100:1)	s-diphenylcarbazone	isolated unsaturated esters prior to assay by gas chromatography	177 233
22	p-Phenylazophenacyl esters of fatty acids	Silica Gel G	pet. ether-EtOEt (85:15)	colored compounds	diagnostic	419

TABLE 11.14. LIPIDS—GLYCERIDES

	Compound	Adsorbent	Developer	Visualization	Comments	Ref.
1	Glycerides	Silica Gel G impregnated with $AgNO_3$	$CHCl_3$-HOAc (99.5:0.5)	dibromo-R-fluorescein	separation according to degree of unsaturation	16
2	Glycerides	Silica Gel G	$CHCl_3$-benzene (70:30)	conc. H_2SO_4	separation of the glyceride fraction from other fractions	64
3	Glycerides	Silica Gel G impregnated with undecane	a. $CHCl_3$-MeOH-H_2O (5:15:1) (for diglycerides) b. acetone-CH_3CN (7:3) (for triglycerides)	Rhodamine B	diagnostic	182
4	Glycerides	Silica Gel G	a. "Skellysolve" F-EtOEt (70:30) b. (10:90) for monoglycerides c. (70:30) for diglycerides d. (90:10) for triglycerides e. (60:40)(35:65)(85:15)	50% H_2SO_4	a. quantitative b. quantitative based upon ozonalysis and periodate oxdation	311 310
5	Glycerides	plaster-of-Paris-bound silicic acid	gradient elution system of pet. ether-EtOEt varied between (9:1) and (4:6). All contained 0.1% HOAc.	2',7'-dichlorofluorescein	a. diagnostic b. gradient elution	334
6	Glycerides	Silica Gel G	a. 1,2-dichloroethane b. $CHCl_3$ c. 1,2-dichloroethane-MeOH (98:2) d. pet. ether-EtOEt (70:30) e. $CHCl_3$-HOAc (96:4)	a. HIO_4-Schiff reagent b. bromthymol blue	diagnostic	174
7	Monoglycerides	hydroxyl-apatite	methyl isobutyl ketone at 10°	phosphomolybdic acid	diagnostic	155
8	Triglycerides	Kieselguhr G impregnated with petroleum	acetone-CH_3CN (8:2)(7:4)	a. phosphomolybdic acid b. I_2 c. α-cyclodextrin-I_2	a. diagnostic b. multiple development	179

No.	Substance	Adsorbent	Solvent system	Detection	Purpose	Ref.
9	Triglycerides	plaster of Paris impregnated with paraffin (b.p. 240–250°)	a. acetone-CH₃CN (8:2) b. propanoic acid-CH₃CN (6:4) plus 0.5% Br₂ by vol.	Sudan Black B	a. diagnostic b. bromination on layers	180
10	Triglycerides	Kieselguhr G impregnated with tetradecane	a. acetone-CH₃CN (8:2) 80% sat. with tetradecane b. propanoic acid-CH₃CN (6:4) 80% sat. with tetradecane plus 0.5% Br₂ by vol.	a. I₂ b. phosphomolybdic acid	a. diagnostic b. bromination on layer	186
		Kieselguhr G impregnated with paraffin (b.p. 240–250°) or Silicone oil	c. acetone-CH₃CN (8:2) d. MeOH-CH₃CN (5:4) e. MeOH-CH₃CN-CH₃CF₂CN (5:4:1.5) f. solution e saturated with silicone oil	c. Rhodamine B d. I₂ e. phosphomolybdic acid	diagnostic	183
11	Glycerides of milk fat (lipolyzed)	Silica Gel G	pet. ether-EtOH-HOAc (90:10:1)		preparative separation prior to assay by gas chromatography	178
12	Glycerides of linseed oil	plaster-of-Paris-bound silicic acid	gradient elution from pet ether to pet. ether-EtOEt (1:1)	conc. H₂SO₄	a. diagnostic b. quantitative c. used to find optimum reaction conditions	335
13	C¹⁴ and tritium assay of tripalmitin and fatty acids	Silica Gel G	pet. ether-EtOEt-HOAc (90:10:1)	a. I₂ b. 2,7'-dichlorofluorescein	a. quantitative b. preparative	364
14	Alkoxydiglycerides				diagnostic	212
15	Acetoglycerides	silicic acid	"Skellysolve" F-EtOEt (92:8)	I₂	diagnostic	130
16	Glycerides of the Swiss Pharmacopeia	Kieselguhr G impregnated with paraffin	HOAc	a. I₂ and benzidine b. Rhodamine B and KOH	diagnostic	6
17	Glycerides from plasma	Silica Gel G	pet. ether-methyl ethyl ketone-HOAc (84:15:1)	a. 50% H₂SO₄ b. osmium tetroxide c. Rhodamine 6 G	diagnostic	459

TABLE 11.15. LIPIDS—GLYCOLIPIDS

	Compound	Adsorbent	Developer	Visualization	Comments	Ref.
1	Glycolipids	Silica Gel G	a. PrOH-NH₄OH (12% NH₃)(4:1) b. 1,2-dichloroethane-MeOH (49:1) c. CHCl₃-96% HOAc (95:5) all consecutively	diphenylamine	a. diagnostic b. stepwise technique	174
2	Glycolipids	Silica Gel G	CHCl₃-MeOH-H₂O (60:35:8) (65:25:4)	a. Rhodamine B b. Dragendorff's reag. c. Bial's reagent d. diphenylamine	diagnostic	427 432

TABLE 11.16. LIPIDS—PHOSPHCLIPIDS AND SULFOLIPIDS

	Compound	Adsorbent	Developer	Visualization	Comments	Ref.
1	Cephalins and lecithins	Silica Gel G	CHCl₃-MeOH-H₂O (11:5:1)	phosphomolybdic acid-SnCl₂ on layer "smoked" with dichloro-dimethylsilane	diagnostic	185
2	Sphingosines, etc.	silicic acid on walls of test tubes	a. CHCl₃ b. NH₃/MeOH-CHCl₃(20:80) (30:70) (NH₃/MeOH is MeOH-H₂O-NH₄OH (28% NH₃) (93:5:2))	I₂	diagnostic	219
3	Lecithin and colamine-cephalin	Silica Gel G	CHCl₃-MeOH-H₂O (65:25:4)	a. Rhodamine B b. Dragendorff's reag. c. ninhydrin	quantitative	430
4	Misc. phospholipids	Silica Gel G	CHCl₃-MeOH-H₂O (60:35:8) (65:25:4)	a. Rhodamine B b. Dragendorff's reag. c. ammonium molybdate-HClO₄ d. ninhydrin	diagnostic	427 432
5	Serum phospholipids	plaster-of-Paris-bound silicic acid	CHCl₃-MeOH-H₂O (80:25:3)	2',7'-dichlorofluorescein	diagnostic	423
6	Lecithins, cephalins and sphingomyelins	Silica Gel G with 10% (NH₄)₂SO₄	CHCl₃-H₂SO₄/MeOH (80:20) (H₂SO₄/MeOH is 0.1 N aqueous H₂SO₄-NₑOH (5:95))	a. I₂ b. 2',7'-dichlorofluorescein c. K₂Cr₂O₇-H₂SO₄	diagnostic	234
7	Cerebron, kerasin and their sulfuric acid esters	Silica Gel G	a. 1,2-dichloroethane b. CHCl₃-HOAc (96:4) c. PrOH-NH₄OH (12.5% NH₃) (8:2)	bromthymol blue	diagnostic	173
8	Beef brain gangliosides	Silica Gel G	PrOH-H₂O (7:3)	a. bromthymol blue b. Ehrlich reagent	preparative	208
9	Cerebral gangliosides	Silica Gel G	BuOH-pyridine-H₂O (3:2:1)	Bial's reagent	diagnostic	197
10	Beef brain gangliosides	Silica Gel G	PrOH-1 N NH₄OH-H₂O (6:2:1)		diagnostic	440

TABLE 11.17. NUCLEOTIDES

	Compound	Adsorbent	Developer	Visualization	Comments	Ref.
1	Misc. nucleotides	collodion-bound "ECTEOLA" cellulose	a. 0.15 M NaCl b. 0.01 N HCl	U.V.	diagnostic	316 317
2	Misc. nucleotides	Cellulose Powder MN 300 G	a. H_2O b. sat. aqueous $(NH_4)_2SO_4$-1 M NaOAc-2-PrOH (80:18:2) c. t-amyl alcohol-formic acid-H_2O (3:2:1) d. BuOH-acetone-HOAc-NH$_4$OH (5% NH$_3$)-H$_2$O (3.5:2.5:1.5:1.5:1)	U.V.	a. diagnostic b. comparison with paper chromatog.	319
3	Misc. nucleotides	a. DEAE-cellulose	dilute aqueous HCl 0.02 to 0.04 N	U.V.	a. diagnostic b. preparative	320
		b. cellulose	sat. aqueous $(NH_4)_2SO_4$-1 M NaOAc-2-PrOH (80:18:2)		c. review	318
		c. ECTEOLA-cellulose	0.06 N HCl			
4	Misc. nucleotides	Cellulose Powder MN 300	a. H_2O for nucleobases b. BuOH-acetone-HOAc-NH$_4$OH (5% NH$_3$)-H$_2$O (4.5:1.5:1:1:2)	U.V.	diagnostic	321
5	Nucleotides, AMP, ADP and ATP	"DEAE-Sephadex" A-25	gradient elution starting with 1.0 N formic acid and adding 10 N formic acid which is 2 M in ammonium formate	fluorescein	diagnostic	82
6	Amino acid esters as models for amino-acylribonucleic acid	see "Proteins, etc.," No. 18				456

TABLE 11.18. PHENOLS, ALCOHOLS AND THEIR DERIVATIVES

	Compound	Adsorbent	Developer	Visualization	Comments	Ref.
1	Acetylene alcohols and glycols					4
2	Chimyl, batyl and selachyl alcohols	see "Lipids-Glycerides," No. 14				212
3	Long-chain aliphatic alcohols	Silica Gel G	a. pet. ether-EtOEt-HOAc (90:10:1) b. pet. ether-EtOEt (20:80) (10:90)(70:30)	50% H_2SO_4	diagnostic	395
4	Cyclohexanol derivatives	Silica Gel G	a. benzene b. benzene-EtOEt (80:20)	H_2O	a. diagnostic b. preparative	128
5	Cardanol and its methylol derivatives	plaster-of-Paris-bound silica gel	EtOAc-toluene (60:40)	diazotized sulfanilic acid	followed course of reaction	11
6	Phenolic acids and esters	see "Carboxylic Acids, etc.," No. 9				69
7	Phenols	a. starch-bound silicic acid b. starch-bound silicic acid kieselguhr (1:1)	a. xylene b. xylene-CHCl₃ (3:1)(1:1)(1:3) c. CHCl₃	diazotized sulfanilic acid followed by KOH	diagnostic	426
8	Pyrocatechol and eugenol derivatives	Silica Gel G, acidic and basic	benzene	SbCl₅ in CCl₄	diagnostic	369
9	Phenols and phenolic acids	starch-bound silicic acid with phosphors	a. "Skellysolve" B-EtOEt (3:7) b. "Skellysolve" B-EtOAc (1:3) c. "Skellysolve" B-acetone (3:1)	U.V.	followed course of reaction	225
10	Phloroglucinol derivatives	see "Miscellaneous," No. 15				380
11	Phenolic aldehydes	see "Aldehydes, etc.," No. 9				396

TABLE 11.18—*Cont.*

	Compound	Adsorbent	Developer	Visualization	Comments	Ref.
12	Phenolic aldehydes, ketones and acids	Silica Gel G	a. benzene-dioxane-HOAc (90:25:4) b. benzene-MeOH-HOAc (45:8:4) c. benzene-MeOH (95:5)	a. diazotized benzidine b. alkaline KMnO₄ c. diazotized sulfanilic acid d. Rhodamine B	a. diagnostic b. quantitative	288 290
13	Phenols and glycols Nitro and amino phenols	a. unbound aluminum oxide with HOAc b. unbound aluminum oxide	a. benzene b. benzene-EtOH mixtures c. CHCl₃ d. EtOEt	paper chromatography reagents	diagnostic	144
14	Phenols	plaster-of-Paris-bound silica gel-oxalic acid	a. hexane-EtOAc (4:1)(3:2) b. benzene-ethyl ether (4:1) c. benzene		diagnostic	113
15	3,5-Dinitrobenzoates of alcohols and phenols	Silica Gel G	a. benzene-pet. ether (1:1) b. hexane-EtOAc (85:15)(75:25) c. toluene-EtOAc (90:10)	colored compounds	does not separate closely related compounds	85
16	3,5-Dinitrobenzoates of alcohols	starch-bound silica gel-bentonite (4:1) with fluorescent material	hexane	U.V.	diagnostic	209
17	3,5-Dinitrobenzoates of butyl and isooctyl alcohols	silica gel		colored compounds		220
18	Phenols in pharmaceuticals	unbound acidic aluminum oxide	a. ether b. benzene-EtOH (95:5)(90:10)	a. KMnO₄-Fe(NO₃)₃ b. KMnO₄	diagnostic	340
19	Phenolic carboxylic acids	Kieselguhr G with Na₂WO₄, Na₂MoO₄ or borax	a. organic layer of BuOH-HOAc-H₂O (4:1:5) b. butyl ether (sat. with H₂O)-HOAc (10:1) c. EtOAc-2-PrOH-H₂O (65:24:11)	Folin Denis Reagent		136

20	Xylenols	Silica Gel G	a. benzene b. benzene-MeOH (95:5)	a. diazotized benzidine b. Echt blue salt	301
21	Alcohols				28
22	Phenols	Silica Gel G and boric acid	EtOH-H$_2$O (80:30) containing 4% boric acid and 2% NaOAc as electrolyte	Diazotized benzidine	a. diagnostic b. electrophoresis	291
23	Phenols	ε-polycaprolactam	a. hexane b. cyclohexane c. benzene d. CHCl$_3$ e. EtOAc	diazotized sulfanilic acid	diagnostic	219a 436a

TABLE 11.19. PROTEINS, AMINO ACIDS AND THEIR DERIVATIVES

	Compound	Adsorbent	Developer	Visualization	Comments	Ref.
1	Amino acids	Silica Gel G	a. EtOH (96%)-H$_2$O (63:37) b. PrOH-H$_2$O (64:36) c. BuOH-HOAC-H$_2$O (60:20:20) d. phenol-H$_2$O (75:25) e. PrOH-NH$_4$OH (34% NH$_3$) (67:33) f. EtOH (96%)-NH$_4$OH (34% NH$_3$) (77:23)	modified ninhydrin	a. diagnostic b. two dimensional	44 277
2	Amino acids	unbound aluminum oxide	a. H$_2$O b. pyridine-H$_2$O (1:1) (80:54) c. BuOH-EtOH-H$_2$O (60:40:40)	ninhydrin	a. diagnostic b. continuous elution c. spotted sample with NaOH	267
3	Amino acids	buffered Silica Gel G (buffered with equal portions of 0.2 *M* KH$_2$PO$_4$ and 0.2 *M* Na$_2$HPO$_4$)	a. EtOH-H$_2$O (70:30) b. EtOH-NH$_4$OH (25% NH$_3$) (4:1) c. EtOH-NH$_4$OH-H$_2$O (7:1:2)	paper chrom. reagents	diagnostic	271
4	Amino acids	Silica Gel G	a. CHCl$_3$-MeOH-NH$_4$OH (17% NH$_3$) (2:2:1) in first direction b. phenol-H$_2$O (75:25 g/g) in second dimension c. methyl ethyl ketone-pyridine-H$_2$O-HOAc (70:15:15:2) for continuous	ninhydrin	a. diagnostic b. continuous development c. two dimensional	99
5	Amino acids	Cellulose Powder MN 300	a. upper phase of BuOH-HOAc-H$_2$O (4:1:5) b. pyridine-methyl ethyl ketone-H$_2$O (15:70:15) c. MeOH-H$_2$O-pyridine (80:20:4) d. six others	ninhydrin	diagnostic	450
6	Amino acids	Silica Gel G	a. PrOH-H$_2$O (1:1) in first direction b. phenol-H$_2$O (10:4) in second direction	ninhydrin	a. diagnostic b. two dimensional	279
7	Amino acids and similar substances	a. Silica Gel G b. Kieselguhr G c. Aluminum Oxide G	a. 440V, 19.6 m. amp. in 0.1 *M* sodium citrate buffer, *p*H 3.8 b. 460V, 12.6 m. amp. in 2 *N* HOAc-0.6 *N* formic acid (1:1) at *p*H 2 c. chromatography using BuOH-HOAc-H$_2$O (3:1:1)	ninhydrin	a. diagnostic b. electrophoresis c. combined electrophoresis and chromatog.	156

8	N-(2,4-Dinitrophenyl)amino acids	a. Silica Gel G b. Silica Gel G with phosphor	a. toluene-pyridine-ethylenechlorohydrin-0.8 N NH$_4$OH (100:30:60:60), upper phase, in first direction b. CHCl$_3$-benzyl alcohol-HOAc (70:30:3) in second direction c. Sol. a in one direction and CHCl$_3$-MeOH-HOAc (95:5:1) in the second direction as continuous chrom. d. Sol. a in one direction and benzene-pyridine-HOAc (80:20:2) in second direction as continuous chrom. e. CHCl$_3$-t-amyl alcohol-HOAc (70:30:3)	a. colored compounds b. transmitted U.V. c. U.V.	a. Layers are all equilibrated with lower phase of Sol. a before use b. continuous development c. two dimensional	45 46
9	C^{14}-tagged N-(2,4-dinitrophenyl)-amino acids	Silica Gel G	a. toluene-pyridine-ethylenechlorohydrin-0.8 N NH$_4$OH (100:30:60:60), upper phase in first direction b. CHCl$_3$-benzylalcohol-glac. HOAc (70:30:3) in second direction	radiographic	a. two dimensional b. layer equilibrated with lower phase of sol. a before use	89
10	3-Phenyl-2-thiohydantoins of amino acids	Silica Gel G	a. CHCl$_3$ b. CHCl$_3$-MeOH (9:1) c. CHCl$_3$-formic acid (100:5) d. CHCl$_3$-MeOH-formic acid (70:30:2) e. Methyl ethyl ketone-pyridine-H$_2$O-conc. HOAc (70:15:15:2)	Cl$_2$-toluidine	diagnostic	46
11	Carbobenzoxy derivatives of amino acids and small peptides	Silica Gel G	a. BuOH-acetone-glac. HOAc-NH$_4$OH (7% NH$_3$)-H$_2$O (4.5:1.5:1:1:2) b. BuOH-glac. HOAc-NH$_4$OH (7% NH$_3$) (5.5:3:1.5) c. BuOH-HOAc-NH$_4$OH (7% NH$_3$)-H$_2$O (6:1:1:2) d. BuOH-glac. HOAc-H$_2$O-pyridine (15:3:12:10) e. in case of two-phase systems, both were used, but layer dipped only in upper phase	a. ninhydrin b. K$_2$Cr$_2$O$_7$ in conc. H$_2$SO$_4$	diagnostic	95
12	Amino acid and dipeptide derivatives	Silica Gel G	CHCl$_3$-MeOH (9:1)	Folin reagent	a. diagnostic b. monitored a synthesis	163
13	Polypeptides (up to five units) and derivatives	Silica Gel G	a. CHCl$_3$-acetone (9:1)(8:2) b. cyclohexane-EtOAc (1:1) c. CHCl$_3$-MeOH (9:1)	morin	diagnostic	341

Table 11.19—*Cont.*

	Compound	Adsorbent	Developer	Visualization	Comments	Ref.
14	Polypeptides (up to ten units) and derivatives	Silica Gel G	a. BuOH sat. with 0.1% NH₄OH b. other systems used in paper chrom.	ninhydrin	a. diagnostic b. monitored a synthesis	424
15	3-Phenyl-2-thiohydantoins of di- and tripeptides	Silica Gel G	heptane-pyridine-EtOAc (5:3:2)	starch-iodine azide	diagnostic	54
16	Proteins as such	polyamide-bound hydroxyl-apatite	potassium phosphate buffers, pH 6.5 of various concentrations	ninhydrin	a. diagnostic b. gradient elution	153
17	Proteins and polypeptides	Sephadex G 25 (moist)	a. 0.05 M NH₄OH b. H₂O	a. Pauly's reagent	a. diagnostic b. determine mol. wt.	82
	Enzymes	"DEAE-Sephadex" A 25	c. gradient elution involving addition of 0.02 M phosphate buffer pH 7.2 (which is also 1 M in NaCl) to the pure buffer	b. DPNH-pyruvic acid	c. gradient elution d. preparative	
18	Carbobenzoxyaminoacyl derivatives of cyclic alcohols	Silica Gel G	CHCl₃-acetone (85:15)	Cl₂ followed by KI and starch	a. monitored course of reaction b. monitored column chrom.	456
19	Metabolic products of tryptophane	Silica Gel G	a. CHCl₃-MeOH-HOAc (75:20:5) b. methyl acetate-2-PrOH-NH₄OH (25% NH₃) (45:35:20)	Ehrlich reagent	a. diagnostic b. urine analysis	87

TABLE 11.20. STEROIDS

	Compound	Adsorbent	Developer	Visualization	Comments	Ref.
1	Seventeen misc. steroids	Silica Gel G	a. benzene b. benzene-EtOAc (9:1)(2:1) c. cyclohexane-EtOAc (9:)(19:1) d. 1,2-dichloroethane e. seven more	SbCl₃ in CHCl₃	diagnostic	416
2	Seventy-nine steroids and sapogenins	unbound aluminum oxide, sometimes impregnated with morin	a. hexane-benzene mixtures b. benzene-EtOEt mixtures c. EtOEt-EtOH mixtures	a. conc. H₂SO₄ b. U.V. c. morin spray	a. diagnostic b. preparative	52
3	Twenty-two misc. steroids	a. starch-bound silicic acid b. Silica Gel G	EtOAc-cyclohexane mixtures	a. SbCl₃ in CHCl₃ b. 2,4-DNPH c. phosphomolybdic acid	diagnostic	13
4	Twenty-seven steroid estrogens	Silica Gel G	a. cyclohexane-EtOAc-EtOH (45:45:10) b. EtOAc-hexane-EtOH (80:15:5) c. EtOAc-cyclohexane (50:50) d. CHCl₃-EtOH (90:10) e. EtOAc-hexane-EtOH-HOAc (72:13.5:4.5:10) f. BuOH sat. with H₂O	a. Folin-Ciocalteau reag. b. Boute reagent c. 2% H₂SO₄ in H₂O-EtOH (1:1)	a. diagnostic b. classification system	221
5	Forty-nine misc. steroids	unbound aluminum oxide	a. benzene-pet. ether mixtures b. benzene-EtOH mixtures	a. SbCl₃ in CHCl₃ b. SbCl₃ in CHCl₃ with 10% SOCl₂	diagnostic	145
6	Twenty-seven misc. steroids	a. unbound aluminum oxide	a. pet. ether-benzene mixtures b. benzene c. benzene-EtOH mixtures	reagents used in paper chromatography	diagnostic	144
	Steroid acids	b. unbound aluminum oxide-HOAc	d. benzene-EtOH (90:10)			

Table 11.20—*Cont.*

	Compound	Adsorbent	Developer	Visualization	Comments	Ref.
7	Steroids from fermentation reactions	Silica Gel G	CHCl₃-acetone mixtures	a. vanillin in H_3PO_4 b. anisaldehyde in H_2SO_4 c. $SbCl_3$ in $CHCl_3$ d. H_3PO_4 e. 2,3,5-triphenyltetrazolium chloride f. $HClO_4$	diagnostic	247
8	Thirteen misc. steroids	a. Silica Gel G with phosphor b. Aluminum Oxide G with phosphor	a. CHCl₃-EtOAc (3:2)(3:1) b. benzene-EtOAc (1:1)(9:1) c. hexane-EtOAc (1:1)	I₂ vapor	a. quantitative b. diagnostic	244
9	Fifty-five misc. steroids	a. starch-bound silica gel b. starch-bound silica gel-NaOH	a. hexane-EtOAc (4:1)(1:1) b. EtOAc c. benzene-2-PrOH (4:1)	a. phosphomolybdic acid b. many others	diagnostic	363
10	Nineteen misc. steroids	plaster-of-Paris-bound "Celite" impregnated, by spraying, with a. formamide b. propylene glycol c. paraffin oil	a. hexane b. hexane-benzene (1:1) c. benzene d. CHCl₃ e. ligroin f. MeOH-H₂O (95:5)	a. H_3PO_4 b. tetrazolium blue c. isonicotinic acid hydrazide	a. diagnostic b. distribution	414
11	Fifteen sterols and sterol derivatives	a. Silica Gel G b. Silica Gel G Kieselguhr G (1:1)	a. cyclohexane-EtOAc-H₂O (600:400:1) (1560:440:1) b. isooctane-CCl₄ (19:1) c. cyclohexane-heptane (1:1)	50% H_2SO_4	diagnostic	27

#	Substance	Adsorbent	Solvent system	Reagent	Application	Ref.
12	Sterols and sterol acetates	a. Kieselguhr G b. Kieselguhr G (impregnated with un-decane)	a. cyclohexane-EtOAc (99.5:0.5) b. HOAc-H2O (92:8)(90:10) c. HOAc-CH3CN (1:3)	phosphomolybdic acid	diagnostic	295
13	Twenty-seven steroidal sapogenins and derivatives	a. Silica Gel G b. Kieselguhr G c. a and b (1:1) d. all equilibrated with water by placing moist filter paper in the chamber	a. CH2Cl2-MeOH-formamide (93:6:1) b. toluene-EtOAc-formic acid (57:40:3) c. cyclohexane-acetone (1:1) d. cyclohexane-EtOAc-E2O (600:400:1) (1000:1000:3) e. CHCl3-MeOH-H2O (185:15:1) (188:12:1) f. three others	50% H_2SO_4	a. diagnostic b. distribution chrom.	26
14	Steroidal sapogenins	Silica Gel G	a. EtOAc b. butyl acetate	chlorosulfonic acid-HOAc (1:2)	diagnostic	405
15	Synthetic steroids	Silica Gel G	a. benzene b. CHCl3 c. CHCl3-MeOH (10:1)(19:1)(97:3)	$SbCl_3$ in $CHCl_3$	diagnostic	67 68
16	Thirty-eight 19-nor-steroids	Silica Gel G	EtOAc-cyclohexane mixtures	$SbCl_3$ in $CHCl_3$	diagnostic	125
17	Estrogens	Silica Gel G	benzene-EtOH (9:1)	$SbCl_5$ in CCl_4	a. diagnostic b. quantitative	394
18	Pregnantriols from urine	unbound aluminum oxide	benzene-EtOH (9:1)	70% H_3PO_4	a. diagnostic b. quantitative	391
19	Estrone derivatives	plaster-of-Paris-bound silicic acid	pentane-EtOAc mixtures	$SbCl_3$ in $CHCl_3$	diagnostic	15
20	Pregnane derivatives	a. aluminum oxide b. Silica Gel Reidel de Haën	a. benzene-CH2Cl2 (2:1) b. cyclohexane-CH2Cl2 (1:2)	I_2 in KI	diagnostic	347
21	Misc. derivatives of pregnanol, cholesterol and sitosterol	Silica Gel G	a. isopropyl ether b. isopropyl ether-EtOAc (5:2) c. benzene	chlorosulfonic acid-HOAc (1:2)	a. diagnostic b. preparative c. monitored course of reaction	408

TABLE 11.20—*Cont.*

	Compound	Adsorbent	Developer	Visualization	Comments	Ref.
22	Pregnandiol	Silica Gel G	CHCl₃-acetone (9:1)	*ortho*-H₃PO₄-phosphomolybdic acid	early test for pregnancy	433 435
23	Cholesterol and its laurate ester	Silica Gel G	benzene-MeOH mixtures	conc. H₂SO₄	quantitative	315
24	Cholesterol	Silica Gel G	hexane-EtOEt-HOAc (50:50:2)	HClO₄	a. quantitative b. microscope slides	296
25	Blood cholesterol and cholesterol esters	Silica Gel G	a. benzene b. benzene-EtOAc (9:1) c. 1,2-dichloroethane d. CHCl₃ e. two others	SbCl₃ in CHCl₃	a. diagnostic b. semiquantitative	415
26	Cholesterol esters	Silica Gel G	isopropyl ether-pet. ether (1:99)	SbCl₃ in CHCl₃	a. diagnostic b. quantitative	460
27	Cholesterol esters	Silica Gel G	benzene-pet. ether (40:60)	50% H₂SO₄	diagnostic	228
28	Cholesterol esters	plaster-of-Paris-bound silicic acid impregnated with paraffin	HOAc	a. I₂ vapor b. SbCl₃ in CHCl₃ c. phosphomolybdic acid d. phosphotungstic acid	a. diagnostic b. reversed phase	249
29	Bile acids, free and conjugated	Silica Gel G	a. HOAc-CCl₄-isopropyl ether-isoamyl acetate-PrOH-benzene (5:20:30:40:10:10) for free acids b. propanoic acid-isoamyl acetate-H₂O-PrOH (15:20:5:10) for conjugate acids	phosphomolybdic acid	diagnostic	154

#	Compound	Adsorbent	Solvent system	Detection	Purpose	Ref.
30	Cholic acid derivatives	Silica Gel G	a. toluene-HOAc-H₂O (5:5:1) upper phase b. BuOH-HOAc-H₂O (10:1:1) c. toluene-HOAc-H₂O (10:10:1)	a. phosphomolybdic acid b. H₂O	a. diagnostic b. quantitative	115
31	Adrenocorticotropic hormones	Silica Gel G	EtOAc-xylene-MeOH (90:5:5)	tetrazolium chloride	diagnostic	30
32	Corticoids from urine	unbound silica gel	CHCl₃-EtOH (95:5)	tetrazolium blue	diagnostic	1
33	Corticosteroids	Silica Gel G (not activated)	CHCl₃-MeOH-H₂O (485:15:1) (188:12:1)(90:10:1)	50% H₂SO₄	diagnostic	25
34	Corticosteroids	plaster of Paris	a. acetone-benzene (1:4) b. EtOH-CHCl₃ (3:97)	alkaline tetrazolium blue	diagnostic	243
35	Cholestane derivatives	Silica Gel G	pet. ether-benzene (9:1)	I₂	diagnostic	361
36	Cholestanol derivatives	Silica Gel G	a. benzene b. benzene-EtOEt (70:30) c. pentane-EtOEt-benzene (20:20:60)	H₂O	quantitative	125
37	Aglycones of oleander glycosides	Silica Gel G	EtOAc-CHCl₃ (9:1)	SbCl₃ in CHCl₃	diagnostic	126
38	Cardinolides	Silica Gel G (not activated)	benzene-EtOH (3:1) sat. with H₂O	a. trichloroacetic acid-chloramine-T b. SbCl₃-acetic anhydride	a. diagnostic b. preparative	322
39	Steroidal compounds involved in tomatin formation	Silica Gel G	EtOAc-cyclohexane (1:1)(3:7)	a. SbCl₃ in chloroform b. 15% H₃PO₄	diagnostic	337 339
40	Digitoxigenin and derivatives	Silica Gel G	CHCl₃-EtOAc (1:1)	trichloroacetic acid-chloramine T	predicted solvents for column chrom.	90
41	Bile acids (free, conjugated) and derivatives	Silica Gel G	a. isoamyl acetate-CCl₄-isopropyl ether-benzene-PrOH-HOAc (4:3:2:1:1:0.5) b. isoamyl acetate-propanoic acid-PrOH-H₂O (4:3:2:1) c. cyclohexane-EtOAc (6:4)	phosphomolybdic acid	a. diagnostic b. microscope slides	152

TABLE 11.20—*Cont.*

	Compound	Adsorbent	Developer	Visualization	Comments	Ref.
42	Steroids from bull testicles	a. plaster-of-Paris-bound silica gel b. plaster-of-Paris-bound aluminum oxide	a. benzene-EtOAc (8:2) b. EtOAc c. butyl acetate d. several others	conc. H_2SO_4-U.V.	diagnostic	272
43	Radioactive andro-stane derivatives	Silica Gel G	cyclohexane-EtOAc (3:2)	radiographic	a. diagnostic b. quantitative c. preparative	349
44	β-Sitosterol from potato beetles	Silica Gel Riedel de Haen	pet. ether-EtOAc-benzene (85:10:5)	$SbCl_3$ in HOAc	diagnostic	348
45	1,3-Cholestanedione methyl ether	Silica Gel G	benzene-EtOEt (4:1)	I_2 vapor	monitored column chrom.	397
46	Aldosterones from urine	Silica Gel G	a. cyclohexane-2-PrOH (7:3) b. $CHCl_3$-glac. HOAc (8:2)	tetrazolium blue	a. two dimensional b. developed in dark c. quantitative	278
47	Sapogenins from *Solanum* species	Kieselguhr G	EtOAc-cyclohexane (7:3)	vanillin in H_3PO_4	diagnostic	336

TABLE 11.21. TERPENOIDS

	Compound	Adsorbent	Developer	Visualization	Comments	Ref.
1	Forty-nine misc. terpenoids	starch-bound silicic acid	hexane	a. fluorescein-Br$_2$ b. H$_2$SO$_4$-HNO$_3$	a. diagnostic b. monitored column	190
2	Fourteen misc. terpenoid	starch-bound silicic acid with phosphors	hexane-EtOAc (85:15)	a. fluorescein-Br$_2$ b. U.V. c. o-dianisidine d. conc. H$_2$SO$_4$ e. bromcresol green f. H$_2$SO$_4$-HNO$_3$	a. diagnostic b. predicted solvents for column chrom. c. monitored column	193 251
3	Twenty-eight oxygenated terpenoids	starch-bound silicic acid	a. hexane-EtOAc (85:15) (10:30) b. CHCl$_3$ (alcohol-free) EtOAc (90:10) (95:5) c. 1-nitropropane-hexane (50:50) d. ethyl carbonate-CHCl$_3$ (15:85) e. hexane-isopropyl formate (70:30) f. four others	a. fluorescein-Br$_2$ b. o-dianisidine c. H$_2$SO$_4$-HNO$_3$ d. conc. H$_2$SO$_4$	a. diagnostic b. chemical reactions on layers	252
4	Twelve misc. terpenoids	unbound alumina	a. pet. ether-benzene mixtures b. benzene c. benzene-EtOH mixtures	reagents used for paper chromatography	diagnostic	144
5	Diterpenoids	silicic acid	hexane-EtOAc (4:1)	KMnO$_4$	a. diagnostic b. monitored column c. review	213
6	Eighteen triterpenoids	synthetic fibrous alumina	a. hexane-benzene (8:1) b. cyclohexane-EtOAc (85:15) c. benzene d. EtOEt e. EtOEt-EtOH (98:2)	a. 2,4-DNPH b. SbCl$_5$ in CCl$_4$ c. Rhodamine B	diagnostic	165

TABLE 11.21—*Cont.*

	Compound	Adsorbent	Developer	Visualization	Comments	Ref.
7	Sixteen triterpenoids	Silica Gel G	a. isopropyl ether-acetone (5:2)(19:1) b. isopropyl ether c. cyclohexane d. benzene e. CH_2Cl_2	chlorosulfonic acid-HOAc	diagnostic	406 407
	Twenty-three triterpene acids		f. sol. a g. sol. a plus 5% pyridine h. EtOAc-MeOH-diethylamine (14:4:3) i. chlorobenzene-HOAc (9:1) j. CH_2Cl_2-pyridine (7:2)			
8	Triterpene acids	Silica Gel G	EtOEt-hexane (1:1)	50% H_2SO_4	diagnostic	421
9	Triterpene acids from *Commiphora glandulosa* Schinz, as methyl esters		$CHCl_3$-EtOAc (4:1)	conc. H_2SO_4	diagnostic	402
10	Carotenoids	a. Silica Gel G-$Ca(OH)_2$ (1:4) b. Silica Gel G-$Ca(OH)_2$ (1:4) impregnated with paraffin	a. benzene-pet. ether (1:1) b. sol. a with 1% MeOH c. MeOH sat. with paraffin	colored compounds	a. diagnostic b. preparative	446 449
11	Isomeric menthols	Silcia Gel G	a. benzene b. MeOH c. benzene-MeOH (95:5)(75:25)	$SbCl_5$ in CCl_4	diagnostic	299
12	Ipomeamarone	starch-bound silica gel	hexane-EtOAc (9:1)	2,4-DNPH	quantitative	2, 76

13	Isophytol and geranyl-linalol	starch-bound silica gel	hexane-EtOAc (85:15)		diagnostic	81
14	Azulene and cadalene	a. starch-bound silica gel b. starch-bound alumina	a. pet. ether b. EtOH	trinitrobenzene	diagnostic	108
15	Terpenoids of mint oils	see "Essential Oils," No. 11				20

TABLE 11.22. VITAMINS

	Compound	Adsorbent	Developer	Visualization	Comments	Ref.
1	Carotenes and fat-soluble vitamins A, D, E, K	unbound aluminum oxide	a. MeOH b. CCl₄ c. xylene d. eleven others	a. 70% HClO₄ b. conc. H₂SO₄	diagnostic	70
2	Carotenes and Vitamin A	unbound aluminum oxide	pet. ether	a. SbCl₃ in CHCl₃ b. colored compounds	a. diagnostic b. quantitative	210 211
3	B vitamins	Silica Gel G with fluorescent material	HOAc-acetone-MeOH-benzene (5:5:20:70)	a. U.V. b. potassium iodoplatinate c. dichloroquinone-chlorimide-NH₃ d. ninhydrin	a. diagnostic b. carried out in dark	116
4	Cyanocobalamin and hydroxycobalamin	Silica Gel G	a. MeOH b. PrOH c. BuOH-HOAc-H₂O (20:5:1) (20:5:5) and others d. BuOH-HOAc-MeOH (20:10:25) e. sixteen others	a. microbiologically b. spectrophotometrically	a. diagnostic b. quantitative	55
5	Vitamins K₂(₂₀), K₂(₃₀) and K₂(₁₀)	Silica Gel G with sodium fluorescein	a. heptane-benzene (1:1) dried and followed by b. benzene	U.V.	a. diagnostic b. radioactive compounds c. quantitative	35
6	Tocopherol mixtures	a. Silica Gel G b. Aluminum Oxide D5	a. CHCl₃ b. benzene	a. ceric sulfate b. phosphomolybdic acid-NH₃	a. diagnostic b. quantitative	354

7	Retinen	a. Silica Gel G b. Silica Gel G impregnated with paraffin	a. pet. ether-benzene mixtures b. MeOH sat. with paraffin	rhodanin	a. diagnostic b. semiquant.	448
8	Fat-soluble vitamins	alumina		a. $HClO_4$-70% b. H_2SO_4-98%		37
9	Ubiquinones	a. Silica Gel G b. Silica Gel G impregnated with paraffin	a. benzene-$CHCl_3$ (1 1) b. acetone-paraffin (sat. with H_2O) (9:1)	a. **Rhodamine B** b. $SbCl_3$ in $CHCl_3$	diagnostic	431
10	**Vitamins**					280

TABLE 11.23. MISCELLANEOUS

	Compound	Adsorbent	Developer	Visualization	Comments	Ref.
1	Benzoquinones from Myriapodes	starch-bound silicic acid	hexane-EtOAc (85:15)		diagnostic	12
2	Antioxidants (phenolic)	unbound polyamide powder	MeOH-acetone mixtures	a. diazotized sulfanilic acid b. phosphomolybdic acid	a. monitored column b. diagnostic	72
3	Antioxidants, synthetic	Silica Gel G	a. benzene b. CHCl$_3$ c. CHCl$_3$-methyl cellosolve (80:20)	a. phosphomolybdic acid b. diazotized sulfanilic acid c. 2,6-dichloroquinone-chlorimide, neutral and buffered	a. diagnostic b. two dimensional c. quantitative	352 353
4	Alkyl phosphenoxides, sulfides, sulfones, and sulfoxides	Silica Gel G	a. acetone b. CHCl$_3$	a. Na$_2$CrO$_7$-H$_2$SO$_4$ b. KMnO$_4$-H$_2$SO$_4$ c. FeCl$_3$ and K$_3$Fe(CN)$_6$	diagnostic	98
5	Thiophene derivatives	a. Silica Gel G b. Aluminum Oxide G	a. benzene-CHCl$_3$ (9:1) b. MeOH c. pet. ether	a. U.V. b. isatin in H$_2$SO$_4$	diagnostic	65
6	Aromatic amines and nitrocompounds	see "Amines," No. 5				110
7	Adulteration of the drug Radix pimpinellae DAB6	Silica Gel G	CHCl$_3$	SbCl$_5$ in CCl$_4$	diagnostic	161
8	Diphenyl in citrus fruits	starch-bound silicic acid with phosphors	pet. ether	U.V.	quantitative	194
9	Polycyclic aromatics	acetylated cellulose powder	MeOH-EtOEt-H$_2$O (4:4:1)	fluorescein	diagnostic	82
10	Nitramine explosives	Silica Gel G	pet. ether-acetone (2:102)	diphenylamine	diagnostic	216

11	Peroxides	starch-bound silica gel	CCl$_4$-acetone (2:1)	a. KI b. ferrous ammonium sulfate and potassium thiocyanate	diagnostic	242
12	Piperidoles, quinololes and cyclohexanediones	unbound aluminum oxide	a. benzene-acetone (1:1) b. acetone-MeOH (3:1)	a. I$_2$ b. U.V.	tested procedure	254
13	Honeybee larval foods	silicic acid	MeOH-CHCl$_3$ (29:71a)	a. p-anisidine b. ninhydrin c. FeCl$_3$ d. I$_2$ e. conc. H$_2$SO$_4$	diagnostic	292
14	Plasticizers (phthalates, phosphates and other esters)	Silica Gel G with fluorescent material	a. isooctane-EtOAc (90:10) b. benzene-EtOAc (95:5) c. butyl ether-hexane (80:20)	a. phosphomolybdic acid b. resorcinol-EtOH-ZnCl$_2$ followed by H$_2$SO$_4$ and KOH c. alcoholic KOH followed by urea d. 2,6-dichloroquinone-chloroimide followed by borax e. five others	diagnostic	293
15	Phloroglucinol-butanones from *Dryopteris*	a. Silica Gel G buffered with NaOAc b. Silica Gel G impregnated with paraffin	a. EtOAc b. MeOH-formic acid-H$_2$O (75:10:15)	Folin-Ciocalteau reagent-NH$_3$	diagnostic	380
16	Chamazulene derivatives and dyes as test substances	a. silicic acid b. starch-bound silicic acid	hexane-EtOAc (9:1)		methods exploration	381
17	Usnic acid	Silica Gel G	a. benzene	a. U.V.	a. diagnostic	437
	Aminopyrine	---	b. MeOH	b. FeCl$_3$	b. on microscope slides	

TABLE 11.23—*Cont.*

	Compound	Adsorbent	Developer	Visualization	Comments	Ref.
18	Neuraminic acid derivatives	Silica Gel G	a. PrOH-1 N NH$_4$OH-H$_2$O (6:2:1) b. PrOH-H$_2$O (7:3)	a. Bial's reagent b. thiobarbituric acid-HIO$_4$-ethylene glycol	diagnostic	127
19	Narcotics in forensic chemistry	Silica Gel G with fluorescent material	piperidine-pet. ether (1:5)	U.V.	diagnostic in urine	92
20	Lumiflavin derivatives	Silica Gel G	a. 2 N HClO$_4$-dimethylsulfoxide-BuOH (2:2:6) b. HOAc-H$_2$O-BuOH (2:2:6)	colored compounds	diagnostic	143
21	Bufadienolides from toad poisons	Silica Gel G	a. EtOAc b. EtOAc-cyclohexane (80:20) c. EtOAc-acetone (90:10) d. EtOAc sat. with H$_2$O	SbCl$_3$ in CHCl$_3$	diagnostic	457
22	Adrenaline and its derivatives	Silica Gel G	CHCl$_3$-MeOH (9:1)	H$_3$PO$_4$-phosphomolybdic acid	a. diagnostic b. quantitative	434
23	Soladulcidin, a nitrogen-containing aglycone from glycosides of *Solanum dulcamara* L.	Silica Gel G	EtOAc-cyclohexane (7:3)	vanillin-H$_3$PO$_4$	diagnostic	338
24	Anthocyanins	polyacrylonitrile-polyamide (7:1)	1-pentanol-PrOH-HOAc-H$_2$O (3:2:1) plus 1–2% 1-heptanol	colored compounds	a. diagnostic b. descending	36
25	Olefins as mercury salts	Silica Gel G	PrOH-triethylamine-H$_2$O (50:25:25)	diphenylcarbazide	diagnostic	309

References

1. Adamec, O., Matis, J., and Galvánek, N., *Lancet*, **81**, (1962I).
2. Akazawa, T., and Wada, K., *Agr. Biol. Chem. (Tokyo)*, **25**, 30 (1961); *Chem. Abstr.*, **55**, 10557 (1961).
3. Akhrem, A. A. and Kuznetsova, A. I., *Doklady Akad. Nauk S.S.S.R.*, **138**, 591 (1961); *Chem. Abstr.*, **55**, 22373 (1961).
4. Akhrem, A. A., Kuznetsova, A. I., Titov, U. A., and Levina, I. S., *Izvest. Akad. Nauk S.S.S.R. Otdel. Khim. Nauk*, 657 (1962).
4a. Amelung, D., and Böhm, P., *Hoppe-Seyler's Z. physiol. Chem.*, **298**, 199 (1954).
4b. Anacker, W. F., and Stoy, V., *Biochem. Z.*, **330**, 141 (1958).
5. Anet, E. F. L. J., *J. Chromatog.*, **9**, 291 (1962).
6. Anker, L., and Sonanini, D., *Pharm. Acta Helv.*, **37**, 360 (1962).
7. Applegarth, D. A., Dutton, G. G. S., and Tanaka, Y., *Can. J. Chem.*, **40**, 2177 (1962).
8. Applewhite, T. H., Diamond, M. J., and Goldblatt, L. A., *J. Am. Oil Chemists' Soc.*, **38**, 609 (1961).
9. Badings, H. T., *ibid.*, **36**, 648 (1959).
10. Baehler, B., *Helv. Chim. Acta*, **45**, 309 (1962).
11. Bakshi, S. H., and Krishnaswamy, N., *J. Chromatog.*, **9**, 395 (1962).
12. Barbier, M., *ibid.*, **2**, 649 (1959).
13. Barbier, M., Jäger, H., Tobias, H., and Wyss, E., *Helv. Chim. Acta*, **42**, 2440 (1959).
14. Barbier, M., Vinogradova, L. P., and Zav'yalov, S. I., *Izvest. Akad. Nauk S.S.S.R. Otdel. Khim. Nauk*, 162 (1961); *Chem. Abstr.*, **55**, 16077 (1961).
15. Barbier, M., and Zav'yalov, S. I., *ibid.*, 1309 (1960); *Chem. Abstr.*, **54**, 22803 (1960).
16. Barrett, C. B., Dallas, M. S. J., and Padley, F. B., *Chem. & Ind.*, (London), 1050 (1962).
17. Barrett, G. C., *Nature*, **194**, 1171 (1962).
18. Barrollier, J., *Naturwissenschaften*, **48**, 404 (1961); *Chem. Abstr.*, **55**, 26557 (1961).

19. Battaile, J., Dunning, R. L., and Loomis, W. D., *Biochim. Biophys. Acta*, **51**, 538 (1961).
20. Battaile, J., and Loomis, W. D., *ibid.*, **51**, 545 (1961).
21. Baumann, U., *Z. Anal. Chem.*, **173**, 458 (1960).
22. Bäumler, J., and Rippstein, S., *Pharm. Acta Helv.*, **36**, 382 (1961).
23. Bäumler, J., and Rippstein, S., *Helv. Chim. Acta*, **44**, 1162 (1961).
24. Berkersky, I., *Anal. Chem.*, **35**, 261 (1963).
25. Bennett, R. D., and Heftmann, E., *J. Chromatog.*, **9**, 348 (1962).
26. Bennett, R. D., and Heftmann, E., *ibid.*, **9**, 353 (1962).
27. Bennett, R. D., and Heftmann, E., *ibid.*, **9**, 359 (1962).
28. Bergel'son, L. D., Dyatlovitskaya, E. V., and Voronkova, V. V., *Doklady Akad. Nauk S.S.S.R.*, **141**, 84 (1961); *Chem. Abstr.*, **56**, 8005 (1962).
29. Berger, J. A., Meyniel, G., and Petit, J., *Compt. Rend.*, **255**, 1116 (1962).
30. Bernauer, W., and Schmidt, L., *Arch. Exp. Pathol. Pharmakol.*, **243**, 311 (1962).
31. Bernhard, R. A., *Nature*, **182**, 1171 (1958).
32. Beroza, M., and Jones, W. A., *Anal. Chem.*, **34**, 1029 (1962).
33. Bickel, H., Gäumann, E., Hütter, R., Sackmann, W., Vischer, E., Voser, W., Wettstein, A., and Zähner, H., *Helv. Chim. Acta*, **45**, 1396 (1962).
34. Bickoff, E. M., Lyman, R. L., Livingston, A. L., and Booth, A. N., *J. Am. Chem. Soc.*, **80**, 3969 (1958).
35. Billeter, M., and Martius, C., *Biochem. Z.*, **334**, 304 (1961).
36. Birkofer, L., Kaiser, C., Meyer-Stoll, H.-A., and Suppan, F., *Z. Naturforsch.*, **17b**, 352 (1962).
37. Blattná, J., and Davídek, J., *Experientia*, **17**, 474 (1961).
38. Bobbitt, J. M., Ebermann, R., and Schubert, M., *Tetrahedron Letters*, 575 (1963).
39. Bobbitt, J. M., Schmid, H., and Africa, T. B., *J. Org. Chem.*, **26**, 3090 (1961).
40. Bobbitt, J. M., Spiggle, D. W., Mahboob, S., von Philipsborn, W., and Schmid, H., *Tetrahedron Letters*, 321 (1962).
41. Boll, P. M., *Chemist-Analyst*, **51**, 52 (1962).
42. Braun, D., and Geenen, H., *J. Chromatog.*, **7**, 56 (1962).
43. Bravo O., R. and Hernández A., F., *ibid.*, **7**, 60 (1962).
44. Brenner, M., and Niederwieser, A., *Experientia*, **16**, 378 (1960).
45. Brenner, M., and Niederwieser, A., *ibid.*, **17**, 237 (1961).
46. Brenner, M., Niederwieser, A., and Pataki, G., *ibid.*, **17**, 145 (1961).
47. Brenner, M., Niederwieser, A., Pataki, G., and Fahmy, A. R., *ibid.*, **18**, 101 (1962).

48. Brenner, M., and Pataki, G., *Helv. Chim. Acta*, **44**, 1420 (1961).
49. Brieskorn, C.-H., and Wenger, E., *Arch. Pharm.*, **293/65**, 21 (1960).
50. Brockmann, H., and Schodder, H., *Ber.*, **74B**, 73 (1941).
50a. Brockmann, H., and Volpers, F., *Chem. Ber.*, **80**, 77 (1947).
51. Bryant, L. H., *Nature*, **175**, 556 (1955).
51a. Bush, I. E., and Willoughby, M., *Biochem. J.*, **67**, 689 (1957).
51b. Cadenas, R. A., and Deferrari, J. O., *Analyst*, **86**, 132 (1961).
52. Černý, V., Joska, J., and Lábler, L., *Collection Czech. Chem. Commun.*, **26**, 1658 (1961).
53. Cerri, O., and Maffi, G., *Boll. Chim. Farm.*, **100**, 940 (1961).
53a. Cerri, O., and Maffi, G., *ibid.*, **100**, 951 (1961).
53b. Cerri, O., and Maffi, G., *ibid.*, **100**, 954 (1961).
54. Cherbuliez, E., Baehler, B., and Rabinowitz, J., *Helv. Chim. Acta*, **43**, 1871 (1960).
55. Cima, L., and Mantovan, R., *Farmaco, (Pavia), Ed. Prat.*, **17**, 473 (1962).
56. Claesson, S., *Arkiv Kemi, Mineral. Geol.*, **23A**, No. 1 (1946).
57. Cochin, J., and Daly, J. W., *Experientia*, **18**, 294 (1962).
57a. Consden, R., Gordon, A. H., and Martin, A. J. P., *Biochem. J.*, **38**, 224 (1944).
57b. Consden, R., Gordon, A. H., and Martin, A. J. P., *Biochem. J.*, **41**, 590 (1947).
58. Coveney, R. D., Matthews, W. S. A., and Pickering, G. B., *Colonial Plant Animal Prod. (Gt. Brit.)*, **5**, 150 (1955).
59. Craig, L. C., Hausmann, W., Ahrens, Jr., E. H., and Harfenist, E. J., *Anal. Chem.*, **23**, 1236 (1951).
60. Craig, L. C., and Post, O., *ibid.*, **21**, 500 (1949).
61. Cremer, E., and Müller, R., *Z. Electrochem.*, **55**, 217 (1951).
62. Cremer, E., and Prior, F., *ibid.*, **55**, 66 (1951).
63. Crowe, M. O'L., *Anal. Chem.*, **13**, 845 (1941).
64. Crump, G. B., *Nature*, **193**, 674 (1962).
65. Curtis, R. F., and Phillips, G. T., *J. Chromatog.*, **9**, 366 (1962).
66. Dahn, H., and Fuchs, H., *Helv. Chim. Acta*, **45**, 261 (1962).
67. Dannenberg, H., and Neumann, H.-G., *Chem. Ber.*, **94**, 3085 (1961).
68. Dannenberg, H., and Neumann, H.-G., *ibid.*, **94**, 3094 (1961).
69. Davídek, J., *J. Chromatog.*, **9**, 363 (1962).
70. Davídek, J., and Blattná, J., *ibid.*, **7**, 204 (1962).
71. Davídek, J., and Davídková, E., *Pharmazie*, **16**, 352 (1961).
72. Davídek, J., and Pokorný, J., *Z. Lebensm. Untersuch.-Forsch.*, **115**, 113 (1961).
73. Davídek, J., Pokorný, J., and Janíček, G., *ibid.*, **116**, 13 (1962).

74. Davídek, J., and Procházka, Ž., *Collection Czech. Chem. Commun.*, **26**, 2947 (1961).

75. Deferrari, J. O., Muchnik de Lederkremer, R., Matsuhiro, B., and Sproviero, J. F., *J. Chromatog.*, **9**, 283 (1962).

76. Demole, E., *Compt. Rend.*, **243**, 1883 (1956).

77. Demole, E., *J. Chromatog.*, **1**, 24 (1958).

78. Demole, E., *Chromatog. Rev.*, **1**, 1 (1959).

79. Demole, E., *J. Chromatog.*, **6**, 2 (1961).

80. Demole, E., *Chromatog. Rev.*, in press.

81. Demole, E., and Lederer, E., *Bull. Soc. Chim. France*, 1128 (1958).

82. Determann, H., Wieland, Th., and Lüben, G., *Experientia*, **18**, 430 (1962).

83. Deters, R., *Chemiker-Z.*, **86**, 388 (1962).

84. Dhont, J. H., and de Rooy, C., *Analyst*, **86**, 74 (1961).

85. Dhont, J. H., and de Rooy, C., *ibid.*, **86**, 527 (1961).

86. Dhopeshwarkar, G. A., and Mead, J. F., *J. Am. Oil Chemists' Soc.*, **38**, 297 (1961).

87. Diamantstein, T., and Ehrhart, H., *Hoppe-Seyler's Z. physiol. Chem.*, **326**, 131 (1961).

88. Döpke, W., *Arch. Pharm.*, **295**, 605 (1962).

89. Drawert, F., Bachmann, O., and Reuther, K.-H., *J. Chromatog.*, **9**, 376 (1962).

90. Duncan, G. R., *ibid.*, **8**, 37 (1962).

91. Dijkstra, G., *Chem. Weekblad*, **57**, 189 (1961).

92. Eberhardt, H., and Freundt, K. J., *Arch. Exp. Pathol. Pharmakol.*, **243**, 310 (1962).

93. Eble, J. N., and Brooker, R. M., *Experientia*, **18**, 524 (1962).

94. Egger, K., *Z. Anal. Chem.*, **182**, 161 (1961).

95. Ehrhardt, E., and Cramer, F., *J. Chromatog.*, **7**, 405 (1962).

96. Eisenberg, F., Jr., *ibid.*, **9**, 390 (1962).

97. Endres, H., *Z. Anal. Chem.*, **181**, 331 (1961).

98. Ertel, H., and Horner, L., *J. Chromatog.*, **7**, 268 (1962).

99. Fahmy, A. R., Niederwieser, A., Pataki, G., and Brenner, M., *Helv. Chim. Acta*, **44**, 2022 (1961).

100. Fassina, G., *Boll. Soc. Ital. Biol. Sper.*, **36**, 1417 (1960).

101. Ferrari, M., and Tóth, C. E., *J. Chromatog.*, **9**, 388 (1962).

102. Fiori, A., and Marigo, M., *Nature*, **182**, 943 (1958).

103. Fischer, R., and Lautner, H., *Arch. Pharm.*, **294/66**, 1 (1961).

104. Fontell, K., Holman, R. T., and Lambertsen, G., *J. Lipid Res.*, **1**, 391 (1960).

104a. Frahm, M., Gottesleben, A., and Soehring, K., *Arzneimittel-Forsch.*, **11**, 1008 (1961).

105. Frydman, B. J., Montes, A. L., and Troparevsky, A., *Anales Asoc. Quim. Arg.*, **45**, 248 (1957); *Chem. Abstr.*, **52**, 17622 (1958).

106. Frydman, B. J., Montes, A. L., and Troparevsky, A., *ibid.*, **45**, 257 (1957); *Chem. Abstr.*, **52**, 17622 (1958).

107. Frydman, B. J., Montes, A. L., and Troparevsky, A., *ibid.*, **45**, 261 (1957); *Chem. Abstr.*, **52**, 17622 (1958).

108. Fukushi, S., and Obata, Y., *J. Agr. Chem. Soc. Japan*, **27**, 353 (1953); *Chem. Abstr.*, **50**, 15027 (1956).

109. Fulco, A. J., and Mead, J. F., *J. Biol. Chem.*, **236**, 2416 (1961).

110. Furukawa, T., *Mem. Fac. Educ. Hiroshima Univ.*, **5**, 85 (1957); *Chem. Abstr.*, **52**, 13364 (1958).

111. Furukawa, T., *J. Sci. Hiroshima Univ.*, **Ser. A21**, 285 (1958); *Chem. Abstr.*, **53**, 809 (1959).

112. Furukawa, T., *Nippon Kagaku Zasshi*, **80**, 45 (1959); *Chem. Abstr.*, **54**, 4107 (1960).

113. Furukawa, T., *ibid.*, **80**, 387 (1959); *ibid.*, **54**, 13938 (1960).

114. Gamp, A., Studer, P., Linde, H., and Meyer, K., *Experientia*, **18**, 292 (1962).

115. Gänshirt, H., Koss, F. W., and Morianz, K., *Arzneimittel-Forsch.*, **10**, 943 (1960).

116. Gänshirt, H., and Malzacher, A., *Naturwissenschaften*, **47**, 279 (1960).

117. Gänshirt, H., and Malzacher, A., *Arch. Pharm.*, **293/65**, 925 (1960).

118. Gänshirt, H., and Morianz, K., *ibid.*, **293/65**, 1066 (1960).

119. Gauglitz, Jr., E. J., and Malins, D. C., *J. Am. Oil Chemists' Soc.*, **37**, 425 (1960).

120. Gee, M., *J. Chromatog.*, **9**, 278 (1962).

121. Getz, H. R., and Lawson, D. D., *ibid.*, **7**, 266 (1962).

122. Giacobazzi, C., and Gibertini, G., *Boll. Chim. Farm.*, **101**, 490 (1962).

123. Giddings, J. C., and Keller, R. A., *J. Chromatog.*, **2**, 626 (1959).

124. Gogröf, G., *Pharmazie*, **12**, 38 (1957).

125. Golab, T., and Layne, D. S., *J. Chromatog.*, **9**, 321 (1962).

126. Görlich, B., *Planta Med.*, **9**, 442 (1961).

127. Granzer, E., *Hoppe-Seyler's Z. physiol. Chem.*, **328**, 277 (1962).

128. Gritter, R. J., and Albers, R. J., *J. Chromatog.*, **9**, 392 (1962).

129. Grassmann, W., Hörmann, H., and von Poratatius, H., *Hoppe-Seyler's Z. physiol. Chem.*, **321**, 120 (1960).

130. Gruger, Jr., E. H., Malins, D. C., and Gauglitz, Jr., E. J., *J. Am. Oil Chemists' Soc.*, **37**, 214 (1960).

131. Grüner, S., and Spaich, W., *Arch. Pharm.*, **287**/59, 243 (1954).
132. Guggolz, J., Livingston, A. L., and Bickoff, E. M., *J. Agr. Food Chem.*, **9**, 330 (1961).
133. Gurvich, N. L., *Vsesoyuz. Nauch.-Issledovatel'. Inst. Maslichn. i Efiromasl. Kul't. Vsesoyuz. Akad. Sel'skokhoz. Nauk, Kratkii Otchet*, 154 (1956); *Chem. Abstr.*, 54, 25595 (1960).
134. Habermann, E., Bandtlow, G., and Krusche, B., *Klin. Wochschr.*, **39**, 816 (1961).
134a. Hais, I. M., and Macek, K., "Handbuch der Papierchromatographie," Jena, Gustav Fischer, 1958.
135. Hall, R. J., *J. Chromatog.*, 5, 93 (1961).
136. Halmekoski, J., *Suomen Kemistilehti*, **35B**, 39 (1962).
137. Hansbury, E., Langham, J., and Ott, D. G., *J. Chromatog.*, **9**, 393 (1962).
138. Hansson, J., and Alm, A., *ibid.*, **9**, 385 (1962).
139. Häusser, H., *Arch. Kriminol.*, **125**, 72 (1960).
140. Hecker, E., *Chimia (Aarau)*, 8, 229 (1954).
141. Hefendehl, F. W., *Planta Med.*, 8, 65 (1960).
142. Heftmann, E., "Chromatography," New York, Reinhold Publishing Corp., 1961.
143. Hemmerich, P., *Helv. Chim. Acta*, 43, 1942 (1960).
144. Heřmánek, S., Schwarz, V́., and Čekan, Z., *Pharmazie*, **16**, 566 (1961).
145. Heřmánek, S., Schwarz, V́., and Čekan, Z., *Collection Czech. Chem. Commun.*, **26**, 1669 (1961).
146. Heřmánek, S., Schwarz, V́., and Čekan, Z., *ibid.*, **26**, 3170 (1961).
147. Heyns, K., and Grützmacher, H. F., *Angew. Chem. Intern. Ed., Engl.*, 1, 400 (1962).
148. Hilton, J., and Hall, W. B., *J. Chromatog.*, **7**, 266 (1962).
149. Hirayama, O., *J. Agr. Chem. Soc. Japan*, **35**, 437 (1961).
150. Hirsch, J., *Federation Proc.*, **20**, 269 (1961).
151. Hofmann, A., and Tscherter, H., *Experientia*, **16**, 414 (1960).
152. Hofmann, A. F., *Anal. Biochem.*, 3, 145 (1962).
153. Hofmann, A. F., *Biochim. Biophys. Acta*, **60**, 458 (1962).
154. Hofmann, A. F., *J. Lipid Res.*, 3, 127 (1962).
155. Hofmann, A. F., *ibid.*, 3, 391 (1962).
156. Honegger, C. G., *Helv. Chim. Acta*, **44**, 173 (1961).
157. Honegger, C. G., *ibid.*, 45, 281 (1962).
158. Honegger, C. G., *ibid.*, 45, 1409 (1962).
159. Honegger, C. G., *ibid.*, 45, 2020 (1962).
160. Hörhammer, L., Wagner, H., and Bittner, G., *Deutsche Apotheker*, **14**, No. 4, 1 (1962).

161. Hörhammer, L., Wagner, H., and Lay, B., *Pharmazie*, **15**, 645 (1960).
162. Horowitz, R. M., and Gentili, B., *J. Org. Chem.*, **25**, 2183 (1960).
163. Huguenin, R. L., and Boissonnas, R. A., *Helv. Chim. Acta*, **44**, 213 (1961).
164. Huhnstock, K., and Weicker, H., *Klin. Wochschr.*, **38**, 1249 (1960).
165. Huneck, S., *J. Chromatog.*, **7**, 561 (1962).
166. Isler, O., Rüegg, R., and Schudel, P., *Chimia (Aarau)*, **15**, 208 (1961).
167. Ito, M., Wakamatsu, S., and Kawahara, H., *J. Chem. Soc. Japan, Pure Chem. Sect.*, **74**, 699 (1953); *Chem. Abstr.*, **48**, 3640 (1954).
168. Ito, M., Wakamatsu, S., and Kawahara, H., *ibid.*, **75**, 413 (1954); *Chem. Abstr.*, **48**, 13172 (1954).
169. Izmaïlov, N. A., and Shraïber, M. S., *Farmatsiya (Sofia)*, No. 3, 1 (1938); *Chem. Abstr.*, **34**, 855 (1940).
170. James, A. T., and Martin, A. J. P., *Analyst*, **77**, 915 (1952).
171. Jaspersen-Schib, R., *Pharm. Acta Helv.*, **36**, 141 (1961).
172. Jaspersen-Schib, R., and Flück, H., *Boll. Chim. Farm.*, **101**, 512 (1962).
173. Jatzkewitz, H., *Hoppe-Seyler's Z. physiol. Chem.*, **320**, 134 (1960).
174. Jatzkewitz, H., and Mehl, E., *ibid.*, **320**, 251 (1960).
175. Jeanes, A., Wise, C. S., and Dimler, R. J., *Anal. Chem.*, **23**, 415 (1951).
176. Jensen, A., *Tidsskr. Kjemi, Bergvesen Met.*, **21**, 14 (1961).
177. Jensen, R. G., and Sampugna, J., *J. Dairy Sci.*, **45**, 435 (1962).
178. Jensen, R. G., Sampugna, J., and Gander, G. W., *ibid.*, **44**, 1983 (1961).
178a. Jensen, R. G., Sampugna, J., and Parry, Jr., R. M., *J. Dairy Sci.*, **45**, 842 (1962).
179. Kaufmann, H. P., and Das, B., *Fette u. Seifen*, **64**, 214 (1962).
180. Kaufmann, H. P., and Khoe, T. H., *ibid.*, **64**, 81 (1962).
181. Kaufmann, H. P., and Ko, Y. S., *ibid.*, **63**, 828 (1961).
182. Kaufmann, H. P., and Makus, Z., *ibid.*, **62**, 1014 (1960).
183. Kaufmann, H. P., Makus, Z., and Das, B., *ibid.*, **63**, 807 (1961).
184. Kaufmann, H. P., Makus, Z., and Deicke, F., *ibid.*, **63**, 235 (1961).
185. Kaufmann, H. P., Makus, Z., and Khoe, T. H., *ibid.*, **63**, 689 (1961).
186. Kaufmann, H. P., Makus, Z., and Khoe, T. H., *ibid.*, **64**, 1 (1962).
187. Keulemans, A. I. M., "Gas Chromatography," New York, Reinhold Publishing Corp., 1959.
188. Khanna, K. L., Schwarting, A. E., Rother, A., and Bobbitt, J. M., *Lloydia*, **24**, 179 (1961).
189. Khorlin, A. Y., and Bochkov, A. F., *Izvest. Akad. Nauk S.S.S.R., Otdel. Tekh. Nauk*, 1120 (1962).
190. Kirchner, J. G., and Miller, J. M., *Ind. Eng. Chem.*, **44**, 318 (1952).
191. Kirchner, J. G., and Miller, J. M., *J. Agr. Food Chem.*, **1**, 512 (1953).
192. Kirchner, J. G., and Miller, J. M., *ibid.*, **5**, 283 (1957).

193. Kirchner, J. G., Miller, J. M., and Keller, G. J., *Anal. Chem.*, **23**, 420 (1951).
194. Kirchner, J. G., Miller, J. M., and Rice, R. G., *J. Agr. Food Chem.*, **2**, 1031 (1954).
195. Klavehn, M., Rochelmeyer, H., and Seyfried, J., *Deut. Apotheker-Z.*, **101**, 75 (1961).
196. Klein, S., and Kho, B. T., *J. Pharm. Sci.*, **51**, 966 (1962).
197. Klenk, E., and Gielen, W., *Hoppe-Seyler's Z. physiol. Chem.*, **323**, 126 (1961).
198. Klohr-Meinhardt, R., *Planta Med.*, **6**, 203 (1958).
199. Klohr-Meinhardt, R., *ibid.*, **6**, 208 (1958).
200. Knappe, E., and Peteri, D., *Z. Anal. Chem.*, **188**, 184 (1962).
201. Knappe, E., and Peteri, D., *ibid.*, **188**, 352 (1962).
202. Knight, H. S., and Groennings, S., *Anal. Chem.*, **26**, 1549 (1954).
203. Kochetkov, N. K., Dmitriev, B. A., and Usov, A. I., *Doklady Akad. Nauk S.S.S.R.*, **143**, 863 (1962).
204. Kochetkov, N. K., Zhukova, I. G., and Glukhoded, I. S., *ibid.*, **139**, 608 (1961).
205. Kokoti-Kotakis, E., *Chim. Chronika (Athens, Greece)*, **27**, 59 (1962).
206. Kore, S. A., Shepelenkova, E. I., and Chernova, E. M., *Maslobo in o Zhirovaya Prom.*, **28**, No. 3, 32 (1962).
207. Korte, F., and Vogel, J., *J. Chromatog.*, **9**, 381 (1962).
208. Kuhn, R., Wiegandt, H., and Egge, H., *Angew. Chem.*, **73**, 580 (1961).
209. Labat, J., and Montes, A. L., *Anales asoc. quim. arg.*, **41**, 166 (1953); *Chem. Abstr.*, **48**, 3637 (1954).
210. Lagoni, H., and Wortmann, A., *Milchwissenschaft*, **10**, 360 (1955).
211. Lagoni, H., and Wortmann, A., *ibid.*, **11**, 206 (1956).
212. Lawson, D. D., and Getz, H. R., *Chem. & Ind. (London)*, 1404 (1961).
213. Lederer, E., *France Parfums*, **3**, No. 14, 28 (1960); *Chem. Abstr.*, **54**, 14579 (1960).
214. Lees, T. M., and DeMuria, P. J., *J. Chromatog.*, **8**, 108 (1962).
215. Lehner, H., and Schmutz, J., *Helv. Chim. Acta*, **44**, 444 (1961).
215a. Lemieux, R. V., and Bauer, H. F., *Anal. Chem.*, **26**, 920 (1954).
216. Lennart Harthon, J. G., *Acta Chem. Scand.*, **15**, 1401 (1961).
217. Libosvar, J., Nedbal, J., and Hach, V., *Ceskoslov. Farm.*, **11**, 73 (1962).
218. Lichtenberger, W., *Z. Anal. Chem.*, **185**, 111 (1962).
219. Lie, K. B., and Nyc, J. F., *J. Chromatog.*, **8**, 75 (1962).
219a. Lin, Y. T., Wang, K. T., and Lin, Y. S., *J. Chinese Chem. Soc., (Taiwan)* **9**, 68 (1962).
220. Lipina, T. P., *Zavodskaya Lab.*, **26**, 55 (1960), *Microchem. J.*, **5**, 660 (1961).

221. Lisboa, B. P., and Diczfalusy, E., *Acta Endocrinol.*, **40**, 60 (1962).
222. Livingston, A. L., Bickoff, E. M., Guggolz, J., and Thompson, C. R., *J. Agr. Food Chem.*, **9**, 135 (1961).
223. Lukas, G., *Sci. Pharm.*, **30**, 47 (1962).
224. Lyman, R. L., Bickoff, E. M., Booth, A. N., and Livingston, A. L., *Arch. Biochem. Biophys.*, **80**, 61 (1959).
225. Lyman, R. L., Livingston, A. L., Bickoff, E. M., and Booth, A. N., *J. Org. Chem.*, **23**, 756 (1958).
226. Machata, G., *Wien. klin. Wochschr.*, **71**, 301 (1959).
227. Machata, G., *Mikrochim. Acta*, 79 (1960).
228. Mahadevan, V., and Lundberg, W. O., *J. Lipid Res.*, **3**, 106 (1962).
229. Malins, D. C., *Chem. & Ind. (London)*, 1359 (1960).
230. Malins, D. C., and Mangold, H. K., *J. Am. Oil Chemists' Soc.*, **37**, 576 (1960).
231. Mangold, H. K., *Fette u. Seifen*, **61**, 877 (1959).
232. Mangold. H. K., *J. Am. Oil Chemists' Soc.*, **38**, 708 (1961).
233. Mangold, H. K., and Kammereck, R., *Chem. & Ind. (London)*, 1032 (1961).
234. Mangold, H. K., and Kammereck, R., *J. Am. Oil Chemists' Soc.*, **39**, 201 (1962).
234a. Mangold, H. K., Kammereck, R., and Malins, D. C., *Microchem. J., Symp. Ser.*, **2**, 697 (1962).
235. Mangold, H. K., and Malins, D. C., *ibid.*, **37**, 383 (1960).
236. Mangold, H. K., and Tuna, N., *Federation Proc.*, **20**, 268 (1961).
237. Marbet, R., and Saucy, G., *Chimia (Aarau)*, **14**, 362 (1960).
238. Marcuse, R., *J. Chromatog.*, **7**, 407 (1962).
239. Mariani, A., and Mariani-Marelli, O., *Rend. ist. super Sanità*, **22**, 759 (1959); *Chem. Abstr.*, **54**, 11374 (1960).
240. Marigo, M., *Minerva medicolegale*, **81**, 70 (1961).
241. Martin, A. J. P., and Synge, R. L. M., *Biochem. J.*, **35**, 1358 (1941).
242. Maruyama, K., *J. Chem. Soc. Japan, Pure Chem. Sect.*, **77**, 1496 (1956); *Anal. Abstr.*, **4**, 3002 (1957).
243. Matis, J., Adamec, O., and Galvánek, M., *Nature*, **194**, 477 (1962).
244. Matthews, J. S., Pereda V., A. L., and Aguilera P., A., *J. Chromotog.*, **9**, 331 (1962).
245. McGugan, W. A., *Intern. Dairy Congr., 15th, London*, 1959 (pub. 1960), 1534 (1959).
246. Meinhard, J. E., and Hall, N. F., *Anal. Chem.*, **21**, 185 (1949).
247. Metz, H., *Naturwissenschaften*, **48**, 569 (1961).
248. Michalec, C., *Chem. Listy*, **55**, 953 (1961); *Chem. Abstr.*, **55**, 26823 (1961).

249. Michalec, C., Sulc, M., and Mestan, J., *Nature*, **193**, 63 (1962).
250. Miller, J. M., and Kirchner, J. G., *Anal. Chem.*, **23**, 428 (1951).
251. Miller, J. M., and Kirchner, J. G., *ibid.*, **24**, 1480 (1952).
252. Miller, J. M., and Kirchner, J. G., *ibid.*, **25**, 1107 (1953).
253. Miller, J. M., and Kirchner, J. G., *ibid.*, **26**, 2002 (1954).
254. Mistryukov, E. A., *Collection Czech. Chem. Commun.*, **26**, 2071 (1961).
255. Mistryukov, E. A., *J. Chromatog.*, **9**, 311 (1962).
256. Mistryukov, E. A., *ibid.*, **9**, 314 (1962).
257. Montag, A., *Z. Lebensm. Untersuch. u.-Forsch.*, **116**, 413 (1962).
258. Morgan, M. E., *J. Chromatog.*, **9**, 379 (1962).
259. Morgan, M. E., and Pereira, R. L., *J. Dairy Sci.*, **45**, 457 (1962).
260. Morris, L. J., *Chem. & Ind. (London)*, 1238 (1962).
261. Morris, L. J., Hayes, H., and Holman, R. T., *J. Am. Oil Chemists' Soc.*, **38**, 316 (1961).
262. Morris, L. J., Holman, R. T., and Fontell, K., *ibid.*, **37**, 323 (1960).
263. Morris, L. J., Holman, R. T., and Fontell, K., *J. Lipid Res.*, **1**, 412 (1960).
264. Morris, L. J., Holman, R. T., and Fontell, K., *ibid.*, **2**, 68 (1961).
265. Mottier, M., and Potterat, M., *Mitt. Gebiete Lebensm. u. Hyg.*, **43**, 123 (1962).
266. Mottier, M., *ibid.*, **47**, 372 (1956).
267. Mottier, M., *ibid.*, **49**, 454 (1958).
268. Mottier, M., and Potterat, M., *ibid.*, **43**, 118 (1952).
269. Mottier, M., and Potterat, M., *Anal. Chim. Acta*, **13**, 46 (1955).
270. Müller, K. H., and Honerlagen, H., *Mitt. deut. Pharm. Ges.*, **30**, 202 (1960).
271. Mutschler, E., and Rochelmeyer, H., *Arch. Pharm.*, **292/64**, 449 (1959).
272. Neher, R., and Wettstein, A., *Helv. Chim. Acta*, **43**, 1628 (1960).
273. Neubauer, D., and Mothes, K., *Planta Med.*, **9**, 466 (1961).
274. Nicolaus, B. J. R., *J. Chromatog.*, **4**, 384 (1960).
275. Nicolaus, B. J. R., Coronelli, C., and Binaghi, A., *Experientia*, **17**, 473 (1961).
276. Nicolaus, B. J. R., Coronelli, C., and Binaghi, A., *Farmaco (Pavia) Ed. Prat.*, **16**, 349 (1961).
277. Niederwieser, A., and Pataki, G., *Chimia (Aarau)*, **14**, 378 (1960).
278. Nishikaze, O., and Staudinger, H., *Klin. Wochschr.*, **40**, 1014 (1962).
279. Nürnberg, E., *Arch. Pharm.*, **292/64**, 610 (1959).
280. Nürnberg, E., *Deut. Apotheker Z.*, **101**, 268 (1961).

281. Nürnberg, E., *ibid.*, **101**, 142 (1961).
282. Nussbaumer, P. A., *Pharm. Acta Helv.*, **37**, 65 (1962).
283. Nussbaumer, P. A., *ibid.*, **37**, 161 (1962).
284. Onoe, K., *J. Chem. Soc. Japan, Pure Chem. Sect.*, **73**, 337 (1952); *Chem. Zentr.*, **127**, 3958 (1956).
285. Pailer, M., and Kump, W. G., *Arch. Pharm.*, **293**, 646 (1960).
286. Paris, R., *Prod. Pharm.*, **15**, 347 (1960).
287. Paris, R., and Godon, M., *Ann. Pharm. Franc.*, **19**, 86 (1961).
288. Pastuska, G., *Z. Anal. Chem.*, **179**, 355 (1961).
289. Pastuska, G., *ibid.*, **179**, 427 (1961).
290. Pastuska, G., and Petrowitz, H.-J., *Chemiker Ztg.*, **86**, 311 (1962).
291. Pastuska, G., and Trinks, H., *ibid.*, **86**, 135 (1962).
292. Patel, N. G., Haydak, M. H., and Lovell, R., *Nature*, **191**, 362 (1961).
293. Peereboom, J. W. C., *J. Chromatog.*, **3**, 323 (1960).
294. Peereboom, J. W. C., *Chem. Weekblad*, **57**, 625 (1961).
295. Peereboom, J. W. C., and Beekes, H. W., *J. Chromatog.*, **9**, 316 (1962).
296. Peifer, J. J., *Mikrochim. Acta*, 529 (1962).
297. Pertsev, I. M., and Pivnenko, G. P., *Farm. Zhur. (Kiev).*, **16**, 28 (1961).
298. Pertsev, I. M., and Pivnenko, G. P., *ibid.*, **17**, No. 2, 35 (1962).
299. Petrowitz, H.-J., *Angew. Chem.*, **72**, 921 (1960).
300. Petrowitz, H.-J., *Chemiker Ztg.*, **85**, 867 (1961).
301. Petrowitz, H.-J., *Erdoel u. Kohle*, **14**, 923 (1961).
302. Petrowitz, H.-J., and Pastuska, G., *J. Chromatog.*, **7**, 128 (1962).
303. Petschik, H., and Steger, E., *ibid.*, **7**, 135 (1962).
304. Petschik, H., and Steger, E., *ibid.*, **9**, 307 (1962).
305. Pobul, L. Y., Formina, A. S., and Dastereva, Z. A., *Khim. i Tekhnol. Topliv i Masel*, **6**, 55 (1961).
306. Potterat, M., and Mottier, M., *Mitt. Gebiete u. Lebensm. Hyg.*, **44**, 192 (1953); *Chem. Abstr.*, **47**, 8919 (1953).
307. Prey, V., Berbalk, H., and Kausz, M., *Mikrochim. Acta*, 968 (1961).
308. Prey, V., Berbalk, H., and Kausz, M., *ibid.*, 449 (1962).
309. Prey, V., Berger, A., and Berbalk, H., *Z. Anal. Chem.*, **185**, 113 (1962).
310. Privett, O. S., and Blank, M. L., *J. Lipid Res.*, **2**, 37 (1961).
311. Privett, O. S., Blank, M. L., and Lundberg, W. O., *J. Am. Oil Chemists' Soc.*, **38**, 312 (1961).
312. Procházka, Z., *Chem. Listy*, **55**, 974 (1961); *Chem. Abstr.*, **55**, 26823 (1961).
313. Pryor, L. D., and Bryant, L. H., *Proc. Linnean Soc. N.S.Wales*, **83**, 55 (1958).
314. Purdy, S. J., and Truter, E. V., *Chem. & Ind. (London)*, 506 (1962).

315. Purdy, S. J., and Truter, E. V., *Analyst*, **87**, 802 (1962).
316. Randerath, K., *Angew. Chem.*, **73**, 436 (1961).
317. Randerath, K., *ibid.*, **73**, 674 (1961).
318. Randerath, K., *Angew. Chem. Intern. Ed. Engl.*, **1**, 435 (1962).
319. Randerath, K., *Biochem. Biophys. Res. Commun.*, **6**, 452 (1962).
320. Randerath, K., *Nature*, **194**, 768 (1962).
320a. Randerath, K., "Dünnschicht-Chromatographie", Stuttgart, Verlag Chemie, 1962.
321. Randerath, K., and Struck, H., *J. Chromatog.*, **6**, 365 (1961).
322. Reichelt, J., and Pitra, J., *Collection Czech. Chem. Commun.*, **27**, 1709 (1962).
323. Reitsema, R. H., *Anal. Chem.*, **26**, 960 (1954).
324. Reitsema, R. H., *J. Am. Pharm. Assoc., Sci. Ed.*, **43**, 414 (1954).
325. Reitsema, R. H., *ibid.*, **47**, 267 (1958).
326. Reitsema, R. H., Cramer, F. J., and Fass, W. E., *J. Agr. Food Chem.*, **5**, 779 (1957).
327. Reitsema, R. H., Cramer, F. J., Scully, N. J., and Chorney, W., *J. Pharm. Sci.*, **50**, 18 (1961).
328. Rigby, F. L., and Bethune, J. L., *Am. Soc. Brewing Chemists Proc.*, 174 (1955).
329. Ritter, F. J., and Meyer, G. M., *Nature*, **193**, 941 (1962).
330. Rosi, D., and Hamilton, P., *J. Chromatog.*, **9**, 388 (1962).
331. Rosmus, J., and Deyl, Z., *ibid.*, **6**, 187 (1961).
332. Rother, A., Bobbitt, J. M., and Schwarting, A. E., *Chem. & Ind. (London)*, 654 (1962).
333. Ruggieri, S., *Nature*, **193**, 1282 (1962).
334. Rybicka, S. M., *Chem. & Ind. (London)*, 308 (1962).
335. Rybicka, S. M., *ibid.*, 1947 (1962).
336. Sander, H., *Naturwissenschaften*, **48**, 303 (1961).
337. Sander, H., *Z. Naturforsch.*, **16b**, 144 (1961).
338. Sander, H., Alkemeyer, M., and Hänsel, R., *Arch. Pharm.*, **295**, 6 (1962).
339. Sander, H., Hauser, H., and Hänsel, R., *Planta Med.*, **9**, 11 (1961).
340. Šaršúnová, M., and Schwarz, V., *Pharmazie*, **17**, 527 (1962).
341. Schellenberg, P., *Angew. Chem. Intern. Ed. Engl.*, **1**, 114 (1962).
342. Schetty, G., and Kuster, W., *Helv. Chim. Acta*, **44**, 2193 (1961).
343. Schlemmer, W., *Boll. Soc. Ital. Biol. Sper.*, **37**, 134 (1961).
344. Schlemmer, F., and Link, E., *Pharm. Ztg. Ver. Apotheker-Ztg.*, **104**, 1349 (1959).
345. Schlögl, K., Pelousek, H., and Mohar, A., *Monatsh. Chem.*, **92**, 533 (1961).

346. Schorn, P. J., *Glas-Instr.-Tech.*, **5**, 43 (1961).

347. Schreiber, K., and Adam, G., *Monatsh. Chem.*, **92**, 1093 (1961).

348. Schreiber, K., Osske, G., and Sembdner, G., *Experientia*, **17**, 463 (1961).

349. Schulze, P.-E., and Wenzel, M., *Angew. Chem. Intern. Ed. Engl.*, **1**, 580 (1962).

350. Schweiger, A., *J. Chromatog.*, **9**, 374 (1962).

351. Sease, J. W., *J. Am. Chem. Soc.*, **70**, 3630 (1948).

352. Seher, A., *Fette u. Seifen*, **61**, 345 (1959).

353. Seher, A., *Nahrung*, **4**, 466 (1960).

354. Seher, A., *Mikrochim. Acta*. 308 (1961).

355. Seiler, H., *Helv. Chim. Acta*, **44**, 1753 (1961).

356. Seiler, H., *ibid.*, **45**, 381 (1962).

357. Seiler, H., and Kaffenberger, T., *ibid.*, **44**, 1282 (1961).

358. Seiler, H., and Rothweiler, W., *ibid.*, **44**, 941 (1961).

359. Seiler, H., and Seiler, M., *ibid.*, **43**, 1939 (1960).

360. Seiler, H., and Seiler, M., *ibid.*, **44**, 939 (1961).

361. Sigg, H. P., and Tamm, C., *ibid.*, **43**, 1402 (1960).

362. Sims, R. P. A., and Larose, J. A. G., *J. Am. Oil Chemists' Soc.*, **39**, 232 (1962).

363. Smith, L. L., and Foell, T., *J. Chromatog.*, **9**, 339 (1962).

364. Snyder, F., and Stephens, N., *Anal. Biochem.*, **4**, 128 (1962).

365. Spickett, R. G. W., *Chem. & Ind. (London)*, 561 (1957).

366. Stahl, E., *Chemiker Ztg.*, **82**, 323 (1958).

367. Stahl, E., *Fette u. Seifen*, **60**, 1027 (1958).

368. Stahl, E., *Parfuem Kosmetik*, **39**, 564 (1958).

369. Stahl, E., *Arch. Pharm.*, **292/64**, 411 (1959).

370. Stahl, E., *Pharm. Rundschau*, **1**, No. 2, 1 (1959).

371. Stahl, E., *Arch. Pharm.*, **293/65**, 531 (1960).

372. Stahl, E., *Angew. Chem.*, **73**, 646 (1961).

373. Stahl, E., *Chemiker-Ztg.*, **85**, 371 (1961).

374. Stahl, E., *Z. Anal. Chem.*, **181**, 303 (1961).

375. Stahl, E., "Dünnschicht-Chromatographie," Berlin-Göttinger-Heidelberg, Springer-Verlag, 1962.

376. Stahl, E., and Kaldewey, H., *Hoppe-Seyler's Z. physiol. Chem.*, **323**, 182 (1961).

377. Stahl, E., and Kaltenbach, U., *J. Chromatog.*, **5**, 351 (1961).

378. Stahl, E., and Kaltenbach, U., *ibid.*, **5**, 458 (1961).

379. Stahl, E., and Schorn, P. J., *Hoppe-Seyler's Z. physiol. Chem.*, **325**, 263 (1961).

380. Stahl, E., and Schorn, P. J., *Naturwissenschaften*, **49**, 14 (1962).

381. Stahl, E., Schröter, G., Kraft, G., and Renz, R., *Pharmazie*, **11**, 633 (1956).
382. Stahl, E., and Trennheuser, L., *Arch. Pharm.*, **293**/65, 826 (1960).
383. Stanley, W. L., *J. Assoc. Offic. Agr. Chemists*, **42**, 643 (1959).
384. Stanley, W. L., *ibid.*, **44**, 546 (1961).
385. Stanley, W. L., Ikeda, R. M., and Cook, S., *Food Technol.*, **15**, 381 (1961).
386. Stanley, W. L., Lindwall, R. C., and Vannier, S. H., *J. Agr. Food Chem.*, **6**, 858 (1958).
387. Stanley, W. L., and Vannier, S. H., *J. Am. Chem. Soc.*, **79**, 3688 (1957).
388. Stanley, W. L., and Vannier, S. H., *J. Assoc. Offic. Agr. Chemists*, **40**, 582 (1957).
389. Stanley, W. L., Vannier, S. H., and Gentili, B., *ibid.*, **40**, 282 (1957).
390. Stansby, M. E., *Food Technol.*, **15**, 378 (1961).
391. Stárka, L., and Malíková, J., *J. Endocrinol.*, **22**, 215 (1961).
392. Steinegger, E., and van der Walt, J. H., *Pharm. Acta Helv.*, **36**, 599 (1961).
393. Strain, H. H., "Chromatographic Adsorption Analysis," New York, Interscience Publishers, Inc., 1941.
394. Struck, H., *Mikrochim. Acta*, 634 (1961).
395. Subbarao, R., Roomi, M. W., Subbaram, M. R., and Achaya, K. T., *J. Chromatog.*, **9**, 295 (1962).
396. Sundt, E., and Saccardi, A., *Food Technol.*, **16**, 89 (1962).
397. Tamm, C., *Helv. Chim. Acta*, **43**, 1700 (1960).
398. Tate, M. E., and Bishop, C. T., *Can. J. Chem.*, **40**, 1043 (1962).
399. Teichert, K., Mutschler, E., and Rochelmeyer, H., *Deut. Apotheker-Z.*, **100**, 283 (1960).
400. Teichert, K., Mutschler, E., and Rochelmeyer, H., *Z. Anal. Chem.*, **181**, 325 (1961).
401. Thoma, J. A., *Anal. Chem.*, **35**, 214 (1963).
402. Thomas, A. F., and Müller, J. M., *Experientia*, **16**, 62 (1960).
403. Trappe, W., *Biochem. Z.*, **305**, 150 (1940).
404. Truter, E. V., "Thin Film Chromatography," London, Clever-Hume, 1963.
405. Tschesche, R., Freytag, W., and Snatzke, G., *Chem. Ber.*, **92**, 3053 (1959).
406. Tschesche, R., Lampert, F., and Snatzke, G., *J. Chromatog.*, **5**, 217 (1961).
407. Tschesche, R., and Sen Gupta, A. K., *Chem. Ber.*, **93**, 1903 (1960).
408. Tschesche, R., and Snatzke, G., *Ann. Chem.*, **636**, 105 (1960).

409. Tswett, M., *Ber. Deut. Botan. Ges.*, **24**, 316 (1906).

410. Tswett, M., *ibid.*, **24**, 384 (1906).

411. Türler, M., and Högl, O., *Mitt. Gebiete u. Lebensm. Hyg.*, **52**, 123 (1961).

412. Turner, N. C., *Natl. Petrol. News*, **35**, R-234 (1943).

413. Vacíková, Á., Felt, V., and Malíková, J., *J. Chromatog.*, **9**, 301 (1962).

414. Vaedtke, J., and Gajewska, A., *ibid.*, **9**, 345 (1962).

415. Van Dam, M. J. D., *Bull. Soc. Chim. Belges*, **70**, 122 (1961).

416. Van Dam, M. J. D., DeKleuver, G. J., and De Heus, J. G., *J. Chromatog.*, **4**, 26 (1960).

417. Vannier, S. H., and Stanley, W. L., *J. Assoc. Offic. Agr. Chemists*, **41**, 432 (1958).

418. Vioque, E., *Grasas Aceites (Seville, Spain)*, **11**, 223 (1960); *Chem. Abstr.*, **55**, 15057 (1961).

419. Vioque, E., and Holman, R. T., *Anal. Chem.*, **33**, 1444 (1961).

420. Vioque, E., and Holman, R. T., *J. Am. Oil Chemists' Soc.*, **39**, 63 (1962).

421. Vioque, E., and Morris, L. J., *ibid.*, **38**, 485 (1961).

422. Vioque, E., Morris, L. J., and Holman, R. T., *ibid.*, **38**, 489 (1961).

423. Vogel, W. C., Doizaki, W. M., and Zieve, L., *J. Lipid Res.*, **3**, 138 (1962).

424. Vogler, K., Studer, R. O., Lergier, W., and Lanz, P. *Helv. Chim. Acta*, **43**, 1751 (1960).

425. Völksen, W., *Krankenhaus-Apotheker*, **11**, 5 (1961).

426. Wagner, G., *Pharmazie*, **10**, 302 (1955).

427. Wagner, H., *Fette u. Seifen*, **62**, 1115 (1960).

428. Wagner, H., *Mitt. Gebiete u. Lebensm. Hyg.*, **51**, 416 (1960).

429. Wagner, H., *Pharm. Ztg., Ver. Apotheker-Ztg.*, **105**, 1340 (1960).

430. Wagner, H., *Fette u. Seifen*, **63**, 1119 (1961).

431. Wagner H., Hörhammer, L., and Dengler, B., *J. Chromatog.*, **7**, 211 (1962).

432. Wagner, H., Hörhammer, L., and Wolff, P., *Biochem. Z.*, **334**, 175 (1961).

433. Waldi, D., *Klin. Wochschr.*, **40**, 827 (1962).

434. Waldi, D., *Mitt. Deut. Pharm. Ges.*, **32**, 125 (1962).

435. Waldi, D., and Munter, F., *Med. Exptl.*, **3**, 45 (1960).

436. Waldi, D., Schnackerz, K., and Munter, F., *J. Chromatog.*, **6**, 61 (1961).

436a. Wang, K. T., *J. Chinese Chem. Soc. (Taiwan)*, **8**, 241 (1961).

437. Wasicky, R., *Anal. Chem.*, **34**, 1346 (1962).

438. Weicker, H., *Klin. Wochschr.*, **37,** 763 (1959).
439. Weicker, H., and Brossmer, R., *ibid.*, **39,** 1265 (1961).
440. Weicker, H., Dain, J. A., Schmidt, G., and Thannhauser, S. J., *Federation Proc.*, **19,** 219 (1960).
441. Weill, C. E., and Hanke, P., *Anal. Chem.*, **34,** 1736 (1962).
442. Williams, J. A., Sharma, A., Morris, L. J., and Holman, R. T., *Proc. Soc. Exp. Biol. Med.*, **105,** 192 (1960).
443. Williams, T. L., "Introduction to Chromatography," Glasgow, Blackie and Sons, 1947.
444. Winkler, W., and Awe, W., *Arch. Pharm.*, **294,** 301 (1961).
445. Winkler, W., and Lunau, E., *Pharm. Ztg.*, *Ver. Apotheker-Ztg.*, **104,** 1407 (1959).
446. Winterstein, A., *Angew. Chem.*, **72,** 902 (1960).
447. Winterstein, A., and Hegedüs, B., *Chimia (Aarau)*, **14,** 18 (1960).
448. Winterstein, A., and Hegedüs, B., *Hoppe-Seyler's Z. physiol. Chem.*, **321,** 97 (1960).
449. Winterstein, A., Studer, A., and Rüegg, R., *Chem. Ber.*, **93,** 2951 (1960).
450. Wollenweber, P., *J. Chromatog.*, **9,** 369 (1962).
451. Wollenweber, P., *ibid.*, **7,** 557 (1962).
452. Wollish, E. G., Schmall, M., and Hawrylyshyn, M., *Anal. Chem.*, **33,** 1138 (1961).
453. Wulff, H. D., and Stahl, E., *Naturwissenschaften*, **47,** 114 (1960).
454. Wyss-Huber, M., Jäger, H., and Weiss, E., *Helv. Chim. Acta*, **43,** 1010 (1960).
455. Yamamura, J., and Niwaguchi, T., *Kagaku Keisatsu Kenkyusho Hokoku*, **13,** 450 (1960); *Chem. Abstr.*, **56,** 6416 (1962).
456. Zachau, H. G., and Karau, W., *Chem. Ber.*, **93,** 1830 (1960).
457. Zelnik, R., and Ziti, L. N., *J. Chromatog.*, **9,** 371 (1962).
458. Zöllner, N., and Wolfram, G., *Klin. Wochschr.*, **40,** 1098 (1962).
459. Zöllner, N., and Wolfram, G., *ibid.*, **40,** 1101 (1962).
460. Zöllner, N., Wolfram, G., and Amin, G., *ibid.*, **40,** 20 (1962).

Index

199